MARX'S SOCIALISM

The Editor

SHLOMO AVINERI is Chairman of the Department of Political Science and Director of the Levi Eshkol Research Institute at the Hebrew University of Jerusalem. A graduate of the Hebrew University and the London School of Economics, Professor Avineri has also taught at Yale University. He has published numerous articles in scholarly journals and his books in English include *The Social and Political Thought of Karl Marx* and *Karl Marx on Colonialism and Modernization*. He also edited a volume of essays on *Israel and the Palestinians*, and translated Marx's early writings into Hebrew.

During 1971-72 Professor Avineri was a Fellow at the Center for the Humanities at Wesleyan University.

Consulting Editor

DAVID SPITZ
Hunter College, CUNY
POLITICAL THEORY

Marx's Socialism

EDITED BY

Shlomo Avineri

L

LIEBER-ATHERTON
New York 1973

Marx's Socialism
edited by Shlomo Avineri

Address all inquiries to:
Lieber-Atherton, Incorporated
1841 Broadway
New York, New York 10023

Library of Congress Catalog Number 70-159600
ISBN 0-88311-004-0 (cloth); 0-88311-005-9 (paper)

Printed in the United States of America

Contents

Introduction

SHLOMO AVINERI

Much of the controversy surrounding Marx and his vision of socialism occurred at a time when a sizable part of his writings remained unknown to the public. The classical controversies between "reformists" and "revolutionists," between social-democrats and bolsheviks, between Bernstein and Kautsky and between Plekhanov and Lenin were conducted at a time when some of Marx's major theoretical works were unpublished and totally unknown to those engaged in the controversies themselves. Only the publication, in the late 1920s and 1930s, of *The German Ideology*, *The Economic-Philosophical Manuscripts*, and the *Grundrisse*, made it possible to confront the whole of Marx's corpus, and not only the tip, broad as it may have been, of the iceberg. This discovery and publication of Marx's theoretical writings made also much of the classical controversies about Marx obsolete and sometimes wholly irrelevant. These controversies do, of course, retain their historical value in the development of socialist thinking and working class organization, but as a key toward a theoretical understanding of the meaning of Marx's theory, they have lost most of their value.

It is for this reason that the selection in this volume includes only articles by authors who have incorporated Marx's early writings into their interpretation of Marx. These writers, divergent as their own interpretations of Marx would be, do agree that an adequate understanding of Marx's early writings is crucial toward an evolution of an over-all view of Marx's critique of capitalism as well as of his vision of future socialist society. Since Marx's explicit discussions of future society are few and far between, one has to reconstruct his views about future communism out of his critique of the bourgeois world: hence this critique is indispensable to his views on what socialist society would represent.

But if there seems to be a consensus about the necessity of confronting Marx's early writings in order to reach a balanced understanding of his theory, very widely dissenting views are held as to the exact significance and value one should attach to these writings *vis-à-vis* the works of his more "mature" period. This question about the continuity or discontinuity of Marx's thought is also a controversy about the meaning one should attach in Marx's thought to such themes as humanism, alienation, and the like, which figure very strongly in the early writings but later recede into the background.

In the opening piece I try to show that one of Marx's earliest — and hitherto much neglected — theoretical writings, his *Critique of Hegel's "Philosophy of Right,"* shows both the dimensions of his indebtedness to Hegel in matters of political and social theory as well as the continuity of his own thought. Not only does Marx himself refer to the *Critique* in some of his later writings as being instrumental in shaping his mature world view, he also arrives in this early work at some of the fundamental conclusions which would always remain central to his critique of bourgeois society. The later, "mature," Marx is already immanent in this early piece of highly sophisticated theoretical confrontation with Hegel.*

Both Tucker and Miliband deal with Marx as a political theorist. Tucker discusses both Marx and Engels jointly, and it could be argued that some of the discrepancies he points to could be attributed to this lack of differentiation between the two thinkers: it could

---

*Since my article has been first printed, an English translation of the *Critique,* with an extensive and most valuable Introduction by Joseph O'Malley, has been published by Cambridge University Press.

be easily shown that Engels lacked Marx's dialectical grasp of the nature of the political sphere. Nonetheless, Tucker rightly points out that there seems to be a twofold view of the state in Marx — one viewing the state as an organization for the defense of the interests of the ruling class, another ascribing to the state organs (the bureaucracy, the police, the army) an independent role. Miliband also points to this ambivalence, but he seems more aware than Tucker that its very existence is a testimony to the dialectical nature of Marx's theory of the state: this ambivalence can be easily resolved if one keeps in mind that Marx always retained something of the Hegelian notion that the state is an expression of universality. Hence even when the state is expressing class interests in their crudest form, this is always presented as if it were aimed at the common good, at the universal interest, and the guardians of this "common good" never view themselves as mere watchdogs of class interests. And if one looks closely enough at Marx's own texts (and here Engels does present a slightly different picture), Marx always attributes to the state machinery an *imagined*, not a real, independence from class interests.

Both Tucker and Miliband also deal with the way in which the "dictatorship of the proletariat" should be integrated into Marx's political theory; Marx's relationship to anarchism and the anarchists is also touched upon. Miliband is especially emphatic in pointing out that despite Marx's opposition to Bakunin, his theory of the state is totally anti-authoritarian. In this Miliband is justly critical of a well-established tradition which tended to identify Marx with an authoritarian bent because of his opposition to the methods and tactics of the anarchists, and mainly the Russians among them.

In dealing with Marx's theory of the state, Miliband also brings up the most intriguing question of Marx's attitude to non-European political cultures and his theory of the "Asiatic mode of production." This aspect of Marx's thought is dealt with extensively in George Lichtheim's essay, which spurned by Karl A. Wittfogel's *Oriental Despotism* unravels the various dimensions through which Marx dealt with the problems of the non-European societies. Much of what passes for orthodox Marxist writing tends to deal with the non-European world in categories which Marx explicitly reserved for his historical analysis of the West: <u>nowhere did Marx imply that the historical sequences of European history have to be duplicated in the non-Western world</u>.* The complexity of Marx's views, as brought out by Lichtheim, may also serve as a challenge to any theory about the meaning of Marxism for the "Third World."

Donald C. Hodges' article, on the other hand, is much more skeptical about the issue of continuity in Marx. Hodges justly warns students of Marx against seeing only the "young" Marx as the "authentic" Marx; he also warns (and here others may take exception to his views) against scholars "presenting a humanistic image [of Marx] congenial to the academic community." Even if one disagrees with his contention that some of the early writings represent "material from Marx's own wastebasket," <u>Hodges is on safe ground when he claims that the modish preoccupation with alienation should not cause one to overlook the fact that for Marx alienation was always set in a concrete socioeconomic context and was not used as a catch-all phrase aiming to explain that kind of cosmic *Weltschmerz* which some of the less critical writers would today like to attribute to Marx. After all, Marx was a social critic, not a psychological therapist</u>.

While Hodges believes that in his later years Marx regarded the *Economic-Philosophical Manuscripts* as "obsolete and downright misleading," <u>Iring Fetscher shows how a curious coalition of social-democrats and Leninists alike tried to de-emphasize the importance of Marx's early writings</u>. By a careful textual comparison of some of the earlier with the later writings, Fetscher tries to bring out the inherent unity of Marx's thought. The main theme of Marx's achievement is, according to Fetscher, his contention that world history is nothing but the producing of man by man's work, and it is this aspect of Marx's humanism which he tries to establish as the core of his system.

Daniel Bell's article is one of the first attempts in English to gauge the impact of Marx's theory of alienation on the conventional assessment of Marx's thought; it brings out quite successfully many of the

---

*For this, see especially Marx's letter of November 1877 to the Editors of *Otechestvenniye Zapiski,* quoted in Karl Marx, *On Colonialism and Modernization,* ed. S. Avineri (Garden City, 1968), pp. 442-445.

ambiguities in Marx's position and points to some of the problems which subsequent scholarship tried to take up and solve, sometimes in directions differing from Bell's own approach. Thus, Joseph J. O'Malley's essay is a most penetrating attempt to emancipate Marx's concept of "nature" from the positivist, "naturalist" stamp imprinted on it by, mainly, some of Engels' later writings. O'Malley shows how Marx's views of man's nature imply a dynamic concept of the developmental structure of man's potentialities: labor, and history, are thus the corollaries to such a dynamic view of man's nature. In this is also implied the possibility of man's self-emancipation through his own molding of the conditions of his own existence.

The four latter pieces in this collection by Gerald A. Cohen, Robert C. Tucker, Ralph Miliband, and George Lichtheim relate to some of the more specific sociopolitical themes in Marx's work. Cohen presents a most fascinating attempt to synthesize Marx's thinking about class relationships within the conceptual framework of alienation. He argues, against Hodges, that not only the proletarian, but also the capitalist, is alienated within capitalist society. Cohen further maintains that since the capitalist does not even produce, which the worker does, he is even "more distant from being truly human than the worker is."

In this selection, the emphasis has been mostly on Marx, not on Marxism: on the thinker, not the doctrine. This does not imply that Marxism, as it was developed by the various schools of Marx's disciples, is insignificant or secondary if compared to Marx's own thought. But no adequate understanding of the varieties of Marxism can be achieved unless one attempts to confront the complexity, richness — and problematics — of the thought of Marx himself.

I would like to thank Miss Maly Shafrir for helping me in the preparation of this volume.

MARX'S SOCIALISM

1: The Hegelian Origins of Marx's Political Thought

SHLOMO AVINERI

Hegel's impact on Marx's intellectual development has recently achieved a fair amount of attention.[1] We have, of course, Marx's own statements about his indebtedness to Hegel in *A Contribution to the Critique of Political Economy* (1859) and the Afterword to *Das Kapital* (1873).[2] Moreover, Marx's correspondence abounds with allusions to Hegel and strongly laments the lack of an understanding of Hegel in some of his disciples.[3]

Yet until recently very little attention has been devoted to the fact that Marx's first major theoretical work, written in 1843 at the age of twenty-five, is a detailed critique of Hegel's *Philosophy of Right*. Most of the literature which relates Marx to Hegel draws its evidence either from the two essays in the *Deutsch-Französische Jahrbücher* or from the *Economic-Philosophical Manuscripts:* yet Marx's views in these writings are an outcome of his earlier confrontation with Hegel in his *Critique of Hegel's Philosophy of Right*. This critique of § § 261-313 of the *Rechtsphilosophie* had never been published in Marx's lifetime and was printed for the first time by

Originally published in *The Review of Metaphysics*, XXI:1, September 1967, 33-50.

1

David Riazanov in 1927. While the *Economic-Philosophical Manuscripts* of 1844 have achieved widespread recognition, this *Critique* remains relatively unknown, has as yet not been translated into English and remains generally neglected. My argument in this paper will be that a close look at the *Critique* is indispensable for an understanding of Marx's intellectual development, that most of the elements of Marx's later, "mature" social philosophy are already in existence in 1843, and that consequently some of the traditional views about the stages Marx's thought went through have to be radically revised.

But before discussing the main argument of the *Critique* it would be worthwhile to recapitulate some of the prior milestones on Marx's way to Hegel. We know that Marx was introduced to Hegelian philosophy in Berlin not through his studies at the University: in the late 1830s, when Marx studied at Berlin, Hegel was already very much "out"; Schelling was "in." Marx was thus initiated into Hegel's thought by a group of young teaching assistants at the University that was known as the *Doktorenklub*. In a letter to his father written in 1837 Marx recounts how he became drawn into Hegelian philosophy because he felt that Hegel had succeeded in closing the gap between the "is" and the "ought" bequeathed to German philosophy by Kant. Paraphrasing Hegel's *Phenomenology,* Marx tells his father that "if the Gods have dwelt till now above the earth, they have not become its center."[4] A similar critique of pre-Hegelian German idealism is implied in an aphorism of Marx of the same period: "Kant and Fichte reach for ethereal heights, looking there for a distant land, while I just try to comprehend (*begreifen*) what I found on the street."[5]

That Marx thus became attracted to Hegel because he thought he had found his philosophy directly related to concrete life is a key to the understanding of Marx's later critique of Hegel. For when he discusses for the first time his intention of writing a critique of Hegel in 1842, he relates this to Hegel's political philosophy and not to his philosophical system as such. When asked by Ruge to contribute a critique of Hegel to a collection of essays he was about to edit, Marx replies that he will concentrate his attack on the *Philosophy of Right* because "the main thing is to fight against the constitutional monarchy as a hybrid creature, full of internal contradictions and bound to be self-destroying."[6]

Yet Marx never wrote this article, and his *Critique of Hegel's Philosophy of Right* was not written until fifteen months later, after the publication of Feuerbach's *Provisional Theses for the Reformation of Philosophy.*[7] In these *Theses* Feuerbach postulated his transformative method for the critique of speculative philosophy in general and Hegelian speculation in particular. According to Feuerbach, Hegelian philosophy is a "mystification" because it perverts the subject-predicate relationship; by a transformative reading of Hegel that will substitute predicate for subject and vice versa, one can arrive at a philosophy that is adequate to reality.[8] Such a philosophy will, according to Feuerbach, emancipate man from his subservience to the conceptual constructs devised by himself: man, who in Hegel's system is a predicate of spirit, will thus be transformed again into a subject, whereas spirit will become what it has always been, a predicate of man.[9]

Marx's reaction to Feuerbach's *Provisional Theses* was enthusiastic. Early in 1843 he tells Ruge that "I approve of Feuerbach's aphorisms except for one point: he directs himself too much to nature and too little to politics. But it is politics which happens to be the only link through which contemporary philosophy can become true."[10] In the same volume in which Feuerbach printed his *Theses* Marx published an anonymous article which ends with an eloquent appeal for the emancipation of philosophy: philosophy will never be emancipated, Marx argues, unless it passes through the purgatory of a *Feuer-bach.*[11]

When Marx began writing his *Critique* a few months after the publication of Feuerbach's Provisional *Theses,* he actually did follow the implications of his remark to Ruge. His commentary on Hegel's *Philosophy of Right* tries to apply Feuerbach's transformative method to politics. Marx's initial fascination with Hegel was caused by his wish to "realize philosophy" and thus close the gap between social life and its theoretical criteria; his immanent critique of Hegel had the same aim in mind. It was the realm of social life which caused both Marx's adoption and his criticism of Hegel's system.

I

Marx's *Critique of Hegel's Philosophy of Right* is a running commentary of those parts of the *Rechtsphilosophie* dealing with civil society and the state. Since Marx's interest is not to confront Hegel's system as a whole but arrive at a criticism of the system through a discussion of Hegel's political theory, he does not begin at the beginning but plunges *in medias res* at § 261, right in the middle of Hegel's account of political institutions.

Marx's basic technique through the *Critique* is essentially simple: he first copies the relevant paragraph from Hegel and then adds his own commentary, mainly based on Feuerbach's transformative method; but the effect is cumulative. While at the beginning of the *Critique* the criticism seems mild and pedantic, at the end, after wading through dozens of paragraphs, not much of Hegel's political theory and his system is left standing. Seldom in the annals of philosophy has a systematic edifice been so thoroughly bored from within.

A detailed account of the *Critique* will have to be undertaken separately.[1 2] Suffice it to say that Marx subjects Hegel's major ideas about the state to the transformative method: sovereignty, the monarch, assemblies of estates—all are treated by Marx as mystifications, inversions hiding behind their institutional façades true realities that have to be brought out by the inversion of the subject-predicate relationship. Marx further operates with Hegel's basic terms of "civil society" (*bürgerliche Gesellschaft*) and "state": his argument, however, is that they do not relate to each other in the way postulated by Hegel. According to Hegel, civil society is the sphere of individually-oriented activity, the realm of needs and of universal self-interest. Hegel's state transcends self-interest by integrating human consciousness through establishing a system of norms which go beyond the universal egoism of civil society. If civil society is the sphere of universal egotism, Hegel's state is oriented toward universal altruism. Hegel's claim that the state is oriented toward universal goals also places the bureaucracy, the universal class in Hegel's language, in a central position in this political theory.

Marx's main argument against this dialectic of civil society and state is that it fails to give adequate expression to the realities of political and social life. Hegel's philosophy does not claim to give instruction to the world as it ought to be: it prides itself on comprehending actuality, and it is this claim which is taken seriously by Marx and shown to be false; surely no critical device could be more legitimate from Hegel's own position. According to Marx, no actual, historical state ever approximated Hegel's scheme. In Hegel's philosophy the state may be universally oriented: all political institutions in real life, Marx argues, are so organized as to make the state a mere instrument for the interests of civil society *pretending* to be universally-oriented. It was this mystification which Hegel failed to see through and consequently even in Hegel's own system the state is, in the last analysis, a bogey, an "idealism" barely able to cover up the crass interests of civil society working through its universalistic pretensions. Especially in his discussion of the Assembly of Estates, Marx shows how Hegel has to admit that legislation is ultimately determined by the particular interests of civil society and not by any guiding principle of universal applicability.[13]

Two aspects of Marx's attack on Hegel's political theory seem particularly illuminating and it is those that I propose to discuss in the following pages. They are Hegel's notion of the role of the bureaucracy and the nature of property. Both are crucial to the understanding of Marx's development toward evolving a socialist philosophy.

According to Hegel the bureaucracy is the "universal class" (*der allgemeine Stand*); while all the activity of the other classes in society is oriented toward their own self-interest, the civil service aims at acting for the *res publica*, the common good. Hence, Hegel says, "individuals are not appointed to office on account of their birth or native personal gifts. The *objective* factor in their appointment is knowledge and the proof of ability."[14] Like the Platonic Guardian, the Hegelian member of the universal class is neutralized as much as possible from the pressures of the economic sphere and the considerations of civil society; though Hegel's device of a guaranteed fixed income (quite revolutionary, by the way, for early nineteenth-century practices, especially in England) is of course rather less radical than Plato's advocacy of common property for the Guardians; but its aim is identical.

The civil service is thus a class of civil society that is already on its way to transcending civil society through its universalistic orientation. For Marx all this is just pure wishful thinking. As he sees it, the universalistic orientations of the bureaucracy just serve individual bureaucrats as a justification to further their own egotistic self-interest. Consequently, while every other class advocates its own self-interest *openly and legitimately,* the bureaucracy has to resort to mystifications and false explanations, since it is supposed to be oriented toward the common weal. Using the transformative method, Marx tries to show that what really happens is not that the state has a bureaucracy: it is the bureaucracy that has the state in its possession and uses it for its own selfish interest. The universal becomes a means for particularistic ends:

> The bureaucracy possesses the essence of the state, the spiritual being of society; this is its private property. The general spirit of bureaucracy is the official secret, the mystery. . . . Authority is thus the principle of its knowledge, and the deification of authoritarianism is its credo. But within itself this spiritualism turns into a coarse materialism, the materialism of dumb obedience. . . . As far as the individual bureaucrat is concerned, the goal of the state becomes a private goal, a hunt for a higher post and the making of a career. . . . The bureaucrat has in the world a mere object for his handling. . . .[15]

By converting itself from a means to an end, the bureaucracy gives rise to the fiction of an imaginary state, and side by side with the real state there appears the chimera of perfect bureaucratic dedication to the body politic: "The bureaucracy is the illusory state alongside the real state, it is the spiritualism of the state. Everything has, therefore, a double meaning: the real and the bureaucratic one."[16] Bureaucracy identifies, according to Marx, "the interest of the state with particular private goals in such a way as to make the interests of the state into just one particular private goal opposed to other private goals."[17]

But though Marx rejects Hegel's identification of the bureaucracy as a universal class, he still retains the theoretical and operational value of the term "universal class." Marx historicizes the term, and as a dynamic term it looms very large in the evolution of his thought toward the proletariat. The *Critique* itself is silent on this, but in the *Introduction to the Critique of Hegel's Philosophy of Right,* written a few months later and published in 1844 in the *Deutsch-Französische Jahrbücher,* this becomes crucial for the whole structure of Marx's argument. Here Marx uses the idea behind the concept of a universal class in a novel and exciting way. He emancipates the Hegelian universal class from its historical identification with the bureaucracy and makes it into a dynamic concept helping to explain social change. Thus Marx's first theoretical discussion of history in class terms relies heavily on the Hegelian dialectics of seeing one particular class of society as a universal class. Marx explains that historical change is always brought about politically by a class of society which succeeds in identifying, for a period of time, its own interests with the universal interests of society. Such a class will become socially and politically dominant because of the convergence of its interests with those of society: by working for itself it also works, at that particular moment, for society as a whole. In such a way the feudal class became dominant because in the early Middle Ages its interest was identical with the need of society for security and protection; the bourgeoisie, similarly, in fighting the absolutist state also represented a far wider interest that its own. But over time the class interest of the dominant class and the universal interest of society begin to diverge from each other, though the dominant class will still stick to its position and privileges: but it has become a "declining" class, representing nobody except itself; ultimately, it will be replaced by a new class whose particular interest now coincides with the general interests of society.[18]

The Hegelian term thus gains both in historical and dialectical dimensions:

> A section of civil society emancipates itself and attains universal domination; a determinate class undertakes, from its particular situation, a general emancipation of society. . . .
> No class in civil society can play this part unless it can arouse, in itself and in the masses, a moment of enthusiasm in which it associates and mingles with society at large, identifies itself with it, and is felt and recognised as the general representative of this

society. Its aims and interests must genuinely be the aims and interests of society itself, of which it becomes in reality the social head and heart. It is only in the name of general interests that a particular class can claim general supremacy.[19]

It is in this context that Marx introduces the proletariat for the first time into his writings. Marx argues that all hitherto existing classes were of ephemeral nature because they were ultimately based on particular interests. The proletariat, when introduced into Marx's argument, stands for the ultimate universal class, for the class whose particular interest *is* the general interest of society. It is evident that Marx thus arrives at his idea of the proletariat not through an economic study or an historical analysis, but through a series of arguments and confrontations all of which are within the Hegelian tradition and relate to the Hegelian idea of a universal class. The passage where Marx mentions the proletariat for the first time in his writings is full of these universalistic attributes:

A class must be formed which has *radical* chains, a class in civil society which is not a class of civil society, a class which is the dissolution of *all* classes, a sphere of society which has a *universal* character because its sufferings are *universal*, and which does not claim a particular redress because the wrong which is done to it is not a particular wrong but wrong in *general*. There must be formed a sphere of society which claims no traditional status but only a *human* status, a sphere which is not opposed to particular consequences but is *totally* opposed to the assumptions of the German political system; a sphere, finally, which cannot emancipate itself without emancipating itself from *all* other spheres of society, without, therefore, emancipating *all* these other spheres; a class which is, in short, a *total* loss of humanity and which can only redeem itself by a *total* redemption of humanity. This dissolution of society, as a particular class, is the *proletariat*. . . .[20]

Marx goes even further: he sees the proletarian demand for the abolition of private property as nothing else than a positive *universalization* of the situation in which the proletariat already finds itself in present society:

When the proletariat announces the dissolution of the existing social order, it only declares the secret of its own existence, for it is the effective dissolution of this order. When the proletariat demands the negation of private property it only lays down *as a principle for society* what society has already made a principle for the proletariat, and what the latter already involuntarily embodies as the negative result of society.[21]

The proletariat is thus a paradigm for society: both its conditions as well as its demands are significant only inasmuch as they reflect the proletariat's position as a "universal class."[22] Marx's idea of the proletariat is unique as it is nothing else than a further development of a theme that was central to Hegel's political theory: it has very little to do in its origins with economic analysis, nor does it represent at this stage indignation at the revolting conditions to which nineteenth-century proletarians were subjected. All this comes in only later.

II

The second issue on which Marx achieves a major breakthrough in the *Critique* is his discussion of property. Though Marx never discusses property *per se* in this work, a theoretical critique of it is implied in his discussion of one of the less important aspects of Hegel's theory of social classes. This occurs in a most obscure text and has hitherto been almost totally neglected.[23] It is also a typical instance of Marx's blowing up into ridiculous proportions a very minor issue in Hegel: he devotes almost forty pages to three paragraphs (§ § 305-307) in Hegel's *Philosophy of Right*.

The issue is Hegel's justification of primogeniture and entailed estates within the nobility. Hegel's argument is fairly simple and straightforward: the preservation of the noble estate which passes in its entirety from father to first-born son safeguards aristocratic landed property both from the fluctuations of the market and from the arbitrary interference of the state. Thus there emerges a class of gentlemen of independent means who can shoulder with integrity the burdens of public office without involving their own private interests in the affairs of the state.

Marx attacks this plea of Hegel for the aristocratic element in the constitution on several grounds: first, he points out that Hegel's justification of primogeniture violates his own idea of family solidarity. On the one hand Hegel postulates the aristocracy as based on the family, since its property is vested not in any individual but in the family as a series over time of related persons. Yet by excluding from the patrimony all members of the family with the exception of the first-born son, Hegel's aristocratic family is totally lacking in solidarity and love, which Hegel takes to be the basic elements of family life: "That class founded on the family thus lacks the basis for family life, love as the real, active and determining principle. It is family life without spirit, the illusion of family life. In its highest form of development, the principle of private property contradicts the principle of family."[24]

Secondly, Marx argues that Hegel's justification of aristocratic primogeniture contradicts his own concept of property. Marx shows how, in earlier sections of his *Philosophy of Right,* Hegel defined property as the exercise of an unlimited right of the will to dispose of an object. By applying Feuerbach's transformative method, Marx arrives here at a brilliant exposé of what he considers to be the inverted nature of Hegelian thought—and of property:

> We have already pointed out how because of the inalienability of landed property the social nerves of private property were cut. Private property (landed property) is secured against the owner's arbitrary will so that, with the whole sphere of arbitrary will turned from a general human into a specific arbitrary will of private property, private property becomes the subject of the will, the will a mere predicate of private property. Private property is no longer a determined object of will, but will is the determined predicate of private property. . . .
>
> Every first-born son in the succession of the property-owner is the inheritance, the property, of inalienable landed property, the predestined substance of its will and its activity. The subject is the thing and the predicate is the man. The will becomes the property of property. . . . The owner of entailed landed property becomes the serf of the landed estate. . . . The profundity of Germanic subjectivity appears everywhere as the crudity of a spiritless objectivity.[25]

This is the same argument which Marx will later employ in *Das Kapital* when discussing the "fetishism of commodities": man is made into an object of property, his own products become his master. Marx's later argument was of course based on an economic analysis, and thus had a universal scope totally lacking in his critique of primogeniture. But it is within this obscure and sometimes pedantic context that Marx· arrived at his critique of private property, using Feuerbach's inversion of the subject-predicate relationship. In the same way as Marx arrives at the idea of the proletariat through a theoretical confrontation with Hegel, so his first discussion of property is within strict philosophical Hegelian limits. His later economic and historical studies only give substance to ideas already arrived at through philosophical discourse. Marx begins to study economics and history only after his philosophical enquiries have led him to see in the proletariat and in economically-determined relations the solution for his philosophical problems. Hence his lament that other socialists lack firm philosophical foundations; hence also the basic difference between Marx and Engels, despite all the affinity and friendship between the two. Engels arrived at proletarian socialism through economic analysis and an historical study of the actual conditions of proletarian life in industrial centers. Much of the later different approach which always distinguished Marx from Engels can be traced back to this difference in background and intellectual heritage. The humanism of Marx and the economism of Engels have two different intellectual sources, just as the proletariat for Marx is a latter-day version of the Hegelian universal class whereas for Engels it is the Manchester working class. Even when discussing Adam Smith and Ricardo, Marx always subjected them to strict dialectical criticism, while Engels, even when he discussed Hegel, was using him to prove an argument from Manchester economics.[26]

III

The nature of the *Critique* as a commentary largely precludes Marx from developing in detail a positive theory of society. Yet there are enough remarks and hints in the *Critique* to indicate quite clearly the general nature of the society Marx had in mind as an alternative to his contemporary world.

One of the difficulties confronting such an understanding is the traditional view that Marx's theories slowly "evolved" toward materialism and communism and that in 1843 he was neither a materialist nor a communist.[27] We have already seen that Marx's inversion of Hegel's system through Feuerbach's transformative method very clearly classifies him as a "materialist" in 1843; similarly his views on property and his postulate of the proletariat as the universal class trying to universalize its own propertylessness are not those of a leftwing, radical Jacobin democrat, but have to be classified as "socialist" or "communist" ideas.

Marx's paradigm of future society is postulated on his anthropology. Man, according to Marx in the *Critique,* is a "communist being" (*kommunistisches Wesen*).[28] It is significant that this "communist being" has very little to do with common property or with communism as a system of society: yet both are implied in it though it is basically an anthropological and not an economic or social concept. Man's communist being, according to Marx, is the view of man that does not start with an individualistic, atomistic model of man; nor does it juxtapose "man" to "society." It holds that all attributes of man are other-oriented, i.e., are implied in his relationship to other human beings. Man as a father, a farmer, a writer is not a self-enclosed monad, but a set of relationships. Man is thus a *Gemeinwesen,* and the fact that the term means both man in a social relationship as well as a republic and a commune only brings out Marx's message: man's "communist" nature implies a social system where man's activity is not divided between "private" and "public" functions. In *On the Jewish Question,* written later in 1843, Marx aims at the same view of man when he says that in contemporary society man is alienated because he is bifurcated into a *bourgeois* and a *citoyen:* he is supposed to behave egotistically and altruistically at the same time.[29]

It is thus the Hegelian separation of the civil society from the state that stands in the way of man's functioning as a *Gemeinwesen* (or *Gattungswesen,* as he calls it in the *Economic-Philosophical Manuscripts*). The new order of society will have to overcome this dichotomy by abolishing the difference between the state and civil society, i.e., by abolishing these two spheres as separate spheres of human activity. Thus Marx arrives in this early stage of his intellectual development at his postulate of the abolition of the state.

Here again a question of terminology comes up and clearly illustrates the theoretical distinctions between Marx and Engels. While Engels in his writings on the subject talks about the state "dying," or "withering away" (*der Staat stirbt ab*), Marx uses an altogether different term drawing on a very distinct intellectual tradition: for him the term is *"Aufhebung* of the state." This Hegelian term is, of course, the crux of the dialectical system: it implies not only *abolition,* but also *transcendence* and *preservation.*

Marx's *Aufhebung des Staates* can be thus viewed as the ultimate outcome of Hegel's political philosophy: for Hegel, the state should have transcended the particularism and egotism of civil society by establishing a sphere of universality that would be superior to civil society. Marx argues in the *Critique* that a universality that is only one sector, one segment, of the whole texture of social relationships is by itself partial and impotent. In other words, a state that exists side by side with civil society could itself be nothing else than a particularism and will be permeated, as Marx tried to show, by the individually-oriented determinations of civil society. Thus the Hegelian state vitiates the aims of Hegel's political philosophy. Only by abolishing the state as a particular *institution* can the ultimate aim of the Hegelian state, i.e., universality, be truly realized. Marx's abolition of the form of the state is aimed at preserving the universalistic content of Hegel's idea of the state, and Marx's socialism is nothing else than Hegel's political theory ultimately *aufgehoben*— abolished and preserved.

It goes without saying that this interpretation raises some basic questions about the precise institutional and organizational consequences of such an *Aufhebung* of the state: Marx is silent on these, and it would be tempting to probe further into the possibilities, both theoretical and institutional, opened up by such a view. But this cannot be done here: our aim was just to relate Marx's view of the *Aufhebung* of the state to the philosophical tradition from which it originated and which it so brilliantly brought to its ultimate end.

There is however at least one hint in Marx as to the institutional technique that would abolish the state: universal suffrage. But universal suffrage is for Marx something very different from what it is for the democrat: for Marx it is not the best, most legitimate, most desired form of political institutionalization. For him it already transcends the existence of the political state. For where the franchise is no longer dependent upon property qualifications, i.e., where the political ceases to be dependent upon civil society, then the whole framework of the social world is changed. Whereas in the nineteenth-century society the limited franchise only brings out the dependence of the state on property, in "true democracy," predicated upon man's communist being, universal suffrage will have the function of going beyond the state.

> In monarchy, for example, or in a republic as a mere particular form of government, political man still possesses a separate existence beside non-political man, the private individual. Property, contract, marriage, civil society appear here . . . as separate modes of existence beside the political state, as the content to which the political state relates as an organizing form. . . . In democracy the political state . . . is just a special content as well as a special mode of existence of the national. In the monarchy this separate entity, the political constitution, has the significance of the universal which controls and determines all the other separate elements. In democracy the state as a separate element is only a separate element, but as the universal it is the real universal, i.e., not a determination in the separation of the other contents. The modern French have perceived that in the true democracy the political state disappears.[30]

This disappearance of the state is also the disappearance of its contradistinction, civil society:

> The vote is the actual relation of civil society to civil society of the legislative power, to the representative element. Or, the vote is the immediate, direct, not only imagined, but also active relation of civil society to the political state. It goes without saying that the vote is the main political interest of actual civil society. In universal suffrage, both active and passive, civil society has really raised itself for the first time to an abstraction of itself, to political being as its real universal being. But the completion of

this abstraction is also at the same time the abolition (*Aufhebung*) of this abstraction. By positing its political being as its real being, civil society has also shown that its civil, non-political being is inessential. . . . Within the abstract political state the reform of the suffrage advances the dissolution of the political state, as well as the dissolution of civil society.[31]

It is thus the internal dialectics of civil society and its immanent striving after universality that will ultimately bring about this internal change leading to the abolition of both the state and civil society. In later life Marx never postulated his future vision of society on such a linear process, yet the dialectics of the inner change of civil society are always a key to the understanding of his social theory. Marx even persists in his belief that at least in the more developed of the industrial nations, universal suffrage will ultimately lead to socialism: this is the view about the function of universal suffrage in England and the United States.[32] It is in the same spirit that Marx calls in *The Communist Manifesto* the seizure of power by the proletariat "winning the battle of democracy" (*Die Erkämpfung der Demokratie*).[33] In the *Manifesto,* as well as in the *Critique,* this has very little to do with political, even radical, democracy in the traditional meaning of the term.

Our aim in this article has been to show that the basic ingredients of Marx's social philosophy—his critique of civil society and of private property, his idea of the proletariat linked to the universal class and his vision of the *Aufhebung* of the state—were already in existence in 1843 and were actually being crystallized while he was writing the *Critique.* It is further maintained that these basic ingredients of Marx's socialism make no sense outside the specific tradition of Hegelian political philosophy, and that in a way Marx sought to actualize the ultimate postulates of Hegel's *Philosophy of Right.*[34] This could not be done except through a radical break with the Hegelian system and Feuerbach's transformative method gave him the technique for this. But even this radical break with the Hegelian tradition cannot be understood except within the context of the Hegelian philosophy itself.

NOTES

This is an abridged version of a paper read at the Sixth International Hegel Congress, held in Prague, September 4-11, 1966.

1. The most important recent studies in English include: H. Marcuse, *Reason and Revolution,* 2nd edition (New York, 1954); S. Hook, *From Hegel to Marx,* new edition (Ann Arbor, 1962); G. Lichtheim, *Marxism: An Historical and Critical Study,* 2nd revised edition (New York, 1965); N. Rotenstreich, *Basic Problems of Marx's Philosophy* (Indianapolis/New York/Kansas City, 1965); L. Dupré, *The Philosophical Foundations of Marxism* (New York/Chicago/Burlingame, 1966); A. James Gregor, *A Survey of Marxism* (New York, 1965), esp. pp. 3-39. Cf. also J. Plenge, *Marx and Hegel* (Tübingen, 1911); J. Hyppolite, *Etudes sur Marx et Hegel* (Paris, 1955).

2. Marx-Engels, *Selected Works* (Moscow, 1962), I, pp. 362, 456.

3. E.g., Marx to Engels, December 9, 1861 (Marx-Engels, *Selected Correspondence,* trans. by Dona Torr [New York, n.d.], p. 129); Marx to Engels, March 25, 1868 (*ibid.,* pp. 236-237); Marx to Engels, November 7, 1868 (*ibid.,* p. 253). Cf. Liebknecht to Marx, May 13, 1870 in W. Liebknecht, *Briefwechsel mit Karl Marx und Friedrich Engels,* ed. G. Eckert (The Hague, 1963), p. 100.

4. Marx to his father, November 10, 1837 (*MEGA,* I 1/2, p. 218).

5. *Ibid.,* p. 42. For some extremely interesting remarks about Marx's early verse, see William M. Johnston, "Karl Marx's Verse of 1836-1837 as a Foreshadowing of His Early Philosophy," *Journal of the History of Ideas,* XXVIII: 2 (April-June, 1967), 259-268. Cf. also P. Demetz, *Marx, Engels and the Poets* (Chicago/London, 1967), pp. 47-49.

6. Marx to Ruge, March 5, 1842 (Marx-Engels, *Werke* [Berlin, 1963], XXVII, p. 397).

7. L. Feuerbach, "Vorläufige Thesen zur Reformation der Philosophie," in *Anekdota zur neuesten deutschen Philosophie und Publizistik* (Zurich and Winterthur, 1843), II, pp. 65f.

8. *Ibid.,* p. 71.

9. Cf. Rotenstreich, *op. cit.,* pp. 5-18.

10. Marx to Ruge, March 13, 1843 (*Werke,* XXVII, p. 417).

11. *Werke,* I, p. 27.

12. See my *The Social and Political Thought of Karl Marx* (Cambridge, 1968), ch. I.

13. *Werke,* I, pp. 267-268, 328.

14. *Hegel's Philosophy of Right,* trans. T. M. Knox (Oxford, 1942), § 291.

15. *Werke,* I, pp. 249-250.

16. *Ibid.,* p. 249.

17. *Ibid.,* p. 250. This view of the bureaucracy as an imaginary universality persists in all of Marx's later writings, especially in his account of the emergence of the French bureaucratic system in "Eighteenth Brumaire of Louis Bonaparte" and "The Civil War in France"; cf. Marx-Engels, *Selected Works* (Moscow, 1962), I, pp. 333, 518. See also the detailed draft of "The Civil War in France" which includes much material which was not included in the published version; printed in *Archiv Marksa i Engelsa* (Moscow, 1934), III (VIII), pp. 320-322. Marx had a similar analysis of the function of bureaucracies in business corporations: see his description of the structure of the East India Company in his article "The

Government of India," published in the *New York Daily Tribune*, July 20, 1853; reprinted in K. Marx, *Articles on India*, 2nd edition (Bombay, 1951), pp. 57-58.

18. K. Marx, *Early Writings*, trans. T. B. Bottomore (London, 1963), p. 56.

19. *Ibid.*, pp. 55-56. Two years later Marx argues on the same lines in *The German Ideology* (trans. R. Pascal [New York, 1960], pp. 40-41): "For each new class which puts itself in the place of one ruling before it, is compelled, merely in order to carry through its aims, to represent its interests as the common interest of all members of society put in an ideal form; it will give its ideas the form of universality. . . . The class making a revolution appears from the very start . . . not as a class but as the representative of the whole of society."

20. *Early Writings*, p. 58. Italics supplied.

21. *Ibid.*, pp. 58-59. In the *Economic-Philosophical Manuscripts* Marx follows the same argument (*ibid.*, pp. 132-133): ". . .The emancipation of society from private property, from servitude, takes the political form of the emancipation of the workers; not in the sense that only the latter's emancipation is involved, but because this emancipation included the emancipation of humanity as a whole. For all human servitude is involved in the relation of the worker to production, and all types of servitude are only modifications or consequences of this relation."

22. In *The Communist Manifesto* Marx calls the proletariat the "national class," representing the interests of the whole body politic and not of any one particular class: the term is different, the attributes are the same. Cf. *Selected Works*, I, pp. 44, 46, 51. See also *The German Ideology*, pp. 25, 75-76. From a totally different viewpoint this universalistic aspect of Marx's 'redemptive' message has been recently discussed by Père Gaston Fessard, S.J. in *Marx and the Western World*, ed. N. Lobkowicz (Notre Dame, 1967), pp. 361-362.

23. There is one notable exception, L. Dupré, *op. cit.*, pp. 103-105, where this is discussed at some length.

24. *Werke*, I, pp. 303-304.

25. *Ibid.*, pp. 305, 311.

26. Engels' ignorance of Hegel is sometimes unbelievable. The only quotation from Hegel brought by him in his *Ludwig Feuerbach and the End of German Classical Philosophy* is obviously quoted from memory and is so badly distorted that one wonders what understanding Engels must have had of Hegel if that is the way in which he remembered his theory of identity (*Selected Works*, II, p. 361). On the other hand, Engels was well aware of the contribution of Hegel to what he sometimes called "philosophic communism."

27. The orthodox Social Democratic historiography of Marx bears most of the responsibility for this view, which was then uncritically accepted and defended by the Leninists. Cf. Franz Mehring, *Karl Marx, The Story of His Life*, English trans. (Ann Arbor, 1962), p. 73.

28. *Werke*, I, p. 283. Marx also refers to 'socialized man' (*der sozialisierte Mensch*) in another instance of the same discussion (*ibid.*, p. 231).

29. "Civil society and the state are separated from one another. The citizen of the state and the member of civil society are also separated. Man has to effect an essential schism with himself" (*ibid.*, p. 281). Cf. *Early Writings*, p. 20.

30. *Werke*, I, pp. 231-232.

31. *Ibid.*, pp. 230-231.

32. Cf. Marx's article "The Chartists" in the *New York Daily Tribune* of August 25, 1852. "The carrying out of Universal Suffrage in England would, therefore, be a far more socialistic measure than anything which has been honoured with that name on the Continent. Its inevitable result, here, is the political supremacy of the working class." See also Marx's Amsterdam Speech of 1872, as quoted in *The First International: Minutes of Hague Congress of 1872*, ed. H. Gerth (Madison, 1958), p. 236: "We do not deny that there are countries like England and America, and if I am familiar with your institutions, Holland, where labour may attain its goal by peaceful means."

33. *Selected Works*, I, p. 53.

34. It is amazing to find out how little attention this element has received in orthodox Communist literature, where the references to Hegel's impact usually follow Engels' dogmatic account in *Ludwig Feuerbach*. Only recently have some Soviet and other Eastern European studies become aware of the relevance of Hegel's *Philosophy of Right* to the understanding of Marx. See e.g., A. A. Piontkowskij, "Zur Frage der Politischen Wertung der Hegelschen Rechtsphilosophie," in *Studien zur Hegels Rechtsphilosophie in USSR* (Moskau, 1966; in mimeograph), pp. 1-24; Milan Sobotka, "Die idealistische Dialektik der Praxis bei Hegel," *Acta Universitatis Carolinae*, IX (Praha, 1965); Milan Sobotka, "Freiheit und Eigentum in Hegels Rechtsphilosophie," *Filosofický Časopis*, XIV:4 (1966), pp. 483-492; Ivan Dubsky, "Hegels Arbeitsbegriff und die idealistische Dialektik," *Rozpravy Československé akademie věd*, LXXI: 14 (1961). See also Adam Schaff, *Marxismus und das menschliche Individuum*, translated from Polish by Erna Reifer (Wien, 1965).

2 : *The Young Marx*
A Reappraisal

DONALD C. HODGES

A new lease on life has recently been given to Marx studies in this country. Scholars are reinterpreting the later works of Marx in terms of his earlier writings and presenting a humanistic image of them congenial to the academic community.[1] It is well known how Marx's writings have come under fire as a result of public distortion and academic misconceptions, not to mention their internal weaknesses and the fact that several of his predictions have gone awry. Unfortunately, the second renascence of Marx scholarship has taken on the character of a salvage operation designed to preserve not only his enduring contribution to the methods of the social sciences but also materials from Marx's own wastebasket.

Myopic commentators have made far too much of the content of Marx's early work at the expense of his method. Furthermore, they have contributed more to the revival of obsolete formulations that Marx himself had abandoned and less to the development and application of his materialistic-critical outlook. As a matter of fact, some of his immediate followers made a similar mistake, prompting him to

Originally published in *Philosophy and Phenomenological Research*, XXVII:2, December 1966, 216-229.

declare that, for all he knew, he was not a Marxist.[2] Since he out-grew the humanistic content of his earlier works, we are confronted with the irony of his current apologists adopting a position alien to Marx himself. Paradoxically, their professed sympathy for his early writings has not prevented them from being anti-Marxist on matters of fundamental import to Marx, the political economist and soci-ologist.

Especially noteworthy among recent would-be scholars of Marx-ism is the absence of an awareness both of the historical significance of what they are doing and of any distinction between the historical Marx and their humanistic image of him. First of all, I am distressed by the efforts of commentators to reconstruct the historical Marx without considering the social conditions and biases of their own attempts at reconstruction. And, secondly, I am increasingly ir-ritated by recent philosophical attempts to make his early human-ism, if we are to call it that, respectable in the light of ethical culture and the mental health movement. In any case, the rash of recent literature on Marx's views concerning alienation is a challenge to the critic to set matters straight. Consequently, I should like, first, to consider the historical significance of current reinterpretations of Marxism in this country and, second, to reconsider the alleged humanism of the young Marx as presented in his *Economic and Philosophic Manuscripts of 1844.*[3]

I

There have been two brief periods since the Great Depression in which Americans have witnessed a renascence of Marx studies on their own soil. The first was during the middle thirties and early forties during which Marx, the economist and political scientist, seemed to many to offer the only warranted explanation of the Great Depression and the only practical solution to its problems of cyclical crisis and unemployment. The second occurred only recent-ly during the close of the fifties when the publication of the first English translation of Marx's early *Economic and Philosophic Manu-scripts* coincided with increasing affluence and the prospect of a return of Asiatic Marxism to the humanism of the European tradition.

Each of these revivals has encouraged and developed a different image of Marx. The most recent wave of scholarship has focused upon Marx's investigation of personal crises and dehumanization rather than economic dislocation and growth in underdeveloped countries. In response to the intensified drive toward consumption, humanists have interpreted Marx's early manuscripts with an eye to self-alienation and other obstacles to self-fulfillment.[4] While in the newly emerging nations it is Marx, the socialist, rather than the humanist, who is currently enjoying a popular revival, in this country Marx scholarship shows the effects of a quite different preoccupation with studies of anxiety, anomie, and related problems of mental health. And for these problems a diagnosis and a remedy are sought in Marx, the alienist and exorciser of neuroses.

Both the recent and earlier renascences of Marx scholarship have been the work of independent scholars, whose Marxism is of the open variety in contrast to the closed Marxism of the official Socialist, Communist, and Trotskyist spokesmen. The first generation of open Marxists included such names as Vernon Venable, the early Hook, Howard Selsam, Barrows Dunham, Herbert Marcuse, Paul Sweezy, Lewis Feuer, and the early Fromm. The second generation includes some of these along with comparative newcomers like Daniel Bell, Michael Harrington, Robert Tucker, and William Ash. Common to both is an openness to supplementary hypotheses within the framework of Marx's materialist historiography and the political economy predicated upon his labor theory of value.

Open Marxists stop short of criticizing the premises of Marx's model on the basis of which Marx made his several diagnoses. Any other sense of open Marxism is simply misleading. Witness C. Wright Mills' category of plain Marxists in which he apparently includes himself along with Joan Robinson, although neither is ordinarily classified as an open Marxist for the understandable reason that they rejected the premises of Marx's model along with his forecasts.[5] If anything, they used Marx as a springboard rather than a crutch. While they read him with some benefit it was to incorporate what they could into their own independent programs of social research.

Springboard Marxists do not belong to the Marxian tradition, but have used it for their own purposes as the name suggests. In this group may be included Lawrence Dennis, James Burnham, Johannes Alasco, George Orwell, and Michael Young. We should be hard pressed to call any of them socialists in the Marxian sense. Although several of them are or have been professed humanists, it is noteworthy that humanism was not an integral part of the premises of Marx's model of society. Current efforts toward a reassessment of Marx have come from at least two different quarters, notably from Marxists with an open mind and from those non-Marxists who have used Marxism as a springboard. If they have not been equally successful it is because open Marxists have looked to the past while springboard Marxists were riding the wave of the future. Since open Marxism continues to be the victim of cultural lag, efforts to breathe new life into the Marxian model have been less effective than efforts to revise and alter it in the light of contemporary developments.

It has been a matter of principle for each of the major revivals of Marx studies in this country to claim intellectual independence of the U.S.S.R. In fact, however, each has been closely allied to corresponding economic and political developments within the Soviet Union. The first renascence corresponded to the period of the popular front thaw of the middle thirties, the Stalin Constitution of 1936, and the emergence of Russia as an ally of the United States and a major partner in the United Nations. The second corresponds to the Khrushchev era of partial liberalization and postrevolutionary coexistence with capitalism. Now that the Soviet Union has arrived at a stage of comparative affluence, appreciation for the humanism of the young Marx is not confined to the West alone.

As a matter of fact, the Soviet Union seems to have led the way in awakening interest in the young Marx. The first English translation of the *Economic and Philosophic Manuscripts* was published in Moscow in 1956, presumably for foreign consumption. A new Russian edition was published during the same year, testifying to the increasing domestic interest in the work. In conjunction with the de-Stalinization campaign in the Soviet Union and the thaw in Eastern Europe, there emerged a new rationale for socialism formulated in the language of Marx's early writings. In place of the former emphasis upon exploitation and the problems of organized labor, attention shifted to the alienation of man in general and to the morality of socialist humanism. The internal shift of interest from production to consumption was paralleled by the intellectuals' shift from Marx's mature writings on political economy to his youthful works on philosophical anthropology and corresponding critique of human culture. As the futility of Marx's focus upon the labor movement became increasingly evident, a new Marx and a novel interpretation of Marxism appeared unrelated to the interests of manual workers.

In comparing the earlier and later renascences of Marx's thought, it is noteworthy that the first was considerably less open-minded than the second. This is largely because the mature Marx was deliberately one-sided and illiberal, even narrow-minded.[6] Consequently, much less reworking of his early thesis concerning alienation has been required to make this humanism palatable to English readers. In part this is because Marx's early writings have something to say about self-development, whereas his mature works concentrate upon the complexities of the economic process. Intellectuals have found the humanist content in the works of the early Marx to be far more congenial to their tastes than the scientific and partisan content of his later works.

However, this humanist image of Marx is a grossly distorted one.[7] There is even a suggestion that contemporary Marx scholars are so wide open that they have begun to depart from the spirit as well as the letter of Marx's own writing. However this may be, there is at least one notable difference between those who used Marxism as a springboard in the thirties and forties and those who currently call themselves open Marxists. The former gave an ideological picture of the Marxist model, but ended by rejecting it. The latter present an ideological picture albeit of Marx's early works, but conclude by accepting it. Distortion of the early Marx is apparently an argument for reviving as well as burying him.

II

I should now like to recover, if not the essential Marx, at least that aspect of his early work that is of lasting importance to the labor movement. The universalistic and largely academic image of his youthful contributions tends to minimize their partisan character. Furthermore, in an historical epoch in which the labor movements of the affluent societies have bartered themselves for a mess of potage, there is a special need to reassess these contributions to a philosophy of the proletariat.

In Marx's early writings we find at least two distinct intellectual enterprises and corresponding critiques of human alienation. On the one hand, Marx set himself the general critical and philosophical task of unmasking self-alienation in its secular forms through a critique of the ideological content of law, ethics, politics, economics, etc.[8] On the other hand, he also became increasingly preoccupied with the revolutionary and practical task of exposing the alienation of the laborer. The Marx who was interested in reification made a major contribution to the sociology of knowledge of which he is now acknowledged as the father.[9] The other Marx, concerned specifically with problems of vital concern to the trade unions, went a different route by laying the foundations of a social science for the working-man.

The young Marx was clearly a humanist, and it is to him that the new revisionists of Marxism have turned. However, in attempting to make a similar case for the humanism of the later Marx they do more than stretch a point. Philosophical platitudes concerning the alienation of humanity, Marx wrote, are a weak substitute for the economic criticism of bourgeois society.[10] In the *Communist Manifesto* humanism was considered not as a proletarian but as a bourgeois doctrine stemming from the French Revolution and Enlightenment. The failure of the humanists lay in representing the "interests of human nature, of man in general, who belongs to no class, has no reality, and subsists only in the realm of philosophical fantasy."[11]

The focus of the young Marx's concern is now widely believed to have been a critique of human alienation. This term "alienation" has become broad enough to include hostility toward a customary environment or associations, loss of contact with things and an inability to relate to other people, even loss of self-control, not to mention ideological thinking and the reification of ideas. Under the rubric of "alienation" is currently included not only the conveyance of property to another and, in a broader sense, the transfer of a right or claim but also mental disorders and illusions of various kinds. The universe of economic theory in which things are personified, the conditions of production are converted into entities, and the social elements of wealth are ossified and isolated also typifies a form of "alienation." However, to focus upon any one of these usages in characterizing the concern of the young Marx is to miss precisely those forms of alienation that most interested him, notably, the estrangement of the producers from their own labor, from the products of their labor, from themselves or some aspect of themselves in their capacity as laborers, and from other men.

In the *Economic and Philosophic Manuscripts of 1844* we see that Marx was as much concerned to criticize alienation in the form of the exploitation of the producers as to criticize different forms of ideological thinking. Throughout the 1840s the goal of humanist enlightenment was subordinated by Marx to the goal of changing the world and emancipating the workers in particular. Dissatisfied with a purely philosophical struggle against darkness and superstition, the fetishism of social institutions and ideologies, he turned increasingly to an attack upon the proprietary classes. Not ignorance, but human oppression became the core of his continuing interest in alienation.

A corresponding shift of interest can be seen in his early and later approaches to the estrangement of the laborer from his conditions of work.[12] In the early manuscripts he seems to have been primarily concerned with the dehumanization of the laborer, with the absence of meaning in work, and with the fragmentation of life-activity under the division of labor. Subsequently, he appears to have been more interested in the laborer's loss of a part of his product, and in that portion of his energies uncompensated by his employers. The dehumanization of labor could be rectified only by abolishing the division of labor; the uncompensated appropriation of his energies only by the abolition of exploitation.

Marx's slogan, "the emancipation of the workers," was loose enough to cover both goals. Although we find the mature Marx more concerned with the abolition of exploitation, the young Marx was by no means indifferent to it.[13] Turning away from a general pre-occupation with the alienation of self-consciousness and of the abstract, nonhistorical individual, Marx stressed the estrangement of the laborer from the capitalistic mode of production. While using the Feuerbachian vocabulary of "man, the species being," "naturalism," "humanism," "humaneness," and so forth, he gives to these terms a partisan content. Instead of man in general, the laborer in particular becomes the focus of the 1844 manuscripts.

Recent interpreters of the young Marx have been led astray by his obscure adaptation of Feuerbach's language. Thus the mistakes typical of current humanistic interpretations come from attributing both an ethical and a psychological content to the earlier writings. In the first place, Marx's criticisms of bourgeois property are interpreted as "ethical evaluations of the degree to which social structures realize an ideal of authentic being, i.e., nonestranged or unalienated existence."[14] In this light the original purpose of Marx's social theory was to analyze the conditions of moral as well as social development—his interest in the phenomenon of estrangement was primarily an ethical one.[15] Secondly, Marx's discussion of estrangement in the *Economic and Philosophic Manuscripts* is interpreted as a contribution to the social psychology of industrial society. The successful businessman who wishes to treat his workers in a Christian manner is cited as a prime example of self-alienation. Thus the individual, and it could be anyone, becomes the center of an institutional conflict represented by conflicting value-patterns. Considering the resulting efforts at rationalization, we have here "a paradigm case of a *socially-induced* neurosis—the state of alienation or estrangement."[16]

In criticism of the moralistic image of these manuscripts, it is noteworthy that Marx's discussion of alienation conspicuously lacks a normative vocabulary. Despite occasional references to man's real or authentic life, he has literally nothing to say concerning the rights and duties of man.[17] For the young Marx there is an alienation of the laborer's product, but no inalienable right to the equivalent of his labor. Here Marx parts company with his predecessor Locke, for whom there was such a right. As a matter of fact, Marx goes beyond the realist Hobbes in denying even a right to self-preservation. As much as the term self-alienation suggests a corresponding inalienable right of personality, there is no such right acknowledged by Marx.

Although the worker is alienated, he lacks the right to be free. This is precisely Marx's point. For the only effective rights are legal ones, and lacking these the worker's only hope is to organize in the struggle to secure protection. Any other talk about rights is evidence not only of impotence, but also of dependence upon a quasi-magical authority that has no power. Ethics is hardly an effective substitute for action.

Efforts to psychologize Marx's early manuscripts are objectionable on other grounds. Marx was not an alienist, and to attribute to him an interest in dissolving neuroses or in promoting mental health in general is to travel the altogether different road that Freud took. If anything, the neuroses and mental ailments of the workers' employers were regarded as a divisive and demoralizing factor, as an asset rather than a liability. The last thing Marx had in mind was to benefit the alienators and exploiters of mankind. Although he used in his manuscripts the Feuerbachian language of humanism he was not in any ethical usage of the term a humanist. On the contrary, Marx's variety of humanist was a revolutionary communist bent on annulling the forms of bourgeois property underlying the alienation of the laborer.[18] Although he also had kind words for what he called the positive humanism of the future, he noted that its effectiveness depends upon the prior annulment of bourgeois property.[19] Let us not forget that the counterpart of the alienated worker was not for the young Marx an alienated bourgeois. On the contrary, "such freedom as exists in capitalist society is enjoyed by the owners of the means of production and entails as its logical antithesis the slavery of the proletariat."[20] Paradoxically, the writer just quoted laments the fact that Marx's discussion of alienation was so narrowly limited at the same time that he belabors the thesis of the young Marx's alleged humanism.

Besides these misguided efforts to moralize and psychologize upon the early contributions of Marx, current discussions of his *Economic and Philosophic Manuscripts* are misleading in imputing to him a theory of alienation which, as I have already intimated, is applicable to the human situation as such rather than to the special conditions of the laborer under capitalism. As a result, critics almost invariably ignore Marx's distinction between the alienated activities that degrade some men and the alienated conditions that upgrade others.

A careful reading of the *Economic and Philosophic Manuscripts,* as I hope to show, reveals that Marx was concerned not with the sources of social pathology in general, but with the alienation of the worker in particular. Not only does this work contain the elements of a theory of class struggle, but also a discussion of alienation that was subsequently to be developed into a full-fledged theory of economic exploitation. Contrary to the current consensus concerning the work, Marx's discussion of alienation is set within the framework of an economic theory rather than a social psychology, a political economy of labor rather than a psychology of personality and human growth.

Humanists sympathetic to the young Marx have compared the early manuscripts with the later ones and noted the radical differences in terminology, viz., the abandonment of the language of alienation and humanism for the language of exploitation and socialism. These differences in terminology are sometimes taken as symptomatic of a fundamental difference in content. Regardless of disagreements on this question, however, the tendency of critics is to exaggerate the significance of Marx's remark that "the emancipation of the workers contains universal human emancipation."[21] For most of them the alienation of the worker was less at stake for Marx than the whole of human alienation. The employers, it has been said, are no less alienated than the workers, although their alienation takes a different form. Anomie, deviant behavior, homelessness, uprootedness, loneliness, isolation, anxiety, boredom, despair, and the quest for identity are currently regarded as forms of alienation to be found at all levels of society, although some forms are more typical of one group than another.[22] The question is whether Marx was concerned with such a wide range of behavioral disorders, which have since been lumped under the general heading of "alienation."

Unlike current uses of the term, Marx's usage was first and foremost economic. He distinguished four different kinds of alienation for the laborer: from his product; from his laboring activity; from his uniquely human capacities; and from his fellow men. Whether or not there are other kinds of alienation, the *Manuscripts* were concerned with elucidating chiefly those forms of estrangement concealed by the abstractions of classical political economy.[23] The first two forms are clearly economic, and it is also comparatively evident that they are not relevant to mankind or individual men, but only to a particular class of men. However, Marx's interpreters are almost unanimous in agreeing that the third and fourth kinds of alienation pertain to all human beings. A major source of confusion is linguistic. For the terms themselves, self-alienation and alienation of mankind, do not exclusively refer to the class of modern laborers. Hence the impression that it is not solely the laborer but individual man who is estranged, that the human condition and not simply the life of the average worker is alienated as a whole.

Consider Marx's discussion of self-alienation. In addition to estranging the laborer from his product and from his laboring activity, the labor process also alienates him from his own body that must serve another, and from his unique capacities of speech and ratiocination that become his means for obtaining employment. Instead of working for the delight of creating something original and pleasing to himself, he must subordinate his own interests as a human being to the requirements of the labor process.[24] He suffers from personal impoverishment; he must live in order to labor instead of laboring for the sake of individual fulfillment. For Marx, in other words, the laborer more than anyone else tends to become self-alienated.

Furthermore, through alienating his labor-power, he is more likely to become estranged from other men: "An immediate consequence of the fact that man is estranged from the product of his labor, from his life activity, from his species being is the *estrangement of man from man*. . . . What applies to a man's relation to his works, to the product of his labor and to himself, also holds of a man's relation to the other man, and to the other man's labor and object of labor."[25] The laborer is estranged from his employers for reasons obvious enough, and he is estranged from his fellow laborers with whom he must compete for jobs. Since he is estranged from his own person as a laboring being, he is also alienated from the dwarfed and brutalized personalities of other laborers, who likewise exist in order to serve others.

In the manuscripts of 1844, alienation involves a specific economic transaction between an alienor and an alienee. The latter is the beneficiary of the transaction, for whom alienation is the necessary condition of appropriation. As a result of this transaction, the worker also finds himself alienated from his vital energies and productive activities (self-alienation) and from the lives and activities of other persons (social alienation). These two forms of alienation are pre-eminently economic. Consequently, they might appear to lack universal human significance. The annulment of the condition of alienated labor means first and foremost the economic and social emancipation of workers and their dependents from the conditions of human servitude. Yet more than their own emancipation and that of their families is at stake in this act of annulment. For, according to Marx, every relation of servitude is but a modification and consequence of the alienated role of the worker in production.[26]

"Till now we have only considered this relationship [of alienation] from the standpoint of the worker. . . ."[27] The question is how Marx also considered it from the standpoint of nonworkers. Appropriation and alienation are opposite sides of the same coin: for every one who alienates his property, his labor, his life-activity, there is someone else who appropriates them. The worker's product is self-alienated; it is also other-appropriated. The worker alienates his energies; the bourgeois acquires them for his own use. Far from being self-alienated, the bourgeois is self-possessed. The alienor of his own energies is self-alienated, not the alienee. Corresponding to Marx's fundamental division of capitalist society into property-owners and propertyless workers is a division into alien persons and alienated men.[28]

In considering the relation of alien persons to the alienated workers, Marx notes the following: first, what appears to the worker as a personal activity of alienation appears to the nonworker as an impersonal condition of existence and as a natural state of affairs; second, what the worker suffers directly in his own person as a consequence of alienation may be witnessed by the nonworker, but cannot be directly experienced by him; and third, what the worker does against himself in his alienated activity is also done to him by the nonworker, although the nonworker does not injure himself in injuring the worker.[29] At this point the first manuscript breaks off unfinished, so that it is difficult to know precisely what Marx intended by this brief outline. At most, we can say that one man's alienation implies another's act of appropriation, and that the laborer's bondage is a condition of freedom for the owners. Thus the young Marx: "If the worker's activity is a torment to him, to another it must be *delight* and his life's joy."[30] Although the worker may be the last to admit it, not the gods but other men possess this alien power over him. Since these other men stand outside and above the labor process, they are obviously not victimized by the laws of political economy expressing the estrangement of the worker in his object. Although Marx goes on to note that the emancipation of workers from their activity of alienation implies universal human emancipation, in the context in which he makes this statement it is clear that it is not the owners and buyers of labor-power who are liberated by this act, but only people in a servile relation to others, i.e., "the whole of human servitude."[31]

But are the proprietary classes not also in a kind of servitude to bourgeois property? Are they not in some sense slaves to the power of money? Money, says Marx, is "the alienated ability of mankind."[32] The question is: "Whose abilities"? Surely not the abilities of the proprietary classes, but rather those of the producers. Let us grant that you cannot buy the same kind of love with money that you can elicit by becoming yourself an affectionate person. The abilities I purchase from others seldom issue in the same degree of satisfaction as those I cultivate myself. Nonetheless, "by possessing the property of appropriating all objects, money is thus the object of eminent possession."[33] Money is the pimp between my need and the object of my need; but I am not oppressed by its power unless I lack money, unless I prostitute myself, my life-activity, for the sake of survival or for the dreams that only money can buy.

It is tempting to infer from Marx's language that businessmen, too, are estranged both from their immediate competitors and from their hired hands. Even the most privileged individual may fall under the inhuman sway of money and the corresponding slavery of accumulation. However, money becomes an alien power to Marx's alien person only in the sense of a fetish, when it becomes desired for its own sake and not solely for the power it commands. To the enlightened bourgeois, it is a means and not an end. In any case, the alienation peculiar to the propertied person does not result from the act of alienating his productive capacities to another. Although money is the alienated ability of mankind, it has an altogether different function in the hands of the proprietor than in the hands of wage-earners. For the wage-earner it represents man's "estranged, alienating, and self-disposing *species-nature.* "[34] For the proprietor it represents a surrogate humanity, the abilities of other men that can become one's own through possessing a legal title.[35] Although money expresses the worker's condition of alienation, the ownership of money is for others a condition of freedom.

Over and above the forms of alienation that are common to members of all classes, the laborer must daily perform alienated labor for his employer. The proprietor does not have to choose between human bondage or death by starvation. Furthermore, self-cultivation and enlightenment are safeguards against alienation, and he has the means and leisure to acquire both. At worst, the condition of the bourgeois is a metaphorical servitude like the kind we impute to persons lacking self-control. Although the slavery of the passions has traditionally come under the heading of self-alienation, it is a far cry from the kind of alienation that interested the youthful Marx. In a sense, any person may become self-alienated in consequence of frustrations posed by his individual character and personality. More important to the young Marx, however, were the frustrations arising from the mode of production. Although deformations of character are frequently conditioned by the latter, they raise pre-eminently personal problems rather than social ones.

Perhaps this is why in his mature works Marx focused upon the exploitation instead of upon the alienation of the laborer. At least this is the principal reason why Marxists have neglected and continue to neglect problems pertinent to the individual as an individual rather than as a member of a social class. Recently, in response to the pressures of atheistic existentialism in Poland and France there has arisen a dialogue in which Marxists, too, have offered counsel on such problems of personal interest as the meaning of life, the destiny of man and his responsibility to society.[36] However, they seem to have forgotten that not even the young Marx, at least not the author of the *Economic and Philosophic Manuscripts,* was ever seriously preoccupied with these issues.

We know that very early in his career Marx came to reject his youthful humanism. But there is another sense in which he remained a humanist to the end of his life. Consequently, what he rejected in the *Manuscripts* was not humanism in general, but rather the universalistic humanism of the left Hegelians and Feuerbach in particular.

How important, then, were the *Manuscripts* to the historical Marx? Looking back, he regarded them as theoretically obsolete and downright misleading. In the first place, they still showed traces of his Hegelian apprenticeship and the influence of Feuerbach. And, secondly, they contained only a very rough draft of his first investigations into political economy, which he never bothered to revise. Publishing them could have been embarrassing and, in any case, would have served no useful purpose. The original contribution of his work seems to have been self-clarification for which a publisher was hardly necessary. In effect did Marx not abandon his early work, as he once commented concerning another manuscript, to the gnawing criticism of the mice?

NOTES

1. See, for example, D. Braybrooke, "Diagnosis and Remedy in Marx's Doctrine of Alienation," *Social Research,* XXV:3 (Autumn 1958), 325-345; F. Pappenheim, *The Alienation of Modern Man* (New York, 1959); D. Bell, "Two Roads from Marx: The Themes of Alienation and Exploitation and Workers' Control in Socialist Thought," *The End of Ideology* (New York, 1960), pp. 355-392; R. C. Tucker, *Philosophy and Myth in Karl Marx* (Cambridge University, 1961), pp. 132-176; E. Fromm, *Marx's Concept of Man* (New York, 1961), pp. 43-58; L. D. Easton, "Alienation and History in the Early Marx," *Philosophy and Phenomenological Research,* XXII:2 (December 1961), 193-205; Michael Harrington, "Marx versus Marx," *New Politics* (Fall 1961), pp. 112-123; Dirk J. Struik and Gary L. Chamberlain, "Symposium on the Young Marx," *Science and Society,* XXVII:3 (Summer 1963), 283-320; H. L. Parsons, "The Prophetic Mission of Karl Marx," *Journal of Religion,* XLIV:1 (January 1964), 52-71; H. L. Parsons, "Value and Mental Health

in the Thought of Marx," *Philosophy and Phenomenological Research*, XXIV:3 (March 1964), 355-365; J. O'Neill, "The Concept of Estrangement in the Early and Later Writings of Karl Marx," *Philosophy and Phenomenological Research*, XXV:1 (September 1964), 64-84; W. Ash, *Marxism and Moral Concepts* (New York, 1964), pp. 136-167; E. Fromm, ed., *Socialist Humanism* (New York, 1965); and the international symposium papers on "Marx and the Western World," presented at the University of Notre Dame, April 24-28, 1966.

2. See Engels' letter to Conrad Schmidt, London, August 5, 1890, *Marx and Engels: Basic Writings on Politics and Philosophy*, ed. L. S. Feuer (Garden City, 1959), p. 396.

3. All subsequent page references to this work are to the first complete English edition translated by M. Milligan (Moscow, 1956).

4. For current non-Marxist discussions of the problem of alienation, see the popular anthologies by Eric and Mary Josephson, eds., *Man Alone: Alienation in Modern Society* (New York, 1962), and H. M. Ruitenbeek, ed., *Varieties of Modern Social Theory* (New York, 1963).

5. C. Wright Mills, *The Marxists* (New York, 1962), p. 98.

6. "Manifesto of the Communist Party," in Feuer, *op. cit.*, pp. 33-35.

7. For the current academic counter-thesis that Marx subsequently abandoned his humanist orientation, see D. Bell, "The Rediscovery of Alienation," *Journal of Philosophy*, LVI:24 (November 1959), 933-952; L. S. Feuer, "What is Alienation? The Career of a Concept," *New Politics* (Spring 1962), pp. 116-134; D. C. Hodges, "The Unity of Marx's Thought," *Science and Society*, XXVIII:3 (Summer 1964); and D. C. Hodges, "Marx's Contribution to Humanism," *Science and Society*, XXIX:1 (Winter 1965). This counter-interpretation is about as offensive to the academic community in this country as it is to intellectuals in Western Europe and the U.S.S.R.

8. "Toward the Critique of Hegel's Philosophy of Right," in Feuer, *Marx and Engels, op. cit.*, p. 263. See also Marx's Preface to the *Economic and Philosophic Manuscripts*, pp. 14-20.

9. Irving L. Horowitz, *Philosophy, Science and the Sociology of Knowledge* (Springfield, 1961), pp. 10-11, 32-33, 65, 87; and Irving L. Horowitz, "Social Science Objectivity and Value Neutrality: Historical Problems and Projections," *Diogenes*, No. 39, pp. 24-25.

10. "Manifesto of the Communist Party," *loc. cit.*

11. *Ibid.*, p. 34.

12. See D. Bell, "Two Roads from Marx," *op. cit.*, pp. 362, 367, 386-7.

13. Bell also makes this point, *ibid.*, p. 361.

14. O'Neill, *op. cit.*, p. 69. For a similar thesis see the essays by H. L. Parsons.

15. *Ibid.*, pp. 71, 80, 83.

16. *Ibid.*, pp. 79-80.

17. For further discussion of Marx's ethics and ethical theory see my "Historical Materialism in Ethics," *Philosophy and Phenomenological Research*, XXIII:1 (September 1962); "Socialists in Search of an Ethic," *Studies on the Left*, III:2 (Winter 1963); and "Marxist Ethics and Ethical Theory," *The Socialist Register*, eds. R. Miliband and J. Saville (London, 1964).

18. *Economic and Philosophic Manuscripts*, p. 164.

19. *Loc. cit.*

20. O'Neill, *op. cit.*, p. 78.

21. *Economic and Philosophic Manuscripts*, p. 82.
22. Josephson, *op. cit.;* and Ruitenbeek, *op. cit.*
23. *Economic and Philosophic Manuscripts*, pp. 67-8, 71f.
24. *Ibid.*, p. 76.
25. *Ibid.*, p. 77.
26. *Ibid.*, p. 82.
27. *Ibid.*, p. 80.
28. *Ibid.*, p. 83.
29. *Loc. cit.*
30. *Ibid.*, p. 79.
31. *Ibid.*, p. 82.
32. *Ibid.*, p. 139.
33. *Ibid.*, p. 137.
34. *Ibid.*, p. 139.
35. *Ibid.*, pp. 139-141.
36. See Adam Schaff, *A Philosophy of Man* (New York, 1963), pp. 24-87.

3. The Young and the Old Marx

IRING FETSCHER

INTRODUCTION TO THE PROBLEM

In the old European social democratic parties, Karl Marx was honored as a great economist, as the writer of *Das Kapital,* a book intended to prove the inevitable decline of the capitalistic system with scientific rigor. In the perspective of Lenin's interpretation of Marxism and the activities of the Communist International, Marx appeared to be first of all a political thinker who taught the working class to create its own organization as a basis for the seizure of political power. Under this perspective, the "Critique of the Gotha Programme" was praised as one of Marx's most important contributions. However in the development of the Communist *Weltanschauung* of the Socialist and of Communist parties, Friedrich Engels and even Joseph Dietzgen were far more significant and influential than Marx himself.

In part this view results because the young Marx, that is, Marx the *philosopher,* was almost unknown and absolutely neglected until the

Originally published in Nicholas Lobkowicz (ed.), *Marx and the Western World,* University of Notre Dame Press, 1967, pp. 19-39.

publications of Karl Korsch and Georg Lukács in 1923. The early
writings of Marx, known to some experts, were held to be brilliant
but not genuinely Marxist, and as such they were at best believed to
be significant for our evaluation of the genesis, not for the understanding, of Marx's mature works. In this respect, the words with
which Mehring in his 1918 biography of Marx ended the chapter on
his early writings are characteristic of the then prevailing appreciation of the young Marx:

> Thus in shadowy contours we observe an outline of socialist soci-
> ety beginning to form. In the *Deutsch-Französische Jahrbücher,*
> Marx is still ploughing the philosophic field, but in the furrows
> turned over by his critical ploughshare the first shoots of the
> materialist conception of history began to sprout, and under the
> warm sun of French civilization they soon began to flower.[1]

Consequently the philosophical writings of Marx were understood
as the first steps toward a scientific method of historical materialism
that obviously was not considered to be a philosophy, and thus
Marx's early writings were inevitably considered "immature" whereas even the publications of a socialist as theoretically feeble as
Kautsky were taken to be far-reaching applications of the supposedly scientific method inaugurated by Marx.

Karl Korsch and Georg Lukács had grown up in an entirely different intellectual climate. They not only knew the neo-Kantian
theory of knowledge but also Hegel's philosophy; moreover Lukács
was familiar with the problems of the differentiation between the
natural sciences on the one side and the humanities and the social
sciences on the other through his early contacts with such outstanding representatives of neo-Kantianism as Emil Lask and Max Weber.
The logic of inquiry within these disciplines could no longer be
conceived of as a universally applicable theory, and consequently
difference between causal and/or functional analysis on the one
hand and the interpretation of cultural phenomena in their complete
totality (*Sinnverstehen*) on the other was, from now on, held to be
fundamental. Wilhelm Dilthey, no less than Max Weber, belonged to
the great inspiring masters. Consequently Lukács and Korsch, il-
luminated by the ideas of this most recent epoch of the history of
German philosophy and with the intention of helping the revolu-

tionary consciousness to an adequate and deeper understanding of its own contemporary status, went back to Hegel and the young Marx although they did not and could not know all early writings of Marx at that time.

The reproaches against Lukács and Korsch from the side of the social democratic and Communist orthodox writers were raised as a defense. Not only was the older interpretation of Marx's theory as an economic theory threatened, so also was a general method of historical investigation. Lukács and Korsch insinuated that Marx had cast the problems of the bourgeois philosophy into a more adequate mold with deeper understanding than could have been achieved by the bourgeois philosophers themselves and on a new basis which definitely opened a way for final solution. To the ideologues of the social democratic and Communist parties, it still appeared necessary to emphasize the radical difference between the bourgeois and the proletarian revolution, on the one hand, and the two *Weltanschauungen*, on the other hand. Lukács, and later on Max Horkheimer, Walter Benjamin, Herbert Marcuse and Theodor Adorno even thought that to stress the continuity of the bourgeois and the revolutionary movements was most important because of the fact that the German and Italian bourgeoisie were in the age of fascism about to betray the ideals of their own past. They endeavored to show to the bourgeois intellectuals the gulf between the liberal principles and humanitarian aspirations of the early bourgeoisie and the meaning and scope of the modern barbarianism which grew out, as they thought, of the antagonism of contemporary capitalist society and led to fascism.

Both the dangers of fascism and the reappraisal of Hegel's philosophy led to a new interpretation of Marx's early writings. Humanism, a genuine constituent of Marx's early works, could no longer be taken for granted. It was negated in practice and disavowed in theory by the fascist movements as well as Stalinism. Thus the time was obviously ripe to win the young Marx as an ally in the fight against these forms of rising barbarism.

This in turn necessitated reappraisal of Hegel's philosophy. Therefore the authors just mentioned set out to fight against the myth of Hegel as the Prussian state philosopher. They took up an issue with which Marx and Engels had already dealt but which had again become accentuated by the mystification of Hegel in works like those of Kuno Fischer and other authors of imperial Germany.

While the representatives of positivist neoliberalism denounced Hegel (and with him Rousseau and other modern philosophers of democracy), these authors emphasized the perspicacity with which Hegel had anticipated the pitfalls and inconsistencies of the liberal society and its elementary dynamics and with which he already had seen through the liberal formulation of the rights of man.

The interpretation of Marx's early writings, of course, depended to a great extent on the evaluation of the bourgeois philosophical tradition. Whereas Lukács and Korsch interpreted Marx's intentions as an attempt to solve by a radical theory and revolutionary *praxis* the problems with which the bourgeois philosophy could not come to grips, Marx was, according to the doctrines of Social Democrats and Communists, the founder of a scientific proletarian *Weltanschauung* that they contrasted emphatically with the *Weltanschauung* of the bourgeoisie. Because both political movements, Social Democracy and Communism, intended to create their own *Weltanschauung*—each of course with a specific character—they had to stress the difference between Hegel and the young Marx on the one hand and the old Marx on the other; and consequently, both had to de-emphasize Marx's early writings. To the ideologues of Stalinism, the discussion of and the references to the young Marx were inexpedient because Marx in his early writings spoke of the proletarian revolution and socialism as a means for the realization of a genuinely human society and not as absolute and dogmatic standards. The new Soviet society, labeled socialist by its own ideologues, was threatened to be exposed to criticism based on the characteristics Marx attributed to a truly "human society." This conception obviously and definitely stood, among other things, in sharp contrast to the conception of the state and law as it was propagated by the Stalinist orthodox writers as by many others.

In the light of the motives I have just mentioned, which functioned as an impediment to the incorporation of the young Marx into the theories and doctrines of the labor movement, the rather late and first publication of the important parts of his early writings, above all the *Philosophic and Economic Manuscripts* and the *German Ideology* (both first published in 1932), was less relevant. One should not forget that some of the early writings, like Marx's contribution to the *Deutsch-Französische Jahrbücher* were previously known and that leading social democrats were well informed about Marx's literary bequest without pressing for publication. Not until recently were there signs of a reappraisal of the young Marx in the "socialist" states—a reappraisal which was triggered, however, as Adam Schaff once remarked by the intensive research and studies of Western scholars. Moreover it seems to me that the achieved status of the Soviet society and the perspectives of as well as the planning for a transition to a "real" Communist society nowadays also favor a frank confrontation with the young Marx. The disparity between contemporary socialist states and Marx's conception of a real human society can be more easily described today as the distance between the socialist phase and the terminal Communist stage of the transition. This now sounds more credible than at an early stage of the movement originated by Marx; at that time this transition was still so far removed in time that the distance between socialism and Communism would have been considered only as a contrast.

Undoubtedly we should also consider the fact that the misery in which the working class had to live for decades in capitalist societies was, by and large, done away with by the development of modern techniques and by the political and social interventions of the state, so that the more subtle and more critical arguments of the young Marx were welcomed in those countries as an enrichment to the polemical arsenal of the Communist parties.

THE MEANING OF MARX'S EARLY WRITINGS FOR AN INTERPRETATION OF THE CRITIQUE OF POLITICAL ECONOMY

The historical distance which separates the present from the political, social, and economic problems characteristic of Marx's time has grown so great that we are at least able to come to grips with his critical theory *as a whole*. I do not think that this is due to its obsolescence or outdatedness. Rather I believe that Marx's theory was worn out by the various kinds of interpretation which were placed on parts, rather than on the whole, of his theoretical framework. Consequently it seems to me that, as a consequence, the appreciation of the whole of Marx's writings was best and most successfully provided in those cases where individual critical scholars—without a close party affiliation and, therefore, without any total allegiance to an ideological body of doctrine—turned to Marx. The insight, by the way, that independence from organization and parties is an indispensable precondition for any genuinely scientific work was reiterated many times by Engels, for example, in a letter to August Bebel (April 1, 1891) when he wrote: "You, within the party, need the socialist science and this science cannot prosper without liberty."

The grasping of the meaning of Marx's theory as a whole with all of its complexities and problems has been impeded, among other things, by the fact that his method was reduced to "historical materialism" and that historical materialism was conceived of as a particular case of the application of so-called "dialectical materialism." The mere inclusion of Marx's critical theory into a comprehensive and allegedly scientific *Weltanschauung* made an adequate understanding of all its complexities impossible. Isolated elements of Marx's theory were integrated into the system of a supposedly global materialistic *Weltanschauung* at the very time that Marxist intellectuals were integrated into a hierarchically structured party machine which became more petrified the further the time of revolutionary transition was left behind and the more the movement changed into a new system of domination. Adam Schaff vaguely alluded to these contingencies when he wrote that the epoch of the personality cult had prevented many intellectuals from adequately appreciating Marx's early writings.

After these introductory remarks, let me get down to the substance of the problem and allow me first to state a thesis which I shall try to prove during the remainder of my paper. As in the works of most great thinkers, one unique and central issue can be traced through the whole of Marx's work, i.e., in his scientific investigations and his instructions for *praxis*, one fundamental problem was upper-most during his lifetime. The central problem is the question: *How did it happen that the bourgeois revolution did not achieve its proclaimed aims, and why, despite formally legalized freedoms, individuals came, in the course of the division of labor and modern market mechanism, to be dominated by social processes which prevailed behind their backs and prevented everybody from achieving a status of humanity which could have been realized in the light of the wealth of the society that already existed?*

Marx's central and most important insight was that this new dependence was not the consequence of the bad intentions of individuals or of a particular social group, but rather the inevitable implication of a specific *socioeconomic structure*. More specifically his task consisted, first, in the identification of a social class, which more than any other had to be interested in the transformation of this economic structure; second, in furnishing an irrefutable proof that the dynamics of the contemporary society made this transformation increasingly easier even if one supposed that the minorities possessing interests in the perpetuation of the prevailing order would resist any reorganization of society. The smaller the privileged class, the greater is its *interest in the concealment of the real social conditions* and the less valid is the "bourgeois economics" which, in its "heroic" early phase, had even once advanced a rudimentary critique of political economy on which Marx could build up his own theory.

With these remarks I am trying to indicate the possibility of an interpretation that encompasses Marx's writings as a whole; up to this time the inherent unity of his work has not been proved. I intend to do this by discussing the critical categories that Marx developed in the *Philosophic and Economic Manuscripts* and in his notebook of the midforties and by showing that these categories are still the basis of the critique of political economy in *Grundrisse der Kritik der Politischen Ökonomie* (1857-1858) as well as in *Das Kapital* (1867) and were never disavowed by the old Marx.

In other words I intend to show that an interpretation of the early writings not only helps us to recognize the motives which led Marx to write a critique of political economy (*Das Kapital*) but also, in addition, that the critique of political economy implicitly and, in part, even explicitly, still contains that same critique of alienation and reification which was the very topic of his early writings.

Alienation and Reification in the Works of 1844

The manuscripts of 1844 had, by and large, been planned as a critique of political economy. In his introduction Marx wrote that he wanted to publish successively brochures containing his critiques of law, ethics, politics and so forth and that he intended finally to approach the whole subject once again in a separate work.[2]

The starting point in this first attempt at a critique of political economy was the critical study of the "political economy" to which Marx was led mainly by Engels' "Outlines." As for the method to be used, Marx referred here (as in the introduction to his "Critique of the Hegelian Philosophy of Right") to Ludwig Feuerbach; moreover an explicit reference to Hegel's *Phenomenology of Mind* evidences an influence which can be traced even to the point of the manuscripts' whole literal formulations.

"Critique of political economy" at this time and later always meant first a critique of the capitalist economy accepted as absolutely rational by bourgeois economists and second, a critique of the corresponding theoretical self-consciousness. In Marx's mind, this critique did not first of all and exclusively lead to a moral condemnation in the name of some absolute ethical norms. Rather it was intended as proof of the deficiencies of the capitalist and all preceding modes of production, measured against and based on the standards of a truly human society, which had now objectively become possible because of the scientific and technological knowledge and wealth that the most developed nations had secured. Marx praised the historical achievements of capitalism for its superiority over all preceding modes of production and to a corresponding extent criticized its limitations, the obstruction of further human progress.

The early writings stress the limitations, the repressions, the inhumanity and the shortcomings of capitalism much more than any appreciation of its achievements, it is true. But it would be completely wrong to insinuate that in 1844 Marx radically and ahistorically condemned capitalism. As the main deficiency of the theoretical self-consciousness of the bourgeoisie Marx considered its inability to grasp that capitalism was a phenomenon that had grown out of history and, consequently, was a relative and surmountable mode of production.

> Political economy starts from the fact of private property but it does not explain it to us. It conceives the *material* process of private property in abstract and general terms . . . which then, serve it as laws. It does not *comprehend* these laws. . . .[3]

That is to say, the bourgeois political economy did not understand that these allegedly *natural* laws grew out of specific *social* relations of both production and property and that these "laws" only reflect human relationships which constituted themselves as quasi-objective and independent patterns, *vis-à-vis* and opposite to the interacting individuals.

In the manuscripts of 1844 Marx searched "for the essential connection between private property, avarice, the separation of labour, capital and landed property, exchange and competition, value and the devaluation of man, i.e., *between this whole alienation and the money-system.*"[4] In this context, "money economy" stands as a metaphor for capitalism in which products (and even individuals) are degraded to the category of pure commodities, the value of which is totally distinct and finds its most complete expression in money (and its more and more abstract forms to the very credit system). As you may remember, Marx begins his discussion with the famous description of alienated labor, and he proceeds in four steps; moreover he refers to the same phenomena under various perspectives.

1. *The alienation of the laborer from the product of his activities* leads to a consolidation of the product as an independent power; as a result this means that:

> The worker becomes all the poorer the more wealth he produces and the more his production increases in power and range. The worker becomes an ever cheaper commodity the more goods he creates. The *devaluation* of the human world increases in direct relation with the *increase in value* of the world of things.[5]

Hegel's conception of the humanization of man through a creative transformation of nature by work stands behind this description. Unlike the animal, man must become what he can be through labor. As an entity with only potential faculties, he can only come to self-consciousness and to a conscious relationship with all other men through an objectification of his powers. But this process, which is the more evident the more perfect man's domination over nature becomes, leads to alienation as soon as the objects created by man stand "alien and hostile," or in opposition to its creators and as soon as the objects are subject to their own patterns of behavior and "coldly" disregard the hopes, wishes, and aspirations of the individuals.

2. The alienation of the worker from his product, from the perspective of the working class, appears as an *alienation of the productive and creative activity itself.* Alienated labor cannot be understood as a proper articulation of one's faculties but as forced labor conceived simply as a means for sheer subsistence. Labor, therefore, does not live up to Marx's requirements; it is not "the satisfaction [of a genuine human] need but only a *means* to satisfy needs external to it [namely labor]." Since labor is not a pleasurable activity but rather one of self-sacrifice and "self-castigation," all human behavior consequently becomes perverted.[6]

At this point Marx's arguments become moral and normative, but he nevertheless considers the standards of his critical appreciation as part of an *historical* analysis and as the *expression of the anticipation of future possibilities, definitely not as a Wesensschau of allegedly eternal and moral norms.*

> From all this, it can be seen that man (the worker) feels himself to be freely active only in his animal functions—eating, drinking and procreating, or at most also in his dwelling and personal adornment—while in his human functions he is reduced to an animal. The animal becomes human and the human becomes animal. Eating, drinking and procreating are, of course, also genuinely human functions. But, considered in abstraction from the sphere of all other human activity and turned into final and sole ends, they are animal.[7]

If a man's productive activities are nothing other than forced labor necessary for subsistence and for that reason external to him, his interests shift entirely to those animal functions (mentioned by Marx); or as we would rather say today, all of his aspirations become absorbed in his wish for further consumption, made possible and imposed on him by modern economy. Moreover this consumption has become more senseless in the same degree that his productive work has become more spiritless.

3. As alienation from his productive activity effected through indirect coercion, or other-directedness, and not on his own initiative and responsibility, the worker becomes *alienated from his species*. To construe man's animal functions as his proper ones means a loss of humanity itself. "Free conscious activity is the species-character of human beings," and "productive life is species-life."[8] *Only man* can fail to realize his real potentialities. His privileged status *vis-à-vis* the animal, which consists in his faculty to turn external nature into his "inorganic body," is converted into a serious disadvantage, because through alienation he is deprived of this "inorganic body."

4. The immediate consequence of this alienation of the worker from his species-life (and of humanity) means the *"alienation of man from other men"* which can most impressively be inferred from the relation between the sexes.

This broad description of alienation can hardly be found in the later works of Marx. But we can assume that he did not question it later and that it is consonant with the brief hints in the *Grundrisse* (1857-1858) and in *Das Kapital* (1867). In contrast to these later works, Marx in 1844 had only a vague idea about the abolition of alienation; in any case he did not then relate the revolutionary *praxis* to the self-antagonism of the capitalistic mode of production as directly as he did in later works. In 1844 his argumentation was as follows: the alienated relation to the labor-product mediately produces the power of one person over others, just as religious alienation produces the power of a heavenly being over its believers. Private property no longer appears as the basis, but as the product and consequence of alienated labor, "just as the gods originally were not the source but the effect of the illusion of man"[9] only much later on this relation becomes an interrelation.

Marx believed that the solution to the problem could be found by putting the question in a different way. No longer did he seek the origin of private property but rather "the relation of *alienated labor* to the evolution of humanity":

> If one speaks of *private property*, one thinks of dealing with something outside man. Speaking of labour, one immediately deals with man. To state the problem in this way includes its solution.[10]

The abolition of an alienated society can be carried out only by the workers, for the "non-worker" it appears only as a state (*Zustand*) of alienation, whereas by the worker himself it is experienced as an *"activity* [Tätigkeit] of alienation."[11] By his alienated mode of production, the worker simultaneously produces himself and his opposite; he becomes a commodity, but as a "self-conscious and self-active commodity"[12] he obtains the basis for abolishing the entire world of commodities. Marx interprets this insight (following Engels) as a consequence of the evolution of economic theories from mercantilism to the physiocrats and the bourgeois political economy to the final socialist criticism. This theoretical development runs parallel to the development of civil society. By 1844 Marx knew that the victory of capitalism over all precapitalistic modes of production was a precondition for the abolition of all alienation.

Marx separated the theories of the *Aufhebung* of alienated society into two or three logically successive forms: into a first form of Communism, which meant only the generalization of private property into Communist property. This leads to *crude Communism*. There is no connection between this way of abolishing private property and the real appropriation of alienated reality. On the contrary all people would be reduced, according to this notion, to the unnatural simplicity of poor people without needs and wants. "Community [in this case] is only a community of labor and equality of salary paid out by the Communist capital, the community as a universal capitalist."[13] The obvious indication of this kind of brute Communism which Marx understood as a primitive generalization of private property is the *Weibergemeinschaft*, the community of women. This

Communism is inhuman, not because it destroys capitalism but because it makes capitalism broader, more radical and more absolute. *It does not transcend capitalistic society but even lags behind some of the more progressive aspects of private property.* Nevertheless Marx thought at this time that at least from the theoretical point of view this kind of Communism was a stage through which one necessarily had to pass.

The second type of Communism, Marx considered, is of a political nature, democratic or despotic. It too remains imperfect and "affected by private property, i.e., the alienation of man."

In its third form alone, "Communism means the positive transcendence of private property and consequently, *a genuine appropriation of the human essence* by and for man." By this Marx meant a society in which all people can freely employ all their manifold and differentiated faculties in order to be able to appropriate their products in the free and many-sided way of "total men." In it, the mere possession of goods no longer prohibits the many-sided and more differentiated forms of appropriating humanized nature. The refined eye, ear, and emotions of all are now able to appropriate the past and present achievements of the human creativity.[14]

A complete description of this unalienated society was furnished by Marx in his *Exzerpthefte,* the notebooks written during this period, where he tried to show how in such a society the productive activities of free individuals are correlated, and how these activities reflect the human species, and not an alien, objectified, and reified world. In it, there would be no more greed, competition, profit-making, cheating, fraud, and exploitation; rather all relationships would be in harmony, and an atmosphere of love would be initiated by free consciousness so that all of man's activities would enrich man.[15]

The Concept of Alienation and Reification as Elaborated in the "Grundrisse der Kritik der Politischen Ökonomie" (1857-1858)

Since the publication of the *Grundrisse,*[16] which were edited in Moscow in 1939 and 1941, it is easier than before to prove the continuity of Marx's thought. These manuscripts date back to the time when Marx prepared the *Kritik der politischen Ökonomie,* published in June 1859, and of which the first volume of *Das Kapital* is but an enlarged and revised version. In the *Grundrisse,* Marx pondered problems and topics he had dealt with in his early writings and made use of the results of his more recent economic studies.

The historical process which led to an extreme alienation of individuals from their social relationships is described here in a more precise way than in 1844. In the money system, the intercourse of individuals with that entire society of which they are a part became completely objectified. Money has become an alien power to them. The individual "carries his social power and his relationship to society in his pocket." Thus "the activity and the product of activity is the *exchange-value,* i.e., a universal in which all individuality and particularity is negated and extinguished."[17] The difference between modern and precapitalistic societies is to be found in the fact that the social character of their productive activity, the participation of the individual in the social production process and the social character of the product today appear alien and contradictory to individuals. On the surface, no relations of personal dependency exist; rather all individuals appear as free; but in reality, everybody is totally subject to alien objective laws (*fremde Sachgesetzlichkeit*) that result from blind social and economic processes. More than ever before, Marx emphasizes, however, at the same time the progressive and necessary character of these social relationships. He contrasts them to the restricted and limited relationships in previous modes of society (for example, to the patriarchal modes of antiquity and the Middle Ages). He welcomes the dissolution of small-group subsistence economies and the development of the worldwide division of labor and the successive exchange of goods in the market as processes through which productivity is enlarged.

> The exchange as mediated through exchange value and money presupposes mutually dependent producers and simultaneously the absolute isolation of their private interests and a division of social labour, the unity and mutual complementarity of which must exist as a quasi-natural relation outside the individuals and independently of them. The pressure upon each other of general

demand and supply mediates the connection of mutually indifferent individuals.[18]

This corresponds very closely to the description of the systems of wants and needs and of the *"Not- und Verstandesstaat"* depicted by Hegel, which allegedly constitutes itself—without the knowledge and will of the individuals—through Adam Smith's "invisible hand." Marx blamed the indifference of people for each other and the impossibility of facing up to their relationship to society; but he clearly saw that the new mode of production was superior to all previous ones and that it simultaneously tended to destroy all genuine social relations, that it isolated the producers (and consumers) and that despite its immense wealth it impoverished people in both literal and figurative senses, i.e., that the increasing specialization of skills and abilities prevented the individual from realizing all of his powers.

Everybody must convert his product (his activity) into an exchange value, into "money," because only in this, and in no other form, is to be found social power and indispensable power over others. From this fact one realizes that "people produce only for society and in society" and that on the other hand their production is not immediately social and not associatively organized. This means that everybody has to sell his product in order that he may take it over in the form of money as an objectification of the social character of his own production. In money, the individual producer acquires, though in alienated form, a part of social productivity; in money he appropriates in alienated form, without knowing it, part of the community. In as much as the division of labor extends over the whole world and leads to a world market (with a worldwide currency), the intercourse of individuals becomes universal. But at the same time, as a result of these interrelations, the dependence of individuals becomes more and more radical; thus, Marx could see in this status the transitory conditions leading to a new form of society and economy.[19]

Moreover we must remember that Marx launched his polemics against any *romantic* glorification of "natural" precapitalistic relations with their local, functional, social, and personal restrictions. *He definitely preferred the worldwide interconnections* of the participants of the capitalist world market. But Marx considered them as transitory and as a necessary precondition to the future subordination of all social relations to the control of associatively organized producers, because he did not conceive any status as something occurring naturally, but as a product of historical *praxis*. Any status had been hitherto achieved in history without being consciously sought for. The present situation constitutes the precondition of a future society in which man, as a whole being, will be a real possibility. Man will no longer be a product of nature but a product of history. In a word, this means *that the total emancipation of man presupposes his total alienation*.

Armed with this historical insight, Marx thought it equally ridiculous to long for the "original plentitude" of primitive social relations or to hold fast to the human emptiness that marks the present. However his essential point was that the *bourgeois consciousness could not overcome the undialectical contrast of romantic aspirations and cynical acceptance of both a rich and an impoverished present*.[20] These contrasts comprise its being, and will, consequently, remain with it to its end.

However progress toward a universal capitalistic mode of production does not appear only as a necessary precondition for the universal promotion of productive capacities; rather it leads to the final point where all personal relations are broken and subjected to the universal basis of new social interrelationships. As soon as most individuals are dominated by "material conditions" or by socially objectified interrelations, and not by other individuals, then the task for mankind is obvious: *to bring these interrelations under mankind's common control and so to break through the course of history, where until now power elites have been circulating without ever facing up to the root cause of dependence and repression*. Surely, as Marx stresses, "individuals are now dominated by abstractions whereas they previously depended on each other," but these abstractions finally bring forth the preconditions on which also all previous modes of domination rested. Throughout history, the dependence of "slaves" on their "masters," has not resulted from the will of the dominating classes but can be explained only by the *primitive modes of production* and the necessities of those limited social conditions (which required specific organizations, as for instance, special military provisions). Whereas in previous stages of history the objective conditions appeared as personal, "in the modern world the personal relations are clearly seen as the pure expression of the modes of production and exchange." In the possibility of such an insight, Marx saw another important advantage of capitalistic society.

As I have already intimated, Marx in the *Grundrisse* elaborated on the notion with which he first dealt in the *Philosophic and Economic Manuscripts*—the notion that "world history is nothing but the producing of man by man's work." More than in the early writings, the positive meaning of the capitalistic mode of production is stressed, but the lines of argumentation are by and large the same as before.

The Fetish Character of the Commodities and the Concept of the Destruction of Alienation *in* Das Kapital

In *Das Kapital,* capitalist society is conceived of as a dialectical totality in which antagonisms, since they tend to transcend present social conditions, are necessary. As with any totality, the parts reflect the whole and every part is governed by the same principles as the whole. What characterizes capitalistic society is the commodity character it attributes to everything. In the societies of Marx's time this process of converting all things into commodities had not yet come to an end, but Marx thought that he could foresee that the process would closely follow this model. The dialectical reconstruction of social entities, which is only possible in so far as societies are truly governed by dialectical processes, does not construct the whole from its parts but presupposes that the parts can only be understood as parts of the whole. This means that the explication cannot properly begin until the analysis has been brought to its end.

In the beginning of *Das Kapital* Marx deals with "the Commodity." Everyone in a capitalistic society is familiar with commodities, but Marx wants to understand them in their historical genesis and becoming and in their structure. In his study of the commodity character of products, his analyses from his early writings are taken for granted.

In the chapter mentioned, Marx analyzes commodity according to four steps: (1) the double character of the commodity is reflected upon; it represents use-value and value. As use-value, it possesses specific qualities; as a value, it has no quality but represents a mere quantity. (2) This character of the product is traced back to labor's own twin qualities, which arise with its division. On the one side, the workers produce particular work (*besondere Arbeit*); on the other, as a result of their general work (*allgemeine Arbeit*), they produce exchange-values. What Marx does is to probe backward from the fixed being to the activities from which it results. (3) Marx shows, historically, how the value-form had developed from the simple and accidental to the money-form until in the money economy the absolute split of use-value from exchange-value has become clearly evident. Now all products of human activities represent only money-equivalents and the general work of society is only able to recognize itself in reification. (4) Marx analyzes the fetish-character of the commodity and its mysteries.

> The mystery of the form of commodity consists in the fact that for individuals it reflects the social character of their own work, as objective qualities of the products of labor themselves, as *social* natural qualities of these things (*gesellschaftliche Naturei-genschaften*) and, consequently, that it mirrors the social relations of the producers to the total work as a social relationship among objects existing outside them.[21]

The commodity character of a product of human activity consists in the phenomenon that this product possesses a value which can be abstractly expressed in money and therefore becomes interchangeable with other products. This quality of exchange and interchangeability appears as a quality of the object itself, a quality which is due to its being a part of the general (world) market, to the laws of which this commodity is subject. In reality, however, these reified relations of things reflect social relations of the producers and the owners of the means of production. "It is only the determinate social relation of individuals which takes the chimerical shape of a relation of objects."[22] This phenomenon, that an entity resulting from the activities of individuals comes to dominate their life, can only be analyzed according to the way Feuerbach saw the relationship between God and man.

To find an analogy, we have to take refuge in the nebulous sphere of the religious world. Here the products of our imagination appear as independent, intelligent and autonomous figures related to man. The same is true in the world of commodities with the products of man's work. This I call the *fetishism* which is attached to the labour-products as soon as they are produced as commodities and which is by consequence, inseparable from the production of commodities."[23]

As soon as people relate themselves to their objects as to a fetish, they begin to attribute some qualities to this dead object which in reality stem from their own life, the power and impotence of their own social relations, for example. In other words, the magic power attributed to the fetish is only real in so far as belief in it makes possible the success of the tribe. But erroneously, this success is attributed to the fetish and not to the organized power of the tribe, just as the interchangeability of the commodity is believed due to the character of the products and not to the division of labor and the market mechanisms. There is a dearth of conscious organization of production in both cases. What Marx calls in this context *fetishism,* he described in his early writings as *alienation.*

Let me quote one more sentence: "Its own social movement possesses for them (the producers of commodities) the form of a movement of objects, which they are controlled by rather than controlling."[24] That the fetishism of commodities, i.e., the mysticism of the commodity world, is only the specific expression of the capitalist mode of production is proved by Marx in his examples of Robinson and of the medieval mode of production. In both of these cases, the measure of labor is regulated by the individual and social needs of specific use-values, i.e., the social character of production is presupposed, whereas in the commodity-producing society the social character of the production of independently producing private workers is constituted in the process of circulation—and there only in alienated form. In the Middle Ages "the social conditions of individuals appeared in their works as their own personal conditions and were not concealed as the social conditions of objects."[25] *The relations were transparent and not mystified.*

However as we have already seen in his manuscripts of 1857,

Marx rejects any romantic glorification of these older modes of production. The commodity-producing society with its alienation is obviously necessary as one transitory stage which lays the material groundwork for a new society. In *Das Kapital* Marx compared this new society to an "association of free people" (a term which he borrowed from Max Stirner and which he mocked many times in other contexts).

> In so far as such an association works with socialized means of production and the individuals consciously organize their individual powers to a social power ... then all determinations of Robinson's mode of production are reiterated ... , but now socially, no longer individually.[26]

The product of such an organized productive activity would immediately be social, and one part of it could remain social and be employed as means of production, whereas other parts could be distributed for the sake of individual consumption. Marx does not reflect in detail on the mode of distribution but considers it dependent on the level of the producers' development. It might be organized along the socialist line of proportional distribution according to the amount of work performed by individuals or along communist lines according to genuine individual needs.

If one looks only at the chapter on the fetish character of commodity, one might believe that Marx expected the *Aufhebung* of alienation to be achieved solely through the common control of production based on the division of labor and that he no longer challenged the principle of the division of labor itself. One could insinuate that Marx considered it sufficient that the sum of all individual labor forces become one social labor force, a situation which could be consonant with maintenance of division of labor. But Marx unmistakably stresses the necessity to overcome the division of labor. His argument in chapter 13 of the first volume of *Das Kapital* —it is true—is based on the revolutionary character of technology and not on the individuals' needs to employ their own potentialities, but eventually it leads to the same conclusion as the early writings:

> If change of special work is carried through rather like some overwhelming natural law, and with the blindly destructive effects of natural law which finds obstacles everywhere, then large

industry because of its catastrophes must make it a life and death matter to accept both the change of jobs and the greatest possible *individuality of the worker as a general social law of production, and to adapt the social conditions to the worker's normal realization.* It becomes a question of life and death to replace the monstrosity of a poor labour population—a reserve held for disposition to meet the varying exploitation needs of capital with the disposal of man for varied jobs; the partial individual (*Teilindividuum*), the bearer of a partial social function, by the *totally developed individual*, for whom many social functions constitute successive modes of activity.[27]

The "total man," whom Marx postulated in his early writings as a contrast-image to the impoverished one-sided, cripple individual who really existed, is here conceived as a necessity to which the capitalist mode of production itself is pushed. This is one of the many observations by which Marx showed himself far ahead of his time, for not until recently was there a widely shared opinion that modern modes of production require a most comprehensive training of the laborer to allow him to adapt himself to the ever changing requirements of industrial production.

SOME FINAL REMARKS

Nobody would deny that the style and the ambiance did change in Marx's writings. There is indeed a difference between the sober explication in *Das Kapital* with its emphasis on theoretical vigor and empirical detail and the critical and moralistically sounding analyses of 1844. But there remains *one fundamental topic* which is the starting as well as the ending point: *the quest to transcend capitalist society toward a more human, free and satisfactory society.* There is no warrant for the conclusion that the old Marx buried the hopes of his youth and abandoned the fulfillment of his aims. His later writings can only be adequately understood in the light of his first writings. If later, the "how" of this transformation and its empirical chances of realization were stressed more strongly than the necessity of the "that" (of which Marx remained too deeply convinced to need stressing), this should not be mistaken for an escape into a general philosophy of history or an exclusive concentration on the analytical restructuring of the modes of the capitalist economy. His intentions, throughout his life, were directed toward a *"critique* of the political economy" and this means the practical critique of capitalist society as much as it does its theoretical conception in the doctrines of the bourgeois economists. Marx did not bring forth a new proletarian economic theory to stand beside the classical bourgeois theories. And the widespread notion of an "economic theory for the proletariat" sometimes sanctioned by Marx and Engels themselves, is, by and large, misleading.

In *Das Kapital* Marx's reflections centered around a critique of those alienated social relations he had already criticized in 1844. If Marx (and particularly Engels later on), were not always conscious of the continuity of this critical approach, this would not amount to a serious objection against my interpretation. *Das Kapital* remains a fragment, and being bound to the galley of his journalistic writings, plagued by illness and lack of genuine enthusiasm, overwhelmed by organizational duties, Marx was no longer able to ponder his work and treat it as a whole. His successors had already begun during his lifetime to pick out pieces of his theoretical reflections which they found expedient for their political and organizational aims. The story of the interpretation of his work was, as in all cases of great thinkers, a story of misinterpretations.

NOTES

1. Franz Mehring, *Karl Marx, The Story of His Life,* Ann Arbor, 1962, p. 73.
2. *MEGA,* I, 3, 33; cf. Karl Marx, *Philosophic and Economic Manuscripts,* trans. M. Milligan, Moscow, 1961, p. 15.
3. *MEGA,* I, 3, 81; cf. trans., p. 67.
4. *Ibid.,* 82; cf. trans., p. 68.
5. *Ibid.,* 83; cf. trans., p. 69.
6. *Ibid.,* 86; cf. trans., p. 72.
7. *Ibid.*
8. *Ibid.,* 88; cf. trans., p. 75.
9. *Ibid.,* 92; cf. trans., p. 80.
10. *Ibid.,* 93; cf. trans., p. 82.
11. *Ibid.,* 94; cf. trans., p. 80.

12. *Ibid.*, 98; cf. trans., p. 85.
13. *Ibid.*, 112; cf. trans., p. 100.
14. *Ibid.*, 114ff.; cf. trans., p. 102ff.
15. *MEGA*, I, 3, 544ff.
16. Karl Marx, *Grundrisse der Kritik der politischen Ökonomie (Rohentwurf)*, Berlin, 1953.
17. *Ibid.*, p. 75.
18. *Ibid.*, p. 76.
19. *Ibid.*, p. 80.
20. *Ibid.*, p. 80ff.
21. *MEW*, XXIII, 86; cf. Karl Marx, *Capital*, Moscow, 1954 ff., vol. I, p. 72.
22. *Ibid.*
23. *Ibid.*
24. *Ibid.*, 89; cf. trans., p. 75.
25. *Ibid.*, 91; cf. trans., p. 77.
26. *Ibid.*, 92; cf. trans., p. 78.
27. *Ibid.*, 511ff.; cf. trans., p. 487. Our italics.

4: The "Rediscovery" of Alienation

DANIEL BELL

There is today, in England and in France, a renewed interest in Marx. One sees this in the pages of the English *Universities and Left Review,* and the French *Arguments*, the magazines of the post-Stalinist left-wing generation in these countries. One hears this in detailed discussion of the writings of the Polish and East German "revisionists," and particularly of the "subterranean" ideas of Georg Lukács, the Hungarian Marxist philosopher, one of the sources of revisionism. One reads this in the literary journals, such as Lucien Goldmann's long essay "La Réification," in the February-March 1959 issue of *Les Temps Moderne.*

This new interest revolves around the theme of alienation. Marx is read not as an economist or political theorist—not for the labor theory of value or the falling rate of profit, not for the theory of the State or even of social classes, and certainly not as the founder of dialectical materialism—but as a philosopher who first laid bare the estrangement of man from an oppressive society. Alienation is taken to be the critical tool of the Marxist method, and the new canon is

Originally published in the *Journal of Philosophy,* LVI:24, November 1959, 933-952.

derived from the early, and in his lifetime unpublished, philosophical manuscripts of Marx. Even non-Marxists accept this new emphasis. Thus in Père Jean-Yves Calvez's comprehensive *La Pensée de Karl Marx,* published in 1956, 440 of a total of 640 pages are devoted to the concept of alienation and its use in social and political analysis.

All of this is rather novel. Rarely in the thirties, for example, when the first burst of Marxist scholarship occurred, did one find in the exegetical and expository writings on Marx a discussion of alienation. In Sidney Hook's pioneer account of Marx's intellectual development, *From Hegel to Marx,* published in 1936, the word "alienation" does not occur *once* in the text. It was not, of course, that Hook was unaware of the idea of alienation and the role it played in Hegelian thought. (His book, based on these early manuscripts, had traced in patient detail Marx's thought to his immediate forebears: to Feuerbach, who, in his discussion of religion, had developed the concept of alienation; to Bruno Bauer, who had emphasized the "critical method" in philosophy; to Moses Hess, who first sketched the picture of humanistic communism; and to the other young Hegelians for whom the relationship of freedom to necessity was the paramount concern.) But the intellectual problem for Hook, as it was for *all* "classical" Marxists, was, first, a defense of the idea of materialism as a viable modern philosophy—and this Hook sought to do by reading Marx uniquely as a naturalist—and, second, to resolve the 'contradiction' between Marx's social determinism (i.e., that one's consciousness and knowledge are shaped by one's existence and class position), and Marx's, and Lenin's, class teleology (or the fact that socialist purpose and goal are instilled into the worker from the 'outside')[1]—and this Hook sought to do by reading Marx as a pragmatist. The intellectual issue for Marxists in the thirties was the validity of historical materialism.

Different times, different *Zeitgeist*. The reason for this change is clear. In Europe today, a school of neo-Marxists, having rejected Stalinism (and, implicitly, historical materialism, which, in its projection of 'higher' stages of society, had been used to justify the Bolshevik use of terror), has gone back to Marx's early writings to find a foundation for a new humanist foundation for Socialism. The revisionist philosophers in Eastern Europe do so to find doctrinal support against the official party theologues. The French post-Stalinists, such as Lucien Goldmann or Edgar Morin, see in the idea of alienation a more sophisticated radical critique of contemporary society than the simplified and stilted Marxist analysis of class. And the young English socialists, such as Charles Taylor of All Souls College, see in the concept of alienation a means of reformulating the idea of community.

While all this is a fresh, and even fruitful, way of making a criticism of contemporary society, it is *not* the "historical Marx." For, as the following analysis argues, Marx had repudiated the idea of alienation divorced from his specific economic analysis of property relations under capitalism, and, in so doing, had closed off a road which would have given us a broader and more useful analysis of society and personality than the Marxian dogmatics which did prevail. While one may be sympathetic to the idea of alienation, it is only further myth-making to read this concept back as the central theme of Marx. As a political effort by the revisionists, bound within the Marxist camp, it may have some polemical value. As a stage of the pilgrim's progress of those coming out of the Marxist forest, it is understandable. As an intellectual effort, it is false. If the concept of alienation is to have any meaning, it must stand on its own feet, without the crutch of Marx. This, then, is the burden of the paper.

I

For the "left-Hegelians," the teachers and colleagues of Marx, the chief task of philosophy was to specify the conditions under which "Man" could achieve his freedom. They accepted the question which Hegel had opened up; they were dissatisfied with his formulation of the problem.

The goal of Man, Hegel had said, was freedom, a condition, he defined, in which man would be self-willed and where his "essence" would become his own possession—in which he would regain his "self." But man was "separated" from his essence and bound by two conditions which seemed inherent in the world: necessity and alienation. Necessity meant a dependence on nature and the acceptance of the limitations which nature imposed on men, both in the sense of the limitation of natural resources and the limitations of physical strength. Alienation, in its original connotation, was the radical dissociation of the "self" into both actor and thing, into a *subject* that strives to control its own fate, and an *object* which is manipulated by others.[2] In the development of science, man could, perhaps, overcome necessity and master nature. But how was one to overcome the Orphic separateness of subject and object? Alienation was an ontological fact, in the structure of grammar as well as of life; for the self was not just an "I" seeking to shape the world according to its intentions, but also a "me," an object whose identity is built up by the pictures that others have of the "me." Thus the condition of complete freedom, in which the self seeks only to be an "I," a shaper of events in accordance with its own will, rather than being shaped by others, is a seeming impossibility. In the face of this irreducible dualism of subject-object, of "I" and "me," how does one achieve the goal of being "self-willed"?

Bruno Bauer, one of the first teachers and friends of Marx, felt that the solution lay in developing a "critical" philosophy which exposed the "mystery" of human relationships (i.e., the *real* motives behind social acts). Most human beings born into the world, said Bauer, simply accept it and are oblivious to the sources of their morals and beliefs, of their rationality and irrationality; they are "determined" by the world. By subjecting all beliefs to criticism, however, men would become self-conscious, reason would be restored to them, and therewith their self-possession. The overcoming of the dualism, therefore, was to be through the achievement of self-consciousness.

Feuerbach, to whom Marx gave credit for making the first real breach in the system of Hegelian abstractions, sought to locate the source of alienation in religious superstition and fetishism. The most radical of all the left-Hegelians, Feuerbach called himself Luther II. Where Luther had sought to demolish an institution that mediated between Man and God, the second Luther sought to destroy God himself. Man would be free, he said, if we could demythologize religion. Man was bound because he took the best of himself, his sensibility, and projected it onto some external object, or spirit, which he called divine.[3] But the history of all thought was a history of progressive disenchantment, and if, finally, in Christianity, the image of God had been transformed from a parochial river deity to a universal abstraction, the function of criticism—using the radical tool of alienation or self-estrangement—was to replace theology by anthropology, to dethrone God and enthrone Man. The way to overcome alienation was to bring the divine back into man, to reintegrate himself through a religion of humanity, through a religion of self-love. Men's relation to each other, said Feuerbach, in first employing terms that, ironically, were adopted later by Martin Buber for religious purposes, had to be on an I-Thou basis.[4] Philosophy was to be directed to life, man was to be liberated from the "spectre of abstractions" and released from the thongs of the supernatural. Religion was only capable of creating "false consciousness." Philosophy would reveal "true consciousness." And, by placing Man rather than God at the center of consciousness, Feuerbach sought to bring the "infinite into the finite."

This uncompromising attack on religion was equally a sharp attack on all established institutions. But beyond that, the spreading use of the concept of alienation had a more radical consequence in the minds of the left-Hegelians, because it initiated a direct break in the history of philosophy by ushering in the period of modernity. In classical philosophy, the ideal man was the contemplative one. Neither the middle ages nor the transitional period to contemporary times (the seventeenth to the mid-nineteenth century) was ever wholly able to detach itself from the ideal of the Stoa. Even Goethe, who gave us in Faust the first modern man, the man of ambition unchained, reverted, in his ethical image of the human ideal, to the Greek. In discussing freedom, however, Hegel had introduced a new principle, the principle of *action;* for man, in order to realize his self, had to strive actively to overcome the subject-object dualism that bound him. In action a man finds himself; by his choices he defines his character. For Hegel, however, the principle of action had remained abstract. In Feuerbach, while the principle of alienation is sharply defined and the source of alienation is located in religion, an abstraction remains because Feuerbach was talking of Man in general. In Marx, action was given specificity in a radical new emphasis on *work*. Man becomes man, becomes alive through work, for through work man loses his isolation and becomes a social or co-operative being, and thus learns of himself; and through work he is able to transform nature as well.[5]

In locating man's alienation in work, Marx had taken the revolutionary step of grounding philosophy in concrete human activity. The road by which he "freed" himself from the Hegelian tyranny of abstraction was a long and difficult one.[6] As a Hegelian, Marx thought first of the alienation of work in terms of idealistic dualities. Man, in working, reifies himself in objective things (i.e., in products which embody his work). This is *labor* (*Arbeit*) and is part of the "alien and hostile world standing over against him." In labor, man is "under the domination, compulsion and yoke of another man." Against this is the state of freedom where man would transform nature, and himself, by free, conscious, spontaneous, creative work. Two things stood in the way of achieving this freedom: the fact that in the alienation of work man lost control over the *process* of work, and lost control, too, of the *product* of his labor.[7] For Marx, therefore, the answer to Hegel was clear: the alienation of man lay not in some philosophical abstraction of Mind, but in the property system. In the organization of work—in labor becoming a commodity—man became an object used by others, and unable, therefore, to obtain satisfaction in his own activity. By becoming himself a commodity, he lost his sense of identity; he lost the sense of "himself."

The extraordinary thing was that Marx had taken a concept which German philosophy had seen as an ontological fact, and had given it a social content. As ontology, as an ultimate, man could only accept alienation. As a social fact, rooted in a specific system of historical relations, alienation could be overcome by changing the social system. But in narrowing the concept, Marx ran two risks: of falsely identifying the source of alienation only in the private property system; and of introducing a note of utopianism in the idea that once the private property system was abolished man would immediately be free.

The question of why men were propertyless turned Marx to economics. For a man whose name is so inextricably linked with the "dismal science," Marx was never really interested in economics. His correspondence with Engels in later years is studded with contemptuous references to the subject and he resented the fact that his detailed explorations prevented him from carrying on other studies. But he continued because, for him, economics was the practical side of philosophy—it would unveil the mystery of alienation—and because he had found in the categories of political economy the material expression of that alienation: the process of economic exploitation.

This development is seen most clearly in the *Economic-Philosophical Manuscripts,* which Marx had written in 1844 at the age of twenty-six. The *Manuscripts,* in the history of Marxist thought, is the bridge from the left-Hegelianism of the early Marx to the Marxism we have come to know. The title itself is both literal and symbolic. Beginning as an anthropology it ends as a political economy. In it one finds the first conceptualization of alienation as rooted in work (rather than in abstract spirit, or religion), and the beginnings of the analysis of property. And in the analysis of property, one finds the direct transmutation, which is so crucial in the development of Marx's thought, of philosophical into economic categories.

In his search for an answer to Hegel's question, Marx had sought to pin down concretely the ways in which the human being was "robbed" of his potential possibilities of realizing his "self." For Feuerbach, religion was the means whereby man was alienated from himself; for in religion man externalized his real "self." For Marx, now, the idea of the "self" had become too abstract. The key to the problem was the nature of work—the process whereby man became a social being—but the question remained as to what barred man from realizing his full nature in work. The answer, he thought, lay in the operation of the property system. But how? In the capitalist system, in the bargain made between worker and employer, the individual was formally free. What, then, was the means whereby a man, unbeknownst even to himself, was alienated and enslaved? Marx found the answer in money. Money is the most impersonal form of value. It is seemingly neutral. A man who has a direct obligation to another, as a serf does to a master, knows directly the source of power over him. But one who sells his labor power for money may feel himself to be free. The product of the laborer can thus be easily "abstracted" into money, and, through the exchange system, be "abstracted" from him.[8]

Money, thus, is the concrete embodiment of the philosophical abstraction which Hegel had described airily as "spirit," and the commodity process the means whereby the laborer, by exchanging his labor power for money, is robbed of his freedom unaware. Political economy became for Marx what religion was for Feuerbach, a means whereby human values are "projected" outside of man and achieve an existence independent of him and over him. And so, alienation, conceived initially by Marx as a process whereby an individual lost his capacity to express himself in work, now became seen as exploitation, or the appropriation of a laborer's surplus product by the capitalist. Thus a philosophical expression which embodies, actually, a socio-psychological insight became transformed into an economic category.

The irony, however, was that in moving from "philosophy" to "reality," from Hegelian phenomenology to political economy, Marx moved from one kind of abstraction to another. In his system, self-alienation became transformed: man as "generic man" (i.e., Man writ large) becomes divided into classes of men.[9] For Marx now, the only social reality is not Man, nor the individual, but economic classes. Individuals and their motives count for nought.[10] The only form of consciousness which can be translated into action—and which can explain history, past, present, and future—is class consciousness.

In *The German Ideology,* written in 1846, the idea of the "self" has disappeared from Marx's writings. Marx now mocks the left-Hegelians for talking of "human nature, of Man in general who belongs to no class, has no reality and subsists only in the realm of philosophical fantasy." In attacking the "true Socialist," Marx writes: "It is characteristic of all these high-sounding phrases about liberation, etc., that it is always 'man' who is liberated . . . it would appear from [their] claims that 'wealth' and 'money' have ceased to exist. . . ."[11]

In *The Communist Manifesto,* the attack is widened, and made cruelly sardonic. The German *literati,* says Marx, "wrote their philosophical nonsense beneath the French original. For instance, beneath the French criticism of the economic functions of money, they wrote 'alienation of humanity'. . . ." And mocking his erstwhile philosophical comrades, Marx speaks scornfully of "this transcendental robe in which the German Socialists wrapped their sorry 'eternal truths' . . . the robe of speculative cobwebs, embroidered with the flowers of rhetoric, steeped in the dew of sickly sentiment."[12]

In saying that there is no human nature "inherent in each separate individual," as Marx does in his sixth theses on Feuerbach, but only social man, and then only classes, one introduces a new *persona*. Marx makes this explicit in his preface to *Capital*, written in 1867: "Here individuals are dealt with only insofar as they are the personifications of economic categories, embodiments of particular class-relations and class interests. My standpoint, from which the evolution of the economic formation of society is viewed as a process of natural history, can, less than any other, make the individual responsible for relations whose creature he socially remains, however he may subjectively raise himself above them."

Thus, individual responsibility is turned into class morality, and the variability of individual action subsumed under impersonal mechanisms. And the ground is laid for the loss of freedom in a new tyranny that finds its justifications in the narrowed view of exploitation which Marx had fashioned.

To sum up the argument thus far: In his early philosophical writings, Marx had seen, against Hegel, that alienation or the failure to realize one's potential as a self, was rooted primarily in work, rather than in the abstract development of consciousness. In the organization of work, men become "means" for the aggrandizement of others, rather than "ends" in themselves. As alienated labor, there was a twofold loss: men lost control over the *conditions* of work, and men lost the *product* of their labor. This dual conception is present, in a different form, in the later Marx: the loss of control of work is seen as *dehumanization*, occasioned by the division of labor and intensified by technology; the loss of product, as *exploitation*, because a portion of man's labor (surplus value) was appropriated by the employer.

But except for literary and illustrative references in *Capital* to the dehumanization of labor and the fragmentation of work, this first aspect, as problem, was glossed over by Marx. In common with some later (bourgeois?) sociologists, Marx felt that there was no solution to the loss of "self" in work inherent in technology. Under communism—in the 'final' society—the division of labor, the cause of dehumanization, would be eliminated so that by variety in work man would be able to develop his varied aptitudes. But these fragmentary discussions take on a utopian hue.[13] In actuality one had to accept not only the division of labor, but hierarchical organization as well. In a polemic against some Italian anarchists who had argued that technology had imposed on man a "veritable despotism," Engels argued that it was utopian to question the nature of authority in a factory: "At least with regard to the hours of work one may write upon the portals of these factories: *Lasciate ogni autonomia, voi che entrate!* [leave, ye that enter in, all autonomy behind!]. If man by dint of his knowledge and inventive genius, had subdued the forces of nature, the latter avenge themselves upon him by subjecting him, in so far as he employs them, to a veritable despotism, independent of all social organization. Wanting to abolish authority in large-scale industry is tantamount to wanting to abolish industry itself, to destroy the power loom in order to return to the spinning wheel."[14]

What became central to *Capital* were the concrete social relationships created by private property, those of employer-and-employee, rather than the processes generated by manufacture. Dehumanization was a creature of technology; exploitation that of capitalism. The solution was simple, if one-sided: abolish private property, and the system of exploitation would disappear. "In contemporary capitalist society men are dominated by economic relations created by themselves, by means of production which they have produced, as if by an alien power . . . ," said Engels. "When society, by taking possession of all means of production and managing them on a planned basis, has freed itself and all of its members from the bondage in which they are at present held by means of production which they themselves have produced but which now confront them as irresistible, alien power; when consequently man no longer proposes, but also disposes—only then will the last alien power which is now reflected in religion vanish. And with it will also vanish the religious reflection itself, for the simple reason that there will be nothing left to reflect."[15]

When critics argued that technological organization might still "deform and debilitate" the worker, the Marxist called this utopian. When skeptics asserted that socialism itself might become an exploitative society, the Marxist had a ready answer: the source of exploitation, and of power, was economic, and political office was only an administrative extension of economic power; once economic power was socialized, there could no longer be classes, or a basis whereby man could exploit man. By this extension it became "clear" that the Soviet Union was a "workers' state," and no basis for exploitation existed. Thus the concept of alienation came, down one road, to a twisted end.

II

Having found the answer to the "mysteries" of Hegel in political economy, Marx promptly forgot all about philosophy. ("The philosophers have only *interpreted* the world differently; the point, however, is to change it," he had scrawled in his *Theses on Feuerbach.*) In 1846, Marx and Engels had completed a long criticism of post-Hegelian philosophy in two large octavo volumes and (except for some gnomic references in the *Critique of the Gotha Programme* in 1875) neither of them returned to the subject until forty years later when Engels, after the death of Marx, was, to his surprise, asked by the *Neue Zeit,* the German Socialist theoretical magazine, to review a book on Feuerbach by C. N. Starcke, a then well-known anthropologist. Engels reluctantly consented and wrote a long review which, slightly expanded, was published two years later in 1888 as a small brochure entitled *Ludwig Feuerbach and the Outcome of Classical German Philosophy.* In writing the review Engels went back to some moldering manuscripts of Marx and found among his papers the hastily scribbled eleven theses on Feuerbach, totaling in all a few pages, which he appended to the brochure. In the Foreword, Engels alludes to the large manuscript (without mentioning even its title,

The German Ideology), and says merely that because of the reluctance of the publishers it was not printed. "We abandoned the manuscript to the gnawings of the mice all the more willingly," wrote Engels, "as we had achieved our main purpose—to clear our own minds."[16] (The gnawing was literal, since many pages, in fact, had been completely chewed up!)

But it is also clear that while, as young philosophy students, the debates with the other young Hegelians were necessary for the purposes of "self clarification," the absorption of both into concrete economic study and political activity had made the earlier philosophical problems increasingly unreal to them. In a letter to his American translator, Florence Kelley Wischnewetzky, in February 1886, Engels writes, apropos of his *Anti-Dühring,* "the semi-Hegelian language of a good many passages of my old book is not only untranslatable but has lost the greater part of its meaning even in German."[17] And in 1893 a Russian visitor to Engels, Alexis Voden, found Engels incredulous when the question of publishing the early philosophical manuscripts was raised. In a memoir, Voden recalled: "Our next conversation was on the early works of Marx and Engels. At first Engels was embarrassed when I expressed interest in these works. He mentioned that Marx had also written poetry in his student years, but it could hardly interest anybody. . . . Was not the fragment on Feuerbach which Engels considered the most meaty of the 'old works' sufficient?" Which was more important, Engels asked, "for him to spend the rest of his life publishing old manuscripts from publicistic works of the 1840s or to set to work, when Book III of Capital came out, on the publication of Marx's manuscripts on the history of the theories of surplus value?" And for Engels the answer was obvious. Besides, said Engels, "in order to penetrate into that 'old story' one needed to have an interest in Hegel himself, which was not the case with anybody then, or to be exact, 'neither with Kautsky nor with Bernstein.' "[18]

In fact, except for *The Holy Family,*[19] a crazy-quilt bag of essays deriding Bruno Bauer and his two brothers, who with their friends constituted the "holy family," none of the early philosophical writings of Marx was published either in his lifetime or that of Engels. Nor is it clear whether the major exegetes, Kautsky, Plekhanov, and

Lenin, were ever aware of their content. None of the questions of alienation appear in their writing. The chief concern of the post-Marxist writers, when they dealt with philosophy, was simply to defend a materialist viewpoint against idealism.

The contemporary 'rediscovery' of the idea of alienation in Marxist thought is due to Georg Lukács, the Hungarian philosopher who did have an interest in Hegel. The idea of alienation, because of its natural affinity to romanticism, had already played an important role in German sociology, particularly in the thought of Georg Simmel, who had been a teacher of Lukács. Simmel, writing about the "anonymity" of modern man, first located the source of alienation in industrial society, which destroyed man's self-identity by "dispersing" him into a cluster of separate roles. Later Simmel widened the concept to see alienation as an ineluctable outcome between man's creativity and the pressure of social institutions (much as Freud's later image of the inescapable tension between instinct and civilization).

Lukács, coming onto Marx after World War I, was able, without knowing of the early *Manuscripts,* to "read back" from Marx into Hegel the alienation of labor as the self-alienation of Man from the Absolute Idea. The Kautsky-Lenin generation had construed Marxism as a scientific, non-moral, analysis of society. But in Lukács' interpretation, Marx's economic analysis of society was turned inside out and became the work, as Morris Watnick put it, "of a moral philosopher articulating the future of man's existence in the accents of a secular eschatology." Lukács' interpretation, which was included in a collection of essays entitled *Geschichte und Klassenbewusstsein* (*History and Class Consciousness*), published in 1923, smacked of idealism to the orthodox Marxists, and Lukács quickly came under fire in Moscow. Among the Communists the book was proscribed, although the work continued to enjoy a *sub rosa* reputation among the Communist intelligentsia, less for its discussion of alienation, however, than for another essay which, in covert form, rationalized the elite position of, and the need for outward submission of, the Communist intellectual to the party. When Lukács fled Germany in the early thirties and took refuge in the Soviet Union, he was forced, eleven years after the publication of the essays, again to repudiate his book, and this time, in an abject act of self-abasement.

Addressing the philosophical section of the Communist Academy in 1934, Lukács stated:

> The mistakes into which I fell in my book *History and Class Consciousness* are completely in line with these deviations [i.e., those attacked in Lenin's *Materialism and Empirio-Criticism*]. . . . I began as a student of Simmel and Max Weber. . . . At the same time the philosophy of syndicalism (Sorel) had a great influence on my development; it strengthened my inclinations toward romantic anti-capitalism. . . . Thus I entered the Communist Party of Hungary in 1918 with a world-outlook that was distinctly syndicalist and idealist. . . .
>
> The book I published in 1923 . . . was a philosophical summation of these tendencies. . . . In the course of my practical party work and in familiarizing myself with the works of Lenin and Stalin, these idealists props of my world-outlook lost more and more of their security. Although I did not permit a republication of my book (which was sold out by that time), nevertheless I first came to full appreciation of these philosophical problems during my visit to the Soviet Union in 1930-31, especially through the philosophical discussions in progress at that time.
>
> Practical work in the Communist Party of Germany, direct ideological struggle . . . against the Social Fascist and Fascist ideology have all the more strengthened my conviction that in the intellectual sphere, *the front of idealism is the front of Fascist counter-revolution and its accomplices, the Social Fascists.* Every concession to idealism, however significant, spells *danger* to the proletarian revolution. Thus, I understood not only the *theoretical falsity,* but also the *practical danger* of the book I wrote twelve years ago. . . .
>
> With the help of the Comintern, of the All-Union Communist Party and of its leader, Comrade Stalin, the sections of the Comintern will struggle . . . for that iron discipline, implacability and refusal to compromise with all deviations from Marxism-Leninism which the All-Union Communist Party . . . achieved long ago. . . .[20]

When the early philosophical works of Marx were unearthed and published, Lukács had the satisfaction of seeing how accurately he had been able to reconstruct the thought of the young Marx.[21] But this did not spare him from attack. The dogma, drawn from Lenin, had become fixed.

The early philosophical writings were published in 1932 in Germany. But in the floodtide of Hitlerism, of the destruction of the Social Democratic and Communist parties, and the dispersal of the German scholarly community, there was little time or incentive to read these inchoate and fragmentary works. In the disillusionments with Stalinism in the late thirties, particularly following the Moscow trials, in some small intellectual radical circles in New York, in the increasing sense of rootlessness felt by a young generation, in the resumption of scholarly activity by a group of German scholars in New York, notably the Frankfurt Institute of Social Research of Max Horkheimer, and the publication of its *Zeitschrift,* first in German and then in English, there arose some small interest in the early writings of Marx, and particularly the idea of alienation. But the application of the idea was psychological and literary and soon found a louder resonance from surprisingly other sources.

The interest in the idea of alienation that unfolded rapidly in the late forties and early fifties came largely from the rediscovery of Kierkegaard and Kafka, and from the sense of despair that both epitomized.

Kierkegaard represented the other great, neglected trunk which had emerged from the deep Hegelian roots. Where the "left-Hegelians" had sought a rational answer to the question of alienation, Kierkegaard argued that none existed. No rational act could overcome the subject-object dualism; any attempt to set rational limits to comprehension end in the "absurd." Only by a "leap of faith" could man establish a relationship with ultimate powers beyond himself. Thus, from ontology, Kierkegaard took the concept of alienation and gave it a religious content; and where Marx had sought to narrow the description of alienation into the exploitative social relationships created by the economic system, Kierkegaard universalized it as an ineluctable, pervasive condition of man.

There were deep reasons for this attraction to the idea of despair—and faith. The sadism of the Nazis, the ruthlessness of war, the existence of concentration camps, the use of terror, had called into question the deepest beliefs of the generation. One could argue, as did Sidney Hook, for example, that the Stalinist terror grew out of the specific historical circumstances which shaped the Russian dictatorship, and that its existence was no indictment of rationalism.

But a more compelling reason—at least, psychologically speaking— seemed to come from the neo-orthodox arguments of Reinhold Niebuhr that such corruption of power was inevitable when men, in their pride, identified their own egos with the demiurge of History, and that rationalism, by encouraging utopian beliefs in man's perfectibility, had left men unarmed against the corruption which lurked in socialism.

From a second source, the "tragic vein" of German sociology, came new, intellectual support for the idea of alienation. In the influence of Karl Mannheim, and later of Max Weber, the idea of alienation merged with the idea of "bureaucratization." The two had absorbed Marx's ideas and gone beyond him. The drift of all society, said Weber, was toward the creation of large-scale organization, hierarchically organized and centrally directed, in which the individual counted for nought. Marx's emphasis on the wage worker as being "separated" from the means of production became, in Weber's perspective, as Gerth and Mills succinctly put it, "merely one special case of a universal trend. The modern soldier is equally 'separated' from the means of violence, the scientist from the means of enquiry and the civil servant from the means of administration." And the irony, said Weber, is that, from one perspective, capitalism and socialism were simply two different faces of the same, inexorable trend.

Out of all this came the impact of the idea of alienation. The intellectual saw men becoming depersonalized, used as a "thing" in the operation of society as a machine; the intellectual himself felt increasingly estranged from the society. The idea of alienation, thus, was a judgment *on* society. It also reflected the self-conscious position of the intellectual *in* the society.

III

The themes of alienation, anomie, bureaucratization, depersonalization, privatization have been common coin in the sociological literature for more than a decade and a half. In the light of all this, the recent attempts to proclaim the theme of alienation in the early

Marx as a great new theoretical advance in the understanding of contemporary society is indeed strange. The reasons for this—which lie in the sociology of knowledge—are fairly simple. There is today a new political generation in England and France—and in the Communist countries of eastern Europe—whose only political perspective had been Marxism. Following the Khrushchev disclosures at the 20th Party Congress and the events in Hungary, this generation became disillusioned about Stalinism. It wants to find its own footing, and, like any generation, has to find it in its own way and in its own language. (Such an attempt is found to be naive and stumbling, yet have some verve and excitement, which is one reason why the *Universities and Left Review* and *Arguments* seem fresh and alive, while *Dissent,* in the U.S., though more sophisticated and worldly-wise, seems weary and stale.) The post-Stalinist radical generation in England and France still wants to think in political terms (and the dissidents and revisionists in eastern Germany and Poland, by the nature of their situation are forced to argue in philosophical categories)—hence the umbilical cords to Marx.[22]

But the difficulty is that there are no apocalyptic ideas or fresh ideological causes. There may be immediate issues such as nuclear tests or educational policy, but no comprehensive political vision which can fire young imaginations and fill the emotional void that obviously exists. The idea of alienation has gained a new edge because of the disorientation of the radical intellectual in the mass society where tradition, avant-garde, and middle-brow culture all jostle each other uneasily—but that is already a far different topic.[23]

Having started out with the idea that in the young Marx there was a double vision of the nature of alienation, I would like to conclude with some brief remarks about the road that Marxism did not take. Marxist thought developed along one narrow road of economic conceptions of property and exploitation, while the other road, which might have led to new, humanistic concepts of works and labor, was left unexplored.

In the transmutation of the concept of alienation, a root insight was lost—that alienation is a consequence of the *organization* of work as well, and that in the effort to give a man a sense of meaning in his daily life, one must examine the work process itself. In manufacture, said Marx, the worker is "deformed into a detail worker," he becomes an appendage to the machine. All this was laid at the door of capitalistic society. Yet there is little evidence that the Communist countries have sought to reverse the process, to explore new combinations of work, to re-examine the engineering process, or to question the concept of efficiency that underlies the contemporary organization of work. If anything, in the intense pressure for production, the lack of free trade union movements and independent agencies, which can act as a control or check on the managers and the State, has meant that the workers in the Communist countries are even more exploited than those in western lands. Technology stands as a "given."

One need not accept the fatalism of the machine process[24]—or wait for new utopias in automation—to see that changes are possible. These range from such large-scale changes as genuine decentralization, which brings work to the workers rather than transporting large masses of workers to the work place, to the relatively minute but important changes in the pace of work, such as extending job cycles, job enlargement, allowing natural rhythms in work, etc. The "flow of demand," to use the sociological jargon, must come from the worker rather than from the constraints imposed upon him. If one believes, for example, that the worker is not a commodity, then one should take the step of abolishing wage payment by the piece, or eliminating the distinction whereby one man gets paid a salary and another an hourly wage. If one accepts the heritage of the humanist tradition, then the work place itself, and not the market, must be the center of determination of the organization of work. The fullness of life can and must be found in the nature of work itself.

NOTES

1. A troublesome issue that still remains unresolved in Marxist theory, for if the intellectuals create the socialist ideology, while the workers, left to themselves, achieve only trade union consciousness, as Lenin maintained, what, then, is the meaning of Marx's statement that existence determines consciousness, and that class fashions ideology?

2. "For freedom," says Hegel in his *Logic,* "it is necessary that we should feel no presence of something which is not ourselves." Finitude is bondage; the consciousness of an object is a limitation; freedom is "that voyage into the open where nothing is below us or above us, and we stand in solitude with ourselves alone."–Hegel's *Logic,* Wallace edition, pp. 49, 66 (cited by Robert Tucker; see footnote 6, below).

3. See Ludwig Feuerbach, *The Essence of Christianity* (New York, Harper Torchbook edition, 1957), p. 30.

4. For a discussion of Feuerbach's use of the I-Thou concept, see the introduction by Karl Barth to *The Essence of Christianity, ibid.,* p. xiii.

5. The key statement of this idea in Marx is to be found, first, in the *Economic-Philosophical Manuscripts of 1844.* An English edition was published in Moscow in 1959. See pp. 67-84, and especially pages 73-77. A more condensed version of this idea is to be found in Part One of *The German Ideology* (New York, International Publishers, 1939), esp. pp. 7-8.

6. A comprehensive exposition of the early views of Marx can be found in Robert C. Tucker, *The Self and Revolution: A Moral Critique of Marx,* unpublished Ph.D. dissertation (Harvard, 1957). This study, revised and expanded, appeared as *Philosophy and Myth in Karl Marx* (New York, Cambridge University Press, 1961). I am indebted to Mr. Tucker for many insights. A lucid discussion of the nature of Marx's early writings can be found in Jean Hippolyte's *Etudes sur Marx et Hegel* (Paris, Librairie Marcel Rivière et Cie, 1955), especially pp. 147-155. An overly simple exposition can be found in H. P. Adams, *Karl Marx in his Early Writings* (London, 1940); a provocative discussion in Hannah Arendt's *The Human Condition* (Chicago, 1958).

7. For a further discussion, see Herbert Marcuse, *Reason and Revolution: Hegel and the Rise of Social Theory* (New York, 1941), pp. 276-277.

8. "Money is the alienated *ability of mankind.* That which I am unable to do as a *man,* and of which, therefore all my individual essential powers are incapable, I am able to do by means of *money.* Money thus turns each of these powers into something which in itself it is not–turns it, that is, into its *contrary."–Economic-Philosophical Manuscripts, op. cit.,* p. 139 (italics in the original).

   It is this conception of money as the hidden mechanism whereby people became exploited (money "the common whore . . . [which] confounds all human and natural qualities") that lay behind Marx's withering analysis of the Jew, as the dealer in money, in economic society. It is this conception, too, that underlay the extraordinarily naive act of the Bolshevik regime in the first days after the October Revolution of abolishing all money in an effort to make the relationship of man to man "direct." The novel implications of this development in Marx's thought, of the *shift* in the early manuscripts from philosophy to political economy, have been explored in great detail by Professor Tucker, *op. cit.*

9. For a neglected discussion of the idea of "generic man" and "historical man" in Marx, see Solomon F. Bloom, *The World of Nations: A Study of the National Implications in the Work of Karl Marx* (New York 1941), Chap. I, pp.1-10.

10. In *The German Ideology* Marx poses the question of how individual self-interest becomes transformed into ideology. "How does it come about," he asks, "that personal interests grow, despite the persons, into class-interests, into common interests which win an independent exist-

ence over against individual persons, in this independence take on the shape of general interests, enter as such into opposition with the real individuals, and in this opposition, according to which they are defined as general interests, can be conceived by the consciousness as ideal, even as religious, sacred interests?"

Having posed the question so concisely, Marx, exasperatingly never goes on to answer it. Sidney Hook, in his article on "Materialism" in the *Encyclopedia of the Social Sciences,* sought to rephrase the problem in these terms: "What are the specific mechanisms by which the economic conditions influence the habits and motives of classes, granted that individuals are actuated by motives that are not always a function of individual self-interest? Since classes are composed of individuals, how are class interests furthered by the non-economic motives of individuals?"

Having rephrased the question even more sharply, Hook, too, left it unanswered. So far no Marxist theoretician has as yet detailed the crucial psychological and institutional nexuses which transform the personifications, or masks of class-role, into the self-identity of the individual.

See *The German Ideology, op. cit.,* p. 203; *E.S.S.,* Vol. X, p. 219; and the discussions by Robert Tucker.

11. *Ibid.,* p. 96.

12. *The Communist Manifesto,* p. 233, in Karl Marx, *Selected Works* (Moscow, 1935), Volume I.

13. In *Capital,* Marx writes powerfully of the crippling effects of the detailed division of labor, and then, in a footnote, quotes approvingly the image of work provided by a French workman who had returned from San Francisco: "I never could have believed, that I was capable of working at various occupations I was employed on in California. I was firmly convinced that I was fit for nothing but letter-press printing. . . . Once in the midst of this world of adventurers, who change their occupation as often as they do their shirt, egad, I did as the others. As mining did not turn out remunerative enough, I left it for the town, where in succession I became typographer, slater, plumber, &c. In consequence of thus finding out that I am fit for any sort of work, I feel less of a mollusk and more of a man." (Marx, *Capital,* Chicago, 1906, Vol. I, Part IV, Section 9, especially pp. 532-535. The footnote is from p. 534.)

14. F. Engels, "On Authority," in *Marx & Engels: Basic Writings on Politics & Philosophy,* edited by Lewis S. Feuer (Anchor Books, New York, 1959), p. 483.

15. Frederick Engels, *Anti-Dühring* (Chicago, 1935), pp. 332-333.

16. Frederick Engels, *Ludwig Feuerbach and the Outcome of German Classical Philosophy,* in Karl Marx, *Selected Works, op. cit.,* Vol. I, p. 147.

17. Engels to Florence Kelley Wischnewetzky, February 25, 1886, in Karl Marx and Frederick Engels, *Letters to Americans* (New York 1953), p. 151.

18. A. Voden, "Talks with Engels," in *Reminiscences of Marx and Engels* (Moscow, undated), pp. 330-331.

19. The first part of *The Holy Family,* subtitled the "Critique of Critical Critique," is devoted to an alleged misreading by Edgar Bauer of Proudhon's work on property. The book then jumps to a detailed analysis of Eugene Sue's *The Mysteries of Paris* and to the alleged misreading of this volume—which is about the sick and wretched of Paris—by a supporter of Bauer who had used the volume to demonstrate the "critical method." The last sections deal with the French Revolution and the rise of French

materialism. In his heavy-handed way, Marx was fond of pinning religious tags on his opponents. Not only are the Bauers called the "holy family" but in *The German Ideology* Max Stirner is called "Saint Max." Although Marx drew most of his ideas from his peers—self-consciousness from Bauer, alienation from Feuerbach, communism from Moses Hess, the stages of property from Proudhon—he was not content simply to synthe-size these ideas, but he had to attack, and usually viciously, all these individuals in the determined effort to appear wholly original.

20. This statement is quoted by Morris Watnick in his study, "Georg Lukács: An Intellectual Biography," *Soviet Survey* (London), No. 24, p. 54. Mr. Watnick's extended discussion of Lukács' ideas can be found in *Soviet Survey*, Nos. 23, 24, 25, 27 (1958-59).

Lukács' book is generally unobtainable here. A chapter from it, under the title "What is Orthodox Marxism," appeared in *The New International*, Summer 1957. Sections of the book have been translated in French, in the review *Arguments* published by Les Editions de Minuit. There are some brief, but penetrating remarks on Lukács—and the prob-lem of the intellectual accepting the soldierly discipline of Communism—in Franz Borkenau's *World Communism* (New York, 1939), pp. 172-175.

21. The early philosophical writings, principally the incomplete *Economic-Philosophical Manuscripts,* and *The German Ideology* were first published (with small sections missing) in 1932 by S. Landshut and J. P. Mayer under the title of *Der historiche Materialismus,* in two volumes. (Some small fragments of the third part of *The German Ideology,* on Max Stirner, had been published by Edward Bernstein in *Dokumente des Sozialismus,* in 1902-03.) A detailed description of the early manuscripts, particularly of *The German Ideology,* was published by D. Riazanov in Vol. I of the Marx-Engels Archiv in 1927. The complete texts are avail-able in the *Marx-Engels Gesamtausgabe* under the direction of V. Adoratski (Berlin, 1932). A new edition of the early papers was pub-lished by S. Landshut in 1953, under the title *Die Frühschriften von Karl Marx.* A complete guide to the works of Marx can be found in Maxi-milien Rubel, *Bibliographie des Oeuvres de Karl Marx* (Paris, 1956).

22. So eager are the young neo-Marxists to maintain a tie to Marxism or to provide some notion of fresh thinking and discovery that such a bright young Scottish philosopher as Alasdair MacIntyre is led to write such farrago as appeared in *The Listener* of January 8, 1959, entitled "Dr. Marx and Dr. Zhivago": "Humanity and the one true bearer of the human essence in our time, the industrial proletariat, has to break through and make new forms. So alienated man remakes and regains himself. This is the picture which the young Marx elaborated, the picture out of which the mature Marxist theory grew. In this picture there is a place for those members of bourgeois society who, humane and sensitive as they are, cling to the ideals and culture they know and therefore cannot make the transition to the new society. Such surely is Zhivago. . . ."

23. One which is explored in my *The End of Ideology* (The Free Press, 1960).

24. For an elaboration of this argument, see my essay "Work and Its Dis-contents: The Cult of Efficiency in America" (Beacon Press, 1956).

5. History and Man's "Nature" in Marx

JOSEPH J. O'MALLEY

In Marx's writings there is a notion of "nature" as applied to man, which is not the notion ordinarily imputed to Marx. This notion is a more fundamental one and offers the possibility of a fresh analysis of certain aspects of Marx's theory on man and society. Up to now it has not been exploited by Marx's American commentators.[1]

All notions proper to Marx's thought find their meaning within the framework of his doctrine of the historical process of production. Accordingly, this essay begins with a general treatment of that process in terms of the factors and dynamisms said to be integral to it. The focus will then turn to Marx's notion of the correlative evolutions of nature and of human nature, as the latter is ordinarily understood in Marx. After that there will be an exposition of the more fundamental sense of nature in regard to man that appears in Marx's writings; this will be accompanied by an indication of the way in which this sense of nature is said to evolve historically and of how it is suggestive of an approach to Marx's social philosophy. A

Originally published in *The Review of Politics,* 28:4, October 1966, 508-527.

brief conclusion will suggest a similarity between this notion of nature utilized by Marx and that of a historical predecessor, without aiming to minimize either the novelty or the significance of its use by Marx.[2]

I

In Marx, the crucial historical reality is the "process of production." He called it the origin or birthplace of history. It is the context within which historiography must locate its objects if historiography is to be valid and if history is to be understood.[3]

"Production" is conceived to be a dynamic process. The activity central to it is "labor." "Labor" is described as the activity ". . . in which man of his own accord starts, regulates, and controls the material reactions between himself and Nature . . . in order to appropriate Nature's productions in a form adapted to his own wants."[4]

"Labor" is spoken of as a "creative force."[5] Its creativity consists in its being an endowment of new forms on natural materials, an endowment by virtue of which those materials become apt to satisfy man's needs.[6]

"Production" is seen to involve a number of factors. These factors of production are also referred to as the "conditions" of production inasmuch as they are all necessary in order that production occur. Generally speaking, there are four factors, or conditions of production. These are living men with needs, society, instruments, and nature.[7]

Man is the laboring "subject" of production; nature, at times used interchangeably with "the earth" (*die Erde*), is the "object" (*Gegenstand*) of production.[8] Nature is called man's "external sensuous world"[9]; it is said to be the source of the materials of production and of man's means of subsistence, and again, man's "primitive toolhouse and larder."[10] It is man's "inorganic body" with which he must remain, by his labor, in a constant, active relationship of exchange.[11]

In addition to man and nature, society and instruments are also said to be essential conditions of production. For Marx production occurs only when men cooperate in their efforts to appropriate the materials of nature which their needs demand: "In order to produce, they enter into definite connections and relations to one another, and only within these social connections and relations does their influence upon nature operate, that is, does production take place."[12] The idea of production by isolated individuals outside of society is said to be an absurdity."[13]

Instruments (*Arbeitsmitteln*) come under the heading of the "objective" conditions of production—as distinct from the "subjective" conditions of production, man and society. An instrument is itself a product, that is, it is natural material formed by human activity to serve as a medium to transmit man's labor power to nature. Instruments are indispensable to the production of the goods immediately suited to answer man's needs. Inasmuch as the instrument is interposed between man and the object (*Gegenstand*) of production it can be said that ". . . the first thing of which the labourer possesses himself is not the *Gegenstand* of labour but its instrument."[14]

The process of production is the totality arising out of, or constituted by the copresence of, these four factors of production. Within that totality the individual factors are said to be "functionally" interrelated. This means that the determinate characteristics of each factor, at any given time and place, are conditioned by the other factors in combination. In short, production is understood by Marx to be a system of "reciprocally interdependent variables."[15] For example, regarding men, the "subjects" of production, it is said by Marx that ". . . what they are . . . coincides with their production, both with *what* they produce and with how they produce"; and inasmuch as the "what" and "how" of production are determined both by the kind of instruments at hand and by ". . . the natural conditions in which man finds himself—geological, oro-hydrographical, climatic and so on—the nature of individuals thus depends on the material conditions determining their production."[16] Thus if man's "nature" is said to be identical with his way of life, then man's "nature" is a function of the other factors of production.

Already the general analysis of the process of production allows of several "definitions" of man, namely, as laborer, as social, and as toolmaker; for man's life activity is said to be productive activity, or labor, and this activity is always social and always involves instruments.[17] Moreover, there is implied a definition of man as "rational animal," where "rational" means purposive and self-aware; for labor is said to be "exclusively human" insofar as it involves the projection of ends to be achieved, a fitting of means to ends, and the ability to attend to the "law" of the *modus operandi* which the plan imposes. Throughout, the laborer is aware of all this, for "the process demands that, during the whole operation, the workman's will be steadily in consonance with his purpose."[18] Thus, too, it is said that, in contrast to animals, man's labor involves the element of freedom.[19]

Two more features of the process of production emerge in the general analysis of it in Marx's writings. The first is its over-all goal or purpose; the second is its evolutionary character. As productive of "use-values," that is, of goods fitted to the satisfaction of man's needs, production aims at man's survival. Production of "use-values" is said to be indirect production of man's life: "By producing their means of subsistence men are indirectly producing their actual material life." This is also spoken of as "the reproduction of the physical existence of the individuals."[20] And since this also requires the production of the means whereby "use-values" are produced, it must be said that the aim of production extends to the continuing formation both of means of subsistence and means of production: "The object of production itself is to reproduce the producer in and together with these objective conditions of his existence."[21]

Productive activity, however, is said to result in something more than the mere physical survival of the producers; as shaped by the existing, objective conditions of production, the activity of production is itself a way of life. As productive activity it results in the continuation of that way of life; production results in the continuation of production. In production, therefore, men are said not only to reproduce their physical life, but also their mode of life, including the social complex in which they cooperatively act on nature. This is not an incidental result. The reproduction of man's physical life requires the reproduction of the conditions of production essential to the making of "use-values"; and the reproduction of those conditions is the reproduction of the mode of life.[22]

While the reproduction of physical life is the primitive aim of production, not all of man's needs are physical needs. The productive activity which aims at the satisfaction of these other, non-physical needs is obviously understood to result in something more in the producer than simple physical existence.[23] So the goal or purpose of production is said to be the sustaining of man's life, but man's life is understood to be more than mere physical existence.

The last feature of the process of production which we will note here is its evolutionary character. Production is not only a process of interchange between man and nature; it is also a historically developing process, an evolving process. Thus, production has a history. In fact, world history is understood to be basically nothing other than the history of production.[24]

The evolution of production is described in various ways: for example, in terms of class struggle, as in the *Communist Manifesto;* or in terms of successive epochs each of which is distinguished by a particular mode of production with its corresponding social form; or again in terms of a progressive dissolution of the primitive relation of the laboring subject to the objective conditions of production.[25]

Within this view of history as being basically the evolution of production, one may focus on any of the individual factors of production and trace its history. But this is valid only so long as the subject of study is understood to be meaningful ultimately within the context of production. This is to do history "materialistically."[26]

At the same time history as the evolutionary development of production is ultimately significant in human terms. Production is human activity which aims at the reproduction of human life. If production is a historically developing process, it is as a process involving the development of man and his world that it is seen to be of ultimate significance. What this means can be seen by treating Marx's notion of production as involving a modification of both man and nature; for the two are said to be changed in the very process of production: "By acting on the external world (*die Natur ausser ihm*) and changing it, [man] at the same time changes his own nature (*seine eigne Natur*). He develops his slumbering powers and compels them to act in obedience to his sway."[27]

II

Marx insisted on the historical character of nature; he criticized as erroneous the separation of nature from history. The crux of this error is said to lie in the failure to see production as the basic historical process: "In the whole conception of history up to the present this real basis of history has either been totally neglected or else considered as a minor matter quite irrelevant to the course of history.... With this the relation of man to nature is excluded from history and hence the antithesis of nature and history is created."[28]

Nature, as the *Gegenstand* of production, is said to be itself historical. Its history is described as a process of change from that "... which first appears to men as a completely alien, all-powerful and unassailable force, with which men's relations are purely animal and by which they are overawed like beasts"[29] to that which "... appears (to man) as his work and his reality."[30] Thus, the "history" of nature is the development of man's environment from the status of raw nature, a complex of nonhuman objects and forces, to the status of human artifact, which is said to express man's perfection and reality in reflecting his developed powers. This historical transformation of nature is spoken of as the progressive "humanization" of nature.[31]

The "humanization" of nature is a result of man's productive activity. To say that man's environment becomes humanized is another way of saying that through man's labor his environment becomes progressively less a complex of "natural objects, which he must reshape to suit his needs, and progressively more a complex of "products" which man's labor has already shaped to that end. Productive activity is said to result in the reproduction both of life and of the conditions of life; and this latter is the transformation of the environment into objects which embody man's activity and purpose:

". . . If this reproduction appears on one hand as the appropriation of the objects by the subjects, it equally appears on the other as the moulding, the subjection, of the objects by and to a subjective purpose; the transformation of the objects into results and repositories of subjective activity."[32]

The complex of "products" which replaces the complex of "natural" objects is constituted of means of subsistence and of production, of instruments and raw materials, all of which are understood to be results of the creativity of labor. Thus is man said to transform his environment, for this complex of artifacts comes progressively, in the course of history, to supplant "raw" nature as the *Gegenstand* of man's life activity.[33]

Correlative with the "humanization" of nature is the "naturalization" of man himself.[34] The "naturalization" of man is understood in terms of a progressive realization in the course of history, of man as such, that is, of man's "species being." This is said to coincide with the emergence of new powers in man, and hence of new modes of human existence and activity. Hegel is praised for having seen the role of labor in this emergence: "The outstanding achievement of Hegel's *Phenomenology* . . . is thus first that Hegel conceives the self-creation of man as a process, conceives objectification as loss of the object, as alienation and as transcendence of this alienation; that he thus grasps the essence of *labor* and comprehends objective man—true, because real man—as the outcome of man's *own labor*. . . . [Hegel] grasps labor . . . as man's *essence* in the act of proving itself. . . ."[35]

For Marx, too, the activity of production entails an objectification of man's powers—the transformation of his environment—which is the correlate of the emergence in man of those powers as realized. Transformed nature manifests man's operative, that is, actually realized powers. Man can read in his environment his own reality and power because his environment has taken on, through the historical development of production, the status of man's own artifact:

It is just in his work upon the objective world, therefore, that man first really proves himself to be a *species being*. This production is his active species life. Through and because of this production, nature appears as *his* work and *his* reality. The object of labor is, therefore, the *objectification of man's species life;* for he duplicates himself not only as in consciousness, intellectually, but also actively, in reality, and therefore he contemplates himself in a world he has created.[36]

It was with this sense of an emergence of man's powers, correlative with the transformation of nature and within the evolution of production, that Marx wrote that ". . . all history is nothing but a continual transformation of human nature. . . ."[37]

There are two ways in which this transformation of human nature can be understood in Marx's writings. This follows from the fact that man's "nature" can be understood in two ways. First, man's "nature" can be understood as coinciding with man's "mode of life" — let us say, his "mode of being."[38] Where this sense of "nature" is applied to man, a distinction can be made between a general human nature and specific expressions of human nature which occur within the process of history as a function of the evolving factors of production. The "transformation of human nature," of which Marx speaks, then means the historical transformation of man's "mode of being" which, ideally, takes the form of a progressive enrichment of that mode of being, and which points toward the achievement of a truly human mode of being.[39]

Nature here is *Wesen;* and where taken in the sense of general human nature includes such notes as "social," "conscious," and "free" — all of which represent features of man's activity which are common to all specific, historical expressions of human nature (*menschliches Wesen*). The definitions of man noted earlier, which Marx accepted, were expressive of these different common features.

There is, however, another, more fundamental, sense in which man's "nature" can be understood in Marx. To this second sense of "nature," and therefore of the "transformation of human nature," in Marx's writings, the succeeding part of this essay will be devoted.

III

The second way in which man's "nature" may be understood in Marx's writings is in reference to that in man which provides both the impetus to, and the orientation of, man's activity. This refers to the complex of "needs" (*Bedürfnisse*) which in man are said to be both the ground of his activity and that by which he is related to his environment. To see the bearing of this doctrine, it is helpful to note the way in which Marx, opposing himself to both Hegel and Feuerbach, described man as related to his objective world.

First, man is not to be understood as "pure activity." This is said to be Hegel's conception of man. Man here is "self-consciousness," pure creative activity; and the world of objects is something "posited" by man (self-consciousness) as a "moment" in his development as self-consciousness. The radical creativity of man, in this view, has as its corollary a conception of the objective world as "utterly without any *independence,* any essentiality vis-à-vis self-consciousness . . . it is mere creature — something *posited* by self-consciousness."[40]

Second, and on the other hand, man is not to be understood as pure passivity. This is said to be Feuerbach's conception of man. Man here is a being who merely contemplates his environment as something simply given, something which determines him and to which he only reacts. Man, in this view, is seen to be in no sense creative of his environment, of his world of objects; and that world, "the object, reality, what we apprehend through our senses, is understood only in the form of *object* or *contemplation* (*Anschauung*). . . ."[41]

It is asserted that Hegel, in conceiving of man as essentially self-consciousness, failed to give adequate weight to man's corporeality, to his physical nature, and hence to his dependence on an independently existing "sensuous" environment. But Feuerbach, on the other hand, "does not understand our sensuous nature as *practical, human-sensuous activity.*"[42] Thus where Hegel erred in taking the *Gegenstand* of man's activity, or nature, to be, in a radical sense, the creature of self-consciousness, Feuerbach erred in failing to see that nature is indeed the historical product of man's "sensuous labor and creation."[43]

Marx sought the middle ground between the two views. Man's true situation is said to involve both an active and a passive relationship to his environment; that is, man is said to be "nature." To conceive of man as "nature" is to conceive of him as immediately related to his environment both actively and passively. In man the focus of this twofold relation is his set of "needs." Man's needs move him to action; they also orient his action. Thus they provide both the dynamism and the intentionality of his existence. By virtue of his needs man is actively oriented toward his environment, nature, as toward the source of the objects of his needs. Man is said to be an "objective" and natural being — to "be nature" — and to "act objectively" because the objective "resides in the very nature of his being." His relatedness to nature is said to consist in his being, at once, actively inclined toward the objects of his needs, and passively drawn to and determined by those objects. "Need" is the key to understanding man's dynamism and intentionality, for a "need" is "the dominion of the objective being in me . . ." and thus is effectively *"passion,* which thus becomes here the activity of my being."[44]

Man is to be understood, then, as an "objective being," a being who is related to a world of objects, because he is a "nature," that is, a structure of dynamic tendencies by virtue of which he is bent on his environment. And his environment is said to be both object of his needs and that which, as object, manifests his reality and his powers:

Man is directly a *natural being.* As a natural being and as a living natural being he is on the one hand endowed with *natural powers of life*—he is an active *natural* being. These forces exist in him as tendencies and abilities—as *instincts.* On the other hand, as a natural, corporeal, sensuous, objective being he is a *suffering,* conditioned and limited creature, like animals and plants. That is to say, the *objects* of his instincts exist outside him, as *objects* independent of him; yet these objects are *objects* that he *needs*— *essential* objects, indispensable to the manifestation and confirmation of his essential powers. To say that man is a *corporeal,* living, real, sensuous, objective being full of natural vigor is to say that he has *real, sensuous, objects* as the objects of his being or of his life, or that he can only *express* his life in real, sensuous objects. . . . *Hunger* is a natural *need;* it therefore needs a *nature* outside itself, an *object* outside itself, in order to satisfy itself, to be stilled. Hunger is an acknowledged need of my body for an *object* existing outside it, indispensable to its integration and to the expression of its essential being.[45]

Man's needs are said to constitute something more than simply physical or psychological phenomena. They are said rather to constitute a dynamic, intentional structure whose significance is "ontological." The "feelings" and "passions" which are the expression of needs "are not merely anthropological phenomena in the narrower sense, but truly *ontological* affirmations of being (of nature). . . ."[46]

The view of man thus established claims to cut across the one-sided views of idealism and all previous materialism. It is said to salvage what is true in each, and to provide the balanced appreciation of man's reality. It is also said to provide the basis for an understanding of world history.[47]

World history is the history of production; and production is the activity of man which is undertaken and carried on in answer to his needs. As providing the impetus to labor, or productive activity, and as providing the orientation of that activity, inasmuch as every need is a tendential relation to specific kinds of objects, man's needs are the primary "condition" of production.[48] As such they are also the primary "condition" of history. The "first premise of all history" is said to be the satisfaction of man's basic needs for food and shelter, and "the first historical act" is said to be the productive act by which they are satisfied.[49] Moreover, man's needs remain the primary motive factor in historical development. They are "a fundamental condition of all history," inasmuch as the satisfaction of man's basic needs through the production of use-values is "the everlasting nature-imposed condition of human existence. . . ."[50]

The dynamism of needs, however, includes the dynamism of growth; the satisfaction of needs is, at once, "the production of new needs."[51] Thus if man is spoken of as a "nature," in the sense of a tendential structure of needs, that "nature" is still said to change. The tendential structure in man by which he is related to his environment — or better, which *is* man, as a being related to his environment — is a structure in process of evolution. This evolution is reflected in the different "modes of life" which evolve within the context of the historical development of production, for any "mode of life" reflects the present and operative needs in man: "The various shaping of material life is, of course, in every case dependent on the needs which are already developed, and both the production and the satisfaction of these needs is a historical process. . . ."[52]

Thus it can be said that man's "nature" differs at one point of history from what it is at another point, meaning by this that the two "modes of life" are different. But more fundamentally it means that man as "nature" is different at one point from what he is at another, that is, that there is a difference in man's tendential make-up. And the difference is explained in terms of the historical development of production.[53]

The evolution of the man *qua* "nature" is thus understood in terms of the emergence of needs. This emergence is seen to be a function of the development of society and the means of production — or, of the development of society and the "humanization" of nature.[54] In Marx's doctrine, this emergence of needs can be understood in two ways.

First, the emergence of needs may be understood in terms of the evolution, as historically and culturally modified, of basic and perennial needs. An instance of this is the need for food: "Hunger is hunger; but the hunger that is satisfied with cooked meat eaten with fork and knife is a different kind of hunger from the one that devours raw meat with the aid of hands, nails, and teeth."[55] For Marx, such modifications constitute real novelty, real difference in the needs in question. The reason is that the character of a need is held to be constituted by the characteristic manner of its gratification. A perennial need allows of a variety of historically and culturally qualified modes of gratification. Each of these is said to be expressive of difference in the existential character of the need.[56]

Second, the emergence of needs may be understood in terms of a more radical novelty. Marx suggested the emergence, within the historical development of production, of wholly new needs as operative impulses to human action. And he suggested that the appearance of these needs, needs which are specifically "human," is what is at stake in the "naturalization" of man: "All history is the preparation for *'man'* to become the object of sensuous consciousness, and for the needs of 'man as man' to become natural, sensuous needs."[57] This emergence of needs, which constitutes the full realization of man's nature, is understood in terms of power and a correlative transformation of the environment, a transformation which represents the development of man's control over both his environment and himself. Speaking of this developed state of man's being as "wealth," Marx wrote:

> ... What is wealth, if not the universality of needs, capacities, enjoyments, productive powers, etc., of individuals, produced in universal exchange? What, if not the full development of human control over the forces of nature—those of his own nature as well as those of so-called "nature"? What, if not the absolute elaboration of his creative dispositions, without any preconditions other than antecedent historical evolution which makes the totality of this evolution—i.e., the evolution of all human powers as such, unmeasured by any previously established yardstick—an end in itself? [58]

The foregoing re-expresses a view which had appeared in Marx's early writings, and which remained basic to his thought, namely, a conception of the evolution of man's nature as a process pointing toward the emergence of specifically human needs:

> We have seen what significance, given socialism, the *wealth* of human needs has, and what significance, therefore, both *a new mode of production* and a new *object* of production have; a new manifestation of the forces of *human* nature and a new enrichment of *human* nature. [59]

Chief among these specifically human needs is a specifically human social need, which is described as a need for "the other human being." Referring to wealth and poverty as ordinarily understood in terms of material possessions, he wrote:

> It will be seen how in place of the *wealth* and *poverty* of political economy comes the *rich human* being and the rich *human* need. The *rich* human being is simultaneously the human being *in need of* a totality of human manifestations of life—the man in whom his own realization exists as an inner necessity, as *need*. Not only *wealth*, but likewise the *poverty* of man—under the assumption of socialism—receives in equal measure a *human* and therefore social significance. Poverty is the passive bond which causes the human being to experience the need of the greatest wealth—the *other* human being. [60]

It has been noted by one of Marx's editors that, in the foregoing passage, Marx attempted to endow the notion of need (*Bedürfnis*) with a social significance.[61] And indeed, an understanding of man's "nature," in Marx, in terms of a dynamic and intentional structure provides a point of departure for an analysis of Marx's social philosophy. The question is, in what sense is man, for Marx, social by nature, that is, what is the character of man's inclination or impulse to social life. An approach utilizing the notion of man's nature which, I suggest, is most fundamental in Marx, would yield, I believe, an interpretation of his social doctrine in which two distinct kinds of "natural" sociality are distinguished in man.

The first would be a "prehuman" sociality consisting of that social impulse present in man's primitive intentional makeup which moves him to cooperative society as a means to the appropriation of nature's products. This would be the inclination to what Marx called "civil society," which he described, following Hegel, as a social complex in which each individual serves as a middleman between every other individual's needs and the "use-values" suited to them.

The second would be a "truly human" sociality consisting in a social impulse which only emerges as a result of the historical development of production. This would be the inclination to the "truly human" society; it is that "need of the greatest wealth – the other human being," noted just above. It is said to be integral to the truly human man; and it would be the catalyst of a truly human society. It would replace self-interest regarding the goods necessary to life – the catalyst of "civil society," according to Marx – as that which holds men together in community.[62]

The historical point of emergence of this second, and truly human, need for society is seen as coinciding with (1) the "naturalization of man," (2) the "humanization of nature," (3) the accomplished "genesis of human society," and (4) the end of human "prehistory." It marks the end of human prehistory because the accomplished emergence of the totality of specifically human needs in individuals is said to mark the appearance in history of a human being who represents "the true resolution of the strife between existence and essence . . . between the individual and the species." The appearance of the truly human man is thus the end of prehuman history, that is, of the history of prehuman man.[63]

The extent to which man's "nature" is understood in terms of the intentional structure constituted by his needs is seen in Marx's appraisal of man in bourgeois society. In bourgeois society, man is said to be "dehumanized." Two types of man are analyzed: the propertyless, or "free," laborer and the propertied bourgeois man. Both are said to lead an inhuman life; and in both cases this inhuman life is understood in terms of a suppression of needs.

The propertyless laborer is said to lead an inhuman life inasmuch as his mode of life is expressive of the subhuman impulses operative in him. As a "nature" he is stultified; his needs are more mean than those of a savage or an animal:

> . . . A dwelling in the *light,* which Prometheus in Aeschylus designated as one of the greatest boons, by means of which he made the savage into a human being, ceases to exist for the worker. Light, air, etc.—the simplest *animal* cleanliness—ceases to be a need for man. . . . None of his senses exist any longer, and not only in his human fashion, but in an *inhuman* fashion, and therefore not even in an animal fashion. . . . It is not only that man has no human needs—even his *animal* needs cease to exist. . . . The savage and the animal have at least the need to hunt, to roam, etc.—the need of companionship.[64]

The laborer leads an inhuman life because his needs have been reduced "to the barest and most miserable level of physical subsistence." He is said to be "an insensible being lacking all needs . . . [whose] activity [is] a pure abstraction from all activity."[65]

But the propertied bourgeois is said also to lead an inhuman life. As a "nature" he is also stultified; the reason given is that in him all human needs are suppressed in favor of the impulse to accumulate monetary wealth. Referring to what he called "the moral ideal" of bourgeois society, Marx wrote:

> Self-renunciation, the renunciation of life and of all human needs, is its principal thesis. The less you eat, drink, and buy books; the less you go to the theater, the dance hall, the public house; the less you think, love, theorize, sing, paint, fence, etc., the more you *save*—the greater becomes your treasure which neither moths nor dust will devour—your *capital*. . . . All passions and all activity must therefore be submerged in *greed*.[66]

Man in bourgeois society is contrasted to the truly human man. The contrast is made most fundamentally in terms of the differences in the needs, or operative impulses, present in each. Inhuman man, as a nature, is a stultified complex of needs, whereas a truly human man is a "universality of needs, capacities, enjoyments, productive powers."

Here, for Marx, is the crucial "contradiction" of the development of production as achieved up to his own day: on the one hand, a set of historically developed, objective forces of production capable of supporting a truly human life for man — that is, the realized means of giving rise to and of answering a quantitatively and qualitatively rich complex of human tendencies; and, on the other hand, a society of men whose lives are seen to be expressive either of subhuman needs alone, or of the single impulse to accumulate monetary wealth. Put more succinctly, the contradiction consists in this: the "humanization" of nature through man's labor has not been accompanied by the "naturalization" of man, but by his denaturalization.[67]

Both processes, "naturalization" and its opposite, are understood in terms of changes in the complex of man's "needs," which constitutes the dynamic and tendential structure of his being. "Naturalization," or the emergent development of human nature, is the enrichment of that complex; denaturalization, or the suppression of human nature, is the impoverishment of that complex. The doctrine is based on a view of man's "nature" as a tendential structure constituted by that complex of operative needs.

I am suggesting, then, that man's "nature" was understood by Marx not simply in the sense of man's empirically describable, historically evolving "mode of life" or mode of being; but in addition, and more fundamentally, in the sense of the dynamic, tendential structure of man's being, by virtue of which he is related to his environment as seeker and agent. "Nature" here means not character or mode of man's activity, but rather the source immanent in man of his activity.

This more fundamental sense of man's "nature," which is found in Marx, can be likened to Aristotle's notion of "nature" (*physis*), where this word signifies that factor (*aitia*) intrinsic to a thing which gives rise to, and in a way sets the limits to, that thing's activities.[68]

With Marx, however, this notion of "nature" is used within the context of a theory of history as a linear process of evolution. Man is said to be in process of evolution; and this evolution is said to consist primarily in a progressive change in man's intentional make-up — a change which admits a real novelty and which is the correlate of man's developing power and control over his environment.

NOTES

1. Certain French commentators, notably J.-Y. Calvez and H. Lefebvre, have exposed the notion. Nevertheless, this paper owes much to the work of American scholars. In addition to the titles cited in the notes below, the following works were especially helpful: M. Bober, *Karl Marx's Interpretation of History* (2nd ed.; New York, 1965); S. Hook, *From Hegel to Marx* (Ann Arbor, 1962); G. Lichtheim, *Marxism: An Historical and Critical Study* (New York, 1961); H. Marcuse, *Reason and Revolution* (2nd ed.; New York, 1954); V. Venable, *Human Nature: The Marxian View* (London, 1946).

2. Scholarly references to Marx's works are ordinarily to the standard German language edition *Karl Marx-Friedrich Engels Historisch-kritische Gesamtausgabe,* ed. Rjazanov and Adoratsky (Moscow & Berlin, 1927-32), usually cited as *MEGA;* or to the *Karl Marx/Friedrich Engels/ Werke* (Berlin, 1953-   ). For the benefit of the general reader references here will be to readily available English renditions of Marx's writings. For Marx's bibliography, see M. Rubel, *Bibliographie des Oeuvres de Karl Marx* (Paris, 1958); and *Supplément à la Bibliographie des Oeuvres de Karl Marx* (Paris, 1960). On the *MEGA,* see also G. Hertel, *Inhaltsvergleichsregister der Marx-Engels Gesamtausgaben* (Berlin, 1957).

3. *The Holy Family,* trans. Dixon (Moscow, 1956), p. 201.

4. *Capital,* trans. Moore and Aveling, ed. Engels (Chicago, 1932), I, 197-198. "Labor" and "production" are sometimes used interchangeably by Marx, as in *Pre-Capitalist Economic Formations,* trans. Cohen (New York, 1965), p. 95. This latter work is a translation of part of a large manuscript composed by Marx in 1857-58 in preparation for his writing of *A Contribution to the Critique of Political Economy* (1859) and *Capital* (Vol. I, 1867). The manuscript was first published in Moscow by the Marx-Engels-Lenin Institute (1939-41) under the title *Grundrisse der Kritik der politischen Oekonomie, Rohentwurf;* it is usually cited as *Grundrisse.* The edition available to Western scholars is that of Dietz Verlag (Berlin, 1953). On the *Grundrisse,* see esp. M. Rubel, "Contribution à l'histoire de la genèse du Capital: Les manuscrits économico-politiques de Karl Marx (1857-58)," *Revue d'Histoire Economique et Sociale,* XXVIII (1950), 169-185; and "Fragments sociologiques dans les inédits de Marx," *Cahiers Internationaux de Sociologie,* XXII (1957), 128-146.

5. *Wage-Labour and Capital,* trans. Anon. (New York, 1933), p. 31.

6. *Capital,* I, 49-50; cf. *The Economic and Philosophic Manuscripts of 1844,* trans. Milligan, ed. Struik (New York, 1964), p. 112; hereafter cited as *1844 Manuscripts.*

7. See esp. *Capital*, I, 197ff.; *The German Ideology*, ed. Pascal (New York, 1965), pp. 16ff.

8. In addition to the page of *Capital* just cited, see also *Pre-Capitalist Economic Formations*, pp. 71, 81; Introduction to *A Contribution to the Critique of Political Economy*, trans. Stone (Chicago, 1904), p. 269; hereafter cited as *Introduction*.

9. *1844 Manuscripts*, p. 109.

10. *Capital*, I, 199-200.

11. *1844 Manuscripts*, p. 112.

12. *Wage-Labour and Capital*, p. 28.

13. *Introduction*, pp. 268, 265-266; and *Pre-Capitalist Economic Formations*, p. 96, on the "stupidity" of taking the "isolated man" as point of departure in analyses of social-economic forms.

14. *Capital*, I, 199-200; cf. *The German Ideology*, pp. 16-17, where Marx states that the satisfaction of a need through productive activity "... implies ... the acquisition of an instrument."

15. Cf. A. G. Meyer, *Marxism: The Unity of Theory and Praxis* (Ann Arbor, 1963), pp. 24ff.

16. *The German Ideology*, p. 7.

17. See, for example, *Capital*, I, 200; *Introduction*, p. 268; *1844 Manuscripts*, pp. 112ff.

18. *Capital*, I, 198.

19. *1844 Manuscripts*, p. 113.

20. *The German Ideology*, p. 7; on "use-values," see *Capital*, I, 41ff., 201.

21. *Pre-Capitalist Economic Formations*, p. 95.

22. *The German Ideology*, p. 7.

23. On production as aimed at the satisfaction of needs other than physical needs, see *Capital*, I, 41-42 and notes; cf. also the view of man elaborated throughout the *1844 Manuscripts*.

24. *The German Ideology*, p. 28: "Our conception of history depends on our ability to expound the real process of production, starting out from the simple material production of life, and to comprehend the form of intercourse connected with this and created by this (that is, civil society in its various stages), as the basis of all history"; also, *ibid.*, pp. 18-19.

25. Preface to *A Contribution to the Critique of Political Economy*, p. 13; *The German Ideology*, pp. 9-13; the notion of history as the progressive dissolution of a primitive property-relation is a principal theme of *Pre-Capitalist Economic Formations*, which also contains a treatment of the different epochal modes of production. In the last analysis all of these ways of describing the evolution of production reduce to different aspects of one historical process.

26. *The Poverty of Philosophy*, trans. Anon. (Moscow, n.d.), esp. pp. 100-111, and the appended letter of December 28, 1846 to P. V. Annenkov, pp. 171ff.; *The Holy Family*, esp. p. 201.

27. *Capital*, I, 198.

28. *The German Ideology*, p. 17.

29. *Ibid.*, p. 19.

30. *1844 Manuscripts*, p. 114.

31. *Ibid.*, pp. 137, 141.

32. *Pre-Capitalist Economic Formations*, p. 86.

33. See *Capital*, I, 199ff.; esp. 202: "With the exception of the extractive industry (which finds its object ready made in nature, as do mining, hunting, fishing, and agriculture when this is carried on in virgin soil), all branches of industry deal with a *Gegenstand* which is already filtered

through earlier labour, is already a product of labour, an object which we term raw material. . . . Animals and plants which we are apt to regard as natural products may not merely be the products of last year's labour, but the result of a gradual transformation which has been going on through many generations, under human control and aided by human labour." These lines express not only the notion of a progressive inter-position of man's own products between himself and raw nature, as a feature of the historical development of production, but also Marx's distinction between what is "natural" (*naturwüchsig*) and what is under human control. He also utilized this distinction in regard to the develop-ment of forms of society and the division of labor; see *The German Ideology*, p. 20, and editor's note 12, p. 201; also Karl Korsch, *Karl Marx* (New York, 1963), pp. 193ff.

34. *1844 Manuscripts*, p. 137.

35. *Ibid.*, p. 177. Marx goes on immediately to criticize Hegel for recognizing only "abstract, mental labor." He also criticized Hegel for conceiving of all objects as nothing other than products of the subject's creative activity. As we shall see, Marx conceived of "object" as being, first, that which is independent of the subject in its existence, and to which the subject is tendentially related. On the relationship of the theories of labor of Hegel and Marx, and the criticism of Hegel's theory by the latter, see H. Niel, "La philosophie du travail chez Hegel et chez Marx. Choix de textes," *Lumière et Vie*, no. 20 (1955), 23-48.

36. *Ibid.*, p. 114. On the notion of "species being" (*Gattungswegen*), see *ibid.*, pp. 112-113. Consciousness and freedom are essential to the "species being" of man; *ibid.*, p. 113: "Man makes his life activity itself the object of his will and of his consciousness. He has conscious life activity. . . . Con-scious life activity distinguishes man immediately from animal life activity. It is just because of this that he is a species being. Or rather, it is only because he is a species being that he is a conscious being, i.e., that his own life is an object for him. Only because of that is his activity free activity."

37. *The Poverty of Philosophy*, trans. Quelch (Chicago, 1910), p. 160.

38. As in *The German Ideology*, p. 7.

39. This is the usual sense in which Marx's notion of man's "nature" is understood; see, for example, Venable's book; Bober, *op. cit.*, pp. 77-81; John Lewis, *The Life and Teaching of Karl Marx* (New York, 1965), pp. 72-73, 75, 78-79; E. Fromm, *Marx's Concept of Man* (New York, 1961), pp. 24-25, 78-79.

40. *1844 Manuscripts*, pp. 178, 180; also *The Holy Family*, p. 254: "*Phenomenology* is therefore quite logical when in the end it replaces human reality by '*Absolute Knowledge*'–*Knowledge*, because this is the only mode of existence of self-consciousness, because self-consciousness is considered as the only mode of existence of man; *absolute* knowledge for the very reason that self-consciousness knows *itself alone* and is no more disturbed by any objective world. Hegel makes man *the man of self-consciousness* instead of making self-consciousness the *self-conscious-ness of man*, of real man, man living in a real objective world and deter-mined by that world. He stands the world *on its head* and can therefore dissolve *in the head* all the limitations which naturally remain in exis-tence for *evil sensuousness*, for *real* man. Besides, everything which *betrays the limitations of general self-consciousness*–all sensuousness, reality, individuality of men and their world—necessarily rates for him as a limit. The whole of *Phenomenology* is intended to prove that *self-*consciousness is the *only reality* and *all reality*."

41. "Theses on Feuerbach," in *The German Ideology*, Thesis I, p. 197.
42. *Ibid.*, Thesis V, p. 198.
43. *The German Ideology*, pp. 35-37.
44. *1844 Manuscripts*, pp. 144, 180-181.
45. *Ibid.*, p. 181.
46. *Ibid.*, p. 165. J.-Y. Calvez comments: "Cette présence du besoin en l'homme est la présence en lui d'une force substantielle, d'une intentionalité fondamentale qui le constitue, d'une dynamisme natif qui soutient son être"; *Le Pensée de Karl Marx* (Paris, 1956), p. 384; on this point, see pp. 380-388; also the treatment in H. Lefebvre, *Le Matérialisme Dialectique* (Paris, 1957), pp. 98ff.
47. *Ibid.*, p. 181. In these early writings Marx called this view of man "naturalism."
48. *Capital*, I, 197; *Introduction*, p. 279: "No wants [needs], no production" (*Ohne Bedürfnis keine Produktion*).
49. *The German Ideology*, pp. 16-17.
50. *Ibid.*, and *Capital*, I, 204-205.
51. *Ibid.*, 17; and *Introduction*, esp. pp. 278ff., where the treatment is in terms of the relationship between "production" and "consumption."
52. *Ibid.*, p. 71.
53. *Capital*, trans. Untermann, ed. Engels (Chicago, 1909), III, 954; "Just as the savage must wrestle with nature, in order to satisfy his wants (*Bedürfnisse*), in order to maintain his life and reproduce it, so civilized man has to do it, and he must do it in all forms of society and under all possible modes of production. With his development the realm of natural necessity expands, because his wants increase; but at the same time the forces of production increase, by which these wants are satisfied."
54. *Wage-Labour and Capital*, p. 33.
55. *Introduction*, p. 279.
56. *1844 Manuscripts*, p. 165; speaking here about the "ontological" significance of needs, and referring to the "feelings" and "passions," which are the affective manifestations of needs, Marx says: "they have by no means merely one mode of affirmation, but rather . . . the distinct character of their existence, of their life, is constituted by the distinct mode of their affirmation. In what manner the object exists for them, is the characteristic mode of their *gratification.*"
57. *1844 Manuscripts*, p. 143.
58. *Pre-Capitalist Economic Formations*, pp. 84-85.
59. *1844 Manuscripts*, p. 147.
60. *1844 Manuscripts*, pp. 143-144. Regarding the reappearance of notions from Marx's early writings in the *Grundrisse*, M. Rubel writes: "Les matériaux contenus dans ces manuscrits sont intéressants à plus d'un titre. Outre qu'ils montrent, malgré leur forme prolixe et les nombreuses redites, le cheminement logico-théorique de la pensée économique de Marx, ils sont très riches en aperçus de tous ordres, historiques, sociologiques et éthiques. Ils présentent à maints endroits ce caractère de *Selbsteverstaendigung*, de ce besoin intime de clarté dont Marx a fait une maxime constante de son travail scientifique. Ils rappellent à beaucoup d'égards les manuscrits dits économico-philosophiques de 1844, ce qui nous montre l'importance qu'il faut attribuer aux idées du jeune Marx et nous permet de mieux saisir l'inspiration fondamentale et la cohésion intime de son oeuvre vaste. . . ."; "Contribution à l'histoire de la genèse du Capital. . . ," pp. 171-172; see also the same author's remarks in

"Marx lecteur (Les carnets d'extraits de Paris, 1844-45)," *La Revue Socialiste*, nouvelle série, no. 5 (November 1946), 529-539.

61. D. Struik, in the edition of the *1844 Manuscripts* cited here; see pp. 244-245.

62. The foregoing is offered more as an indication of the way in which such an analysis of Marx's social doctrine would proceed, than as an adequate treatment. Some of the pertinent references for such a treatment are the following: on the primitive social relationship as a cooperative one, *The German Ideology*, esp. pp. 18-19; on man as naturally *"zoon politikon,"* *Introduction*, pp. 265-268; on "civil society," *The German Ideology*, esp. pp. 26-27, *1844 Manuscripts*, p. 159, and *The Holy Family*, pp. 176, 162-163—but cf. T. Bottomore's rendition of the latter passage in *Karl Marx: Selected Writings in Sociology and Social Philosophy* (New York, 1964), pp. 219-220—and "Theses on Feuerbach." In addition see also: *The German Ideology*, pp. 70ff., *Pre-Capitalist Economic Formations*, pp. 90ff., "On the Jewish Question," in *Karl Marx: Early Writings*, trans. Bottomore (New York, 1965), *The Poverty of Philosophy, passim*, and *1844 Manuscripts, passim*.

63. *1844 Manuscripts*, pp. 137, 142-143; Preface to *A Contribution to the Critique of Political Economy*, p. 13.

64. *Ibid.*, pp. 148-149; also p. 121.

65. *Ibid.*, p. 149; also p. 111: "Man (the worker) only feels himself freely active in his animal functions—eating, drinking, procreating, or at most in his dwelling and in dressing-up, etc.; and in his animal functions he no longer feels himself to be anything but an animal. What is animal becomes human and what is human becomes animal. Certainly eating, drinking, procreating, etc., are also genuinely human functions. But abstractly taken, separated from the sphere of all other human activity and turned into sole and ultimate ends, they are animal functions."

66. *Ibid.*, p. 150; also p. 157: "To be sure, the industrial capitalist also takes *his* pleasures. He does not by any means return to the unnatural simplicity of need; but his pleasure is only a side-issue—recreation—something subordinated to production. . . ." Marx saw the perversity of this state of affairs as consisting in the suppression of human needs in the service of production, rather than, as should be the case, production serving for the satisfaction and development of human needs. Production, rather than the satisfaction and development of man's needs, is said to have become the purpose of labor; or again the life and development of the producer have ceased to be the end of production. Cf. *Pre-Capitalist Economic Formations*, pp. 84-85.

67. This is also expressed by Marx, especially in his early writings, in terms of "alienation" (*die Entfremdung*). The distinction is between labor as *Selbstentfremdung*, and labor as *Selbstbetätigung*. The latter is labor which results in the "naturalization" or fulfillment of the laboring subject; the former is labor which results in the denaturalization of the laboring subject. See *The German Ideology*, pp. 66-68; *1844 Manuscripts*, esp. the Manuscript entitled "Die entfremdete Arbeit"; in the English edition of Struik, pp. 106-119.

68. See, for example, *Metaphysics*, 1015a 15; *Physics*, 192b 6-193a.

6: *Bourgeois and Proletarians*

GERALD A. COHEN

I. Bourgeois and Proletarians

In *The Holy Family* Marx draws an important distinction between the alienation endured by the worker and the alienation endured by the capitalist in bourgeois society:

> The possessing classes and the class of the proletariat present pictures of the same human self-estrangement. But the former class feels at home in and confirmed by this self-estrangement, recognizes its estrangement as its special power, and enjoys in it the semblance of a human existence; the latter feels annihilated in its estrangement, and glimpses in it its impotence and the reality of an inhuman existence.[1]

My first task is to explain what Marx means in this difficult passage, and why he thinks it is true. It is impossible to fulfill this task without drawing upon material from works other than *The Holy Family*. This is because the passage is embedded in a section which throws little light on it, since it uses the distinction to argue

A slightly revised version of the original article which appeared in the *Journal of the History of Ideas*, XXIX:2, April-June 1968, 211-230.

101

that the proletariat is revolutionary and the bourgeoisie conservative, without elaborating the distinction itself. Furthermore, almost the entire text of *The Holy Family* is given over to polemic of an unusually minute, clownish, and altogether dated kind. Serious theoretical discussion occurs only in fragments. I shall therefore explore the meaning of the *Holy Family* passage by paying attention to a characterization of the human essence which is offered in *The German Ideology* and to the doctrine of alienation as it unfolds in the *Paris Manuscripts*. These materials do solve the puzzles in the text I have quoted.[2] I begin with *The German Ideology:*

> Men can be distinguished from animals by consciousness, by religion, or anything else you like. They themselves begin to distinguish themselves from animals as soon as they begin to *produce* their means of subsistence.[3]

I shall treat this as a declaration about man's essence, because one way of fixing the essence of something is by allocating it to its genus and species, its species being determined by the differentia between it and other species of its genus; and it is man's differentia which Marx is providing. Men belong to the genus animal, or at any rate to a genus of which animals are the other species. To ask which species man is is to ask what distinguishes men from (other) animals. Marx's answer is that man himself does the distinguishing. Man makes that part of his essence in virtue of which he is not an animal. This means that it is man's nature to make his nature,[4] that he is by nature a maker, or producer, in the most general sense: he produces what he is.

But Marx is also proposing that man is a producer in a more specific sense. For he performs the act of distinguishing himself from animals—the act which is productive, in a general sense—by engaging in particular acts of production, in the making of things. Those acts are the concrete content of man's universal act of self-creation.

For Marx, a man is self-estranged if his existence is not in conformity with his essence. Since man is really a productive being, he should behave like one in his empirical life,[5] and his empirical life-conditions should promote the possibility of such behavior. Productive activity must be each individual's purpose, his fundamental interest and aim, since essence is the proper end of existence. To be nonalienated, therefore, is to engage in productive activity as an end-in-itself, to use one's powers in order to exercise them, and to exult in manifesting them. The fact that neither capitalist nor worker does this explains the first sentence of the *Holy Family* passage, which asserts that they are both alienated. The capitalist does not produce at all: he is not a producer, but an owner. And the proletarian produces not in order to realize his powers, but for an alien reason: to stay alive.

But why is the bourgeoisie *content* in its self-estrangement, and the proletariat not? The answer falls into two parts: (a) the bourgeoisie, unlike the proletariat, cannot *hope* to escape its alienation; and (b) the bourgeoisie, unlike the proletariat, has no *desire* to escape its alienation.

(a) Capitalists and workers are, respectively, owners and producers. It is possible to be a nonalienated producer, but it is not possible to be a nonalienated owner. It follows that a worker can *hope* to be disalienated: the transformation is no threat to his identity. He is identified as a producer, even though he produces for alien reasons, and, as we shall see, in an alien way.[6] But a capitalist can hope for no salvation from alienation, for "nonalienated owner" is a *contradictio in adjecto.* An owner cannot cease to be alienated without ceasing to be. The capitalist *must* cling to his alienated life, since there can be no nonalienated life for him.

It might be objected that though the capitalist, insofar as he is a capitalist, cannot wish to be disalienated, this need not be true of the man who *is* a capitalist. It appears true of the man only when we focus on one of his aspects: his ownership of capital. But (at least for some purposes) Marx did treat the capitalist abstractly. He developed a phenomenology of the abstract man who is purely an owner, and nothing besides. The lines of this phenomenology will be traced later in the paper. The justification of the abstract perspective will be provided elsewhere. (A brief version of it is given in IV-3, below.)

(b) The contrasting *desires* of capitalist and worker are explicable if the following thesis, to which Marx was committed, is accepted: If a person is aware that the conditions of his life are antagonistic to the realization of his essence, he will be dissatisfied with his life situation. To this must be added the general principle that a man can demand or desire only those states of affairs of which he has some conception. The conjunction of these propositions entails that a man will desire to be disalienated if and only if he is in some way aware that he is alienated. It remains to show that the worker is conscious of his alienation, while the capitalist is not. This will explain their discrepant desires.

I shall introduce the explanation by means of an analogy. Let us say that to be nonalienated is analogous to possessing a fine human body. To be alienated is to lack a fine human body. When the capitalist confronts himself in the mirror, he sees a finely clad body. He does not realize that he lacks a fine body, because he does not even see his body—it does not exist for him: he sees only his clothes. When the worker gazes in the mirror he sees a naked but bruised and misshapen human body. He sees his body, and he sees that it is not fine. And so he desires a fine body, while the capitalist does not.

To interpret the analogy. The worker is forced to labor, and in laboring he confronts his specifically human powers, but is frustrated through being unable to exercise them properly. The capitalist never engages with his powers, even in an alienated way. *His* powers are utterly dormant, because his money exerts power *for* him: it hides his power from him as his clothes hide his body in the analogy. He experiences no frustrating exercise of his faculties, for he does not exercise them at all.

We are now close to what Marx meant when he said that the bourgeoisie have a semblance of a human existence. He did not mean that they are nearer to being really human than are the workers. He meant that their capital, their money, the machines they own, *are* human for them: their possessions take on human powers, in a manner which will be elaborated later. They feel no need to be truly human, for they have the full gamut of human powers in their capital.[7] They have a substitute or *ersatz* humanity. The proletariat lives a truly inhuman life, while the bourgeoisie lives a falsely human life. And this is why the proletariat desires to be truly human and the bourgeoisie does not.

It is because the capitalist has lost all perception of and contact with his essence that he tolerates his alienation. But the worker daily glimpses his essence at a distance from him and experiences his humanity in a distorted form,[8] so that he hopes and desires to live in a nonalienated world.

The idea that the worker possesses his humanity in a warped form while the capitalist has lost his completely can be defended by reference to the well-known characterization of alienation as the circumstance in which man becomes a thing. For the thing which the worker is said to become is a thing very like man—namely, a machine, a thing conceived and described in the vocabulary of human powers. But the thing which the capitalist becomes, as we shall see, is much more grotesque, and quite lacking in human qualities, since it lacks all qualities. The capitalist, it will emerge, is a bearer of properties which he does not have.

I have been trying to illuminate the *Holy Family* passage by means of the notion that the worker is a productive, active being, while the capitalist is not. Additional light is cast in the same direction by Marx's suggestion that whereas the workers really suffer, the capitalists do not. While not systematizing his views on suffering, Marx does reveal an attitude to it in the *Manuscripts*. The topic enters the first paragraph of the work, where Marx, following Adam Smith, speaks of the separation of capital, landed property, and labor, which bourgeois society has wrought. It has sundered factors of production which were more integrated at an earlier period of economic history. (The capitalist division of labor is a fragmentation of what is already a fragment.) And Marx points out that this loss of unity (which for him betokens alienation, since he thinks any incidence of discrete spheres in society does) is *harmful* only for the workers.[9]

Two pages later, he gives an ontological formulation of this thesis:

> ...it should be noted that where both worker and capitalist suffer, the worker suffers in his existence while the capitalist suffers in the profit on his dead Mammon.[10]

Earlier we found that the capitalist does not act on the world. Marx is now contending that he is, equally, not acted on *by* the world: it cannot make *him* suffer. His money insulates him against the impact of things in the world. It is only when his dead Mammon suffers, when his capital is depleted, that he has any relation to suffering, and that relation is completely external. To return to the mirror analogy: his clothes can be violated, but his body cannot be harmed. Sometimes, when he looks in the mirror, he notices that his garments are torn.

This is obviously meant to be true not of particular capitalists, but of an abstract being who is nothing but an owner of money. Yet empirical exemplification of the point is available. For three-dimensional capitalists worry when their fortunes decline, even when there is no chance that the decrease will be great enough to disturb their mode of life in any way. In the Marxian contention, they are upset because they identify themselves with their capital, and they do so because, not being producers, they lack a human identity without it. They can possess human powers and liabilities only derivatively, *through* their capital. The worker, by contrast, suffers directly. He suffers inhumanly, just as he produces inhumanly, but he does suffer and he does produce.

Marx's understanding of the significance of suffering confirms what was urged above: that the workers know that they are alienated, while the capitalists do not. For in Marx's early thought suffering is a mode of knowledge. In later writings he asserts that the workers' misery prevents them from entertaining illusions about their position and sharpens their insight into social processes in general. He appears to think that he who knows the Woe must know the Vale. But in the *Manuscripts* the relation between suffering and knowledge is more intimate and less situational: suffering is itself a *way* of knowing.[11] This result is attained through a series of conceptual assimilations. Suffering *from* something is associated with suffering or undergoing that thing, that is to say, *experiencing* it, which is in turn related to *perceiving* it, that is, gaining knowledge of it. It seems that the English word "suffer" has nuances which stimulate a development of this kind. We have only to think of the interchangeability of locutions like "I suffered many years of torment" and "I knew many years of torment."[12] And the German word *leiden,* which is the one Marx used in the present connection, has similar shadings. So it appears that Marx's idea of suffering helps to explain the vision of reality of which he speaks in the *Holy Family* passage. But I am committed to elucidating that passage by means of his account of the essence of man, and suffering, it seems, failed to enter that account.

It does not enter explicitly, but it is a corollary of the stress on production. Man cannot produce without using his body, without bringing it to bear on things in the world, and in that contact the world acts on man, and must be borne by him. In the Marxian view, activity and passivity entail one another, since each entails and is entailed by commerce with the world: "As soon as I have an object, this object has me for its object."[13] Thus productivity has a passive dimension, and since Marx is prepared to treat any passive relation to the world as a form of suffering, we are able to conclude that suffering is part of man's natural estate.

In sum: the man who works for a living encounters the world both as agent and as patient, though in an alienated way; while the man who owns for a living is separated by what he owns from both active and passive contact with things outside him. In the rest of the paper I shall explore proletarian and bourgeois alienation in greater detail.

II. The Worker's Relation to his Machine

Capital is the link between the worker and the capitalist, since the former works at a machine, which is a physical form of capital, and the latter owns money, which is convertible into capital. I shall discuss the worker's alienation in his relation to the machine, and the capitalist's in his relation to money, since I wish to compare their situations, and capital provides a convenient meeting point for the comparison.[14] This means that I shall neglect certain aspects of alienation, such as man's distance from his fellow man, and his incapacity for sensuous enjoyment of nature. In treating the capitalist, I shall try simply to expound Marx, since exposition of his views on this subject is rarely offered. By contrast, many discussions of the worker's alienation are available. Indeed, often what is presented as an account of man's alienation is restricted to a consideration of the worker. I hope the present paper shows such a procedure to be mistaken. As to the worker, I shall confine myself to three possible criticisms of the relatively familiar Marxian description of his position. They concern (1) product-alienation and process-alienation; (2) aspects of process-alienation; and (3) the dictum that "Man becomes a machine."

1. Product-alienation resides in the fact that what the worker makes is taken from him. The result of his labor does not benefit him: the more he produces, the more impoverished he becomes. In addition, there is alienation "in the process of *production,* within *productive activity* itself."[15] Marx thinks that these two modes of alienation are intimately connected:

> How could the worker stand in an alien relationship to the product of his activity if he did not alienate himself in the act of production itself? The product is indeed only the *résumé* of activity, of production. Consequently, if the product of labour is alienation, production itself must be alienation—the alienation of activity and the activity of alienation. The alienation of the object of labour merely summarizes the alienation in the work activity itself.[16]

This seems unacceptable. "Active alienation" consists in the soul-destroying effects laboring at the machine has on the worker. It seems that these cannot entail product-alienation, since we can consistently suppose that a man controls the product he makes by inhuman toil. If the division of labor removes this possibility, because under its sway there can be no product on which any man has a special claim, the community of workers could still own the goods they slavishly produce: at the very least those goods need not be used, as product-alienation demands, to enslave them further. Isn't Marx just wrong in thinking that from what happens to the worker within the factory one can infer what happens to the product after it leaves the factory?

Marx is also committed to the converse implication, that product-alienation entails process-alienation. (A close reading of the text reveals that he thinks the entailment is mutual. His metaphor of summation alone suggests this, since in one sense series and sum entail one another.) And this proposition seems equally dubious. For we can imagine men who have some dignity in the labor-process, although their products are taken away. Indeed many Marxists concede this, when responding to liberal claims that work has been or can be made enjoyable and fulfilling by arguing that this only conceals alienation, since the product is still taken away from the worker. These defenders abandon Marx when they give this answer, for they separate what he connected.

Notwithstanding these objections, I think the two modes of alienation can be seen to associate naturally with each other. This begins to be clear once we recognize how bizarre it was to suppose that the workers might control the products of the factory in which they slave. For they would have the power to do so only if they owned the factory, and if they owned it, they would not submit themselves to a debasing regimen. If they controlled the product, they would not let the process alienate them. But the man who in fact controls the product is willing to rob the worker of the fruits of his toil. Such a man will naturally make working conditions as exploitative as possible. He shows himself oblivious to the worker's needs in the way he treats the product. Consistency will lead him to shape the man to the needs of the machine in the process of production. One cannot reply that the capitalist would provide salubrious conditions for the worker if he though it profitable to do so. For the capitalist with whom we are concerned is only the agent of the machine. *It is the machine that exploits the worker.* The capitalist exploits him only because he owns the machine. He does not exploit him by means of the machine. (These asseverations are defended in III-3.)

Finally, the worker brings to the factory a consciousness that he is not working for himself, and this affects him negatively in the throes of the labor-process.

It might be thought that the filiation between product- and process-alienation traced here could be short-circuited, in the following way. Product-alienation means that the product is used to enslave the worker, and that means that the product is (or is used to build) a new machine, which facilitates further process-alienation. On this interpretation, the product stays within the factory, or within the factory-system, to increase the agony of industrial life. But this solution to the problem eliminates much of what Marx comprehended in the concept of product-alienation.[17]

2. We have seen that Marx wishes to fuse product-alienation and process-alienation. He also thinks that a number of seemingly separable elements of process-alienation are inextricable from one another. These are listed in the *Manuscripts*[18]: (i) the worker denies himself instead of fulfilling himself, (ii) he feels miserable, (iii) he does not develop his energies, (iv) he is exhausted, (v) he is debased, (vi) he works involuntarily, (vii) his work is not the satisfaction of a need but a means to the satisfaction of his needs, (viii) he works for another.

These indices of alienation take on a certain coherence if we begin with (vii) and use the definition of and principles about human nature which were advanced earlier in the paper. (vii) is outlawed by the definition of man. It therefore entails (v), since "debased" means "dehumanized"; and it entails (iii), since the negation of (iii) is actively in accord with man's essence. Again, we have seen that the worker knows that he is alienated in his work, and that a man will resent what he knows alienates him. This allows us to infer (ii) and (vi). (viii) is licensed by the insistence that no one would impose alienating work conditions on himself. This leaves (i) and (iv). (i) is simply a way of summarizing aspects already dealt with, and (iv) need not be true if physical exhaustion is intended, but it is certainly warranted by the picture I have tried to compose, if emotional exhaustion is allowed to count.

3. In the *Manuscripts* Marx approvingly quotes Wilhelm Schulz, who, one year prior to the time at which Marx was writing, maintained that "the important distinction between how far men work *with* machines or *as* machines has not received attention."[19] Marx addresses himself to this question and selects the second alternative: hence his dictum that *man becomes a machine.* It is perhaps worth registering that he does not mean this literally. He does not think that what is left of the human being is a robot. What he holds is that man is forcibly adapted to fit the machine, rebuilt to accommodate its demands on him.[20] He is accorded the treatment proper to a

machine, and in the factory his behavior resembles that of a machine.

I do not think this famous dictum should be retained by Marxists. I think it should be replaced by a proximate but importantly different formulation. It is better to say that man is transformed into a *tool*, or as Marx says elsewhere, into an appendage of the machine.[21] Here is why the latter terminology is preferable. The craftsman wields a tool. The industrial worker cannot be said to wield a machine, for the machines of modern industry cannot be wielded. Marx wishes to say that the machine wields the worker, since he conceives him as placed at its disposal, to be pushed and pulled. A machine in operation is a system in motion and the man is what is moved. But this makes it impossible to characterize the worker as a machine (as opposed to a machine-part). The same conceptual barrier which prevents us from thinking of the worker as wielding the machine blocks the thought that the worker has become a machine once it is asserted that the machine wields *him*. The machine relates to the worker as the craftsman relates to his tool, and not as the worker ought to relate to the machine, since machines cannot be wielded. If we turn from wielding to the more general concept of controlling, under which it falls, we can then say that the worker ought to control the machine although the machine controls the worker. But if we comprehend this control concretely, then we must allow that what the machine does to the worker is not something the worker can do to the machine.

My rejection of the machine dictum as a succinct label for alienation in the factory is supported by Alan White's enlightening remarks on the meaning of the word "mechanical":

> "Mechanical" describes the manner in which we carry out some continuous train of action, such as knitting or playing the piano. It is typically used of routine or *skilled* performances which from practice we can go through without attention to the details, and, hence, without showing or needing originality or liveliness; in short, like a smoothly functioning machine.[22]

Now this is perhaps not the noblest kind of work given to man. But it is difficult to see how it is possible or why it should be thought

desirable to abolish it, for to do so would be to abridge our reper-
toire of skilled performances. So the machine dictum not only fails
to sum up alienation in the factory; it fails to point at an unambigu-
ously depressing idea. Anyone who insists that all mechanical
activity is alienated or objectionable is being overdemanding and
even silly. But if supreme value lies in realizing men's productive
powers, then it *is* necessary to reject activities in which man resembles not a machine, but a tool.

Marx may have overlooked productive work of the kind White
mentions because of his wavering perception of the difference between human productivity and what appears to be productivity in
animals. He commonly cites advance planning as a distinguishing
factor.[23] But certain *bona fide* skills are acquired just because they
eliminate the need to apply a plan in the course of the work they
enable.

Earlier in this paper I treated the idea that the worker becomes a
machine as a mark of his superiority over the capitalist. That idea
must be abandoned, but the point can still be made, in a different
way. For the worker, though a tool, remains intimately involved in
the productive process[24]; and he is a living tool, never utterly inert.
He is still closer to the essence of man than the capitalist is.

III. The Capitalist's Relation to his Capital

1. At least four images of the capitalist can be found in Marx's
writings: (i) He who owns things instead of producing them, or the
capitalist as *Owner;* (ii) He who accumulates and hoards things instead of enjoying them, or the capitalist as *Miser*[25]; (iii) He who
consumes things instead of producing them, or the capitalist as *Consumer;* (iv) He who is a most stupendously productive individual, as
a member of a class under whose dominion man has changed the
shape of nature.

The first of these conceptions must be treated as dominant and
must be carefully explored if the quotation from *The Holy Family* is
to be understood. It appears irreconcilable with the fourth conception, sketched in *The Communist Manifesto*,[26] of the capitalist as

dynamic director of man's conquest of nature. In *The Holy Family* Marx is suppressing this aspect of the capitalist, and in the *Manuscripts* we see the result of this abstraction: the capitalist becomes a mere appendage of his capital,[27] though he is not appended in the same way as the worker. The legitimacy of the abstraction cannot be considered here. It must suffice to point out that although capitalists are energetic and entrepreneurial in the first phases of capitalism, Marx thought that they would tend to become pure owners, divorced from the productive process, as capitalism developed its distinctive character, so that the first image is more revealing than the fourth.

While (i) appears to exclude (iv), it is plainly compatible with (ii), though it does not entail it. As I expound (i) in detail it may come to seem incompatible with (iii), and (ii) and (iii) are apparently incompatible as they stand. Yet I believe it is possible to entertain an idea of the capitalist which embraces all three elements, in which the profligate life of the self-indulgent bourgeois (iii) is represented as a mode of existence of the capitalist who is a Scrooge (i and ii). This synthesis is articulated in the *Manuscripts*:

> Of course, the industrial capitalist also has his pleasures, . . . but his enjoyment is only a secondary matter . . . it is . . . a *calculated, economic* enjoyment, for he charges his pleasures as an expense of capital and what he squanders must not be more than can be replaced with profit by the reproduction of capital. Thus enjoyment is subordinated to capital and the pleasure-loving individual is subordinated to the capital-accumulating individual.[28]

The enjoyment of the capitalist as consumer is "calculated" and "economic" because he does not surrender himself to it. He cannot give himself up to it, because he remains tied to his money. We must now examine the nature of this tie, the nature of capitalist ownership. We must try to answer the question: What is it to be fundamentally an owner?

2. For Marx, capital cannot exist without a capitalist who owns it. "The concept of capital implies the capitalist."[29] Property must have a human embodiment if it is to be allowed entry into economic equations. But although capital must be possessed by a capitalist, the relation of possession which unites them is most peculiar. For, as I

shall try to show, it follows from the fact that the capitalist owns proper*ty* that he himself lacks proper*ties*.[30] Only someone who is in a certain sense qualityless can qualify for the role of Owner. In the terms of the mirror analogy, there is no body under the capitalist's clothes, but only empty space.

Now for Marx all truly human properties are powers, or propensities to have effects on the world. He forbids us to predicate a feature of a human being unless the standard effects of possessing that feature are realized. A capitalist may appear ugly, but if his money buys beautiful women for him, then, Marx says, he is not ugly, since the effect of ugliness, its power to repel, is annulled by money.[31] This restriction on what is to count as a human feature derives from Marx's view of man as an essentially productive being, through a generalization in which productivity covers *all* powers. It is in this sense of properties that the capitalist has none: his self is not manifested in the world. And the explanation of this is the fact that he owns property, which keeps the world at a distance from him. The workers do operate on the world, in an alienated way, so that they have a dehumanized humanity, but the capitalist's humanity is a void.

Let us turn to the *Manuscripts*:

> The less you *are*, the less you express your life, the more you *have* . . . Everything which the economist takes from you in the way of life and humanity, he restores to you in the form of *money* and *wealth*. And everything which you are unable to do your money can do for you; it can eat, drink, go to the ball and to the theatre. It can acquire art, learning, historical treasures, political power; and it can travel.[32]

We shall shortly consider how money performs for the capitalist, so that he does nothing himself, and therefore lacks a nature, just because he owns capital, which has such a rich nature ("it is the true opulence").[33] But first I want to display how Marx contrasts this form of ownership with the relation the feudal lord enjoys to his property:

> . . .in feudal landownership . . . there is an appearance of a more intimate connexion between the owner and the land than is the

case in the possession of mere *wealth*. Landed property assumes an individual character with its lord, is knightly or baronial with him, has his privileges, his jurisdiction, his political rights, etc. It appears as the inorganic body of its lord.[34]

It is crucial that the landowner does not see his property as something he can sell. Instead, he has entered into an "honorable marriage with his land."[35] If he comes to treat his property as alienable, he possesses it only contingently, since the very same thing could be possessed by another, and he is on the way to being a capitalist, whose ownership can be so abstract, that in some instances neither he nor anyone else can say *what* he owns, but only how *much*. Manors maketh men, but factories maketh owners, and the capitalist merely owns his wealth. He engages in no intimate interaction with what he owns, he never really *has* it, where to have it is to hold it. (I intend that sense of "have" in which it is incorrect to say of an object that I have it when it is neither within my grasp or under my control. In this sense, I do not *have* the spectacles I have left at home.) With the advent of bourgeois society "all personal relationships between the property owner and his property . . . cease."[36] No one is firmly connected with the property he owns and the result is that

the medieval adage, *nulle terre sans seigneur,* is replaced with a new adage, *l'argent n'a pas de maître,* which expresses the complete domination of living men by dead matter.[37]

Let us examine the character of this domination.

3. I have already cited a number of capacities which Marx ascribes to prodigious capital, in its money form. But what is it for my wealth to eat and drink and go to the ball or the theater *for* me? Well, the ball and the theater are essentially social occasions, where men and women get together. Marx means, I think, that money defines who comes, that I come *qua* money-owner, and that I am interested in going only *qua* money-owner. Money attracts me and brings me to these places. It is money which actually pays them a visit, and it drags me along. If eating and drinking are also understood in their social aspects, similar interpretations can be offered.

Chief among the features of capital is its *"power of command* over labor and its products." And Marx tells us that "the capitalist possesses this power, not on account of his personal or human qualities, but as the *owner* of capital" and that "capital itself rules the capitalist."[38] It would thus be a mistake to conceive the capitalist as a human being who forms the intention of controlling the worker and uses his capital to do so. On the contrary, it is capital, the machine, which controls the worker, and the capitalist does so only derivatively and abstractly, as an extension of capital, not because of any personal aspirations or through any individual virtues, such as were needed by feudal lords, who exacted respect through their breeding and bearing.

The way capital wreaks an alchemical transformation on its owner is most strikingly expressed in the following passage:

> What I *am* and *can* do is . . . not at all determined by my individuality. . . . As an individual I am *lame,* but money provides me with twenty-four legs. Therefore, I am not lame.[39] I am a detestable, dishonorable, and stupid man, but money is honored and so also is its possessor. Money is the highest good, and so its possessor is good. Besides, money saves me the trouble of being dishonest; therefore I am presumed honest. I am *stupid,* but since money is *the real mind* of all things, how should its possessor be stupid?[40] . . . I who can have, through the power of money, everything for which the human heart longs, do I not possess all human abilities? Does not my money, therefore, transform all my incapacities into their opposites?[41]

As Bottomore translates the passage, the capitalist has these faculties *through* rather than *by means of* money. (The German preposition is *"durch,"* which can be translated either way.) I believe Bottomore's decision accords with Marx's intentions, for I do not think Marx meant that capital is an *instrument* I use to get what I want. Rather, my capital gets it and has it *for* me, and I have it only *through* my capital. Money shines on my life and makes it bright, but the light in my life is always a reflection. Marx is not saying that a woman falls in love with me because I am rich, or that I entice her by means of my money. Rather, she is attracted *to* my money, she is seduced *by* my money, not by means of it, and it is even my money which satisfies her. Again, when I am honored because of my money, it is my money which is honored, and I only as its keeper. I have neither love nor honor, but complete semblances of both, since my money has both, and my ownership of my money is only a semblance of real possession.[42]

These theses can be called philosophical: it is not easy to establish precise verification-conditions for them. Yet they correspond to some observable tendencies in capitalist society. Some capitalists do have abilities which decay because they have no need or occasion to use them. When society tends to make a healthy body and a healthy mind mere means to survival or enrichment, the powers of mind and body tend not to be used when money can secure whatever they enable a man to get. Thus the ontological topsy-turvy is accompanied by psychobiological corruption.

IV. Concluding Remarks

1. The contrast between bourgeois and proletarian may now be restated. For Marx, human characteristics are powers, and powers are interpreted as capacities to produce. In bourgeois society property is what is produced, so that to have properties is to create property. The worker does create property, in an alienated way; therefore he has properties, of a deformed sort. The capitalist, as mere Owner of property, has no properties. He does not even *have* the property he *owns,* for to have a thing is to be in intimate active contact with it. The capitalist is more distant from being truly human than the worker is. He is not a creator and he is therefore not even a real possessor: he is a sham possessor. The worker is a degenerate creator, and this is thought to be better.

Each is a man who is dominated by a thing, namely capital, whose most immediate form for one is the machine, for the other, money. In the body of the paper I have tried to exhibit the objective differences between the two relations of domination. Now I wish to bring into relief certain more psychological aspects. To that end I propose the following chart of possibilities.

CHART OF PSYCHOLOGICAL POSSIBILITIES

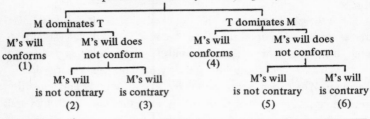

Relation between Man and Thing
(worker and machine — i.e., capital;
capitalist and money — i.e., capital)

M dominates T

M's will conforms (1)

M's will does not conform

M's will is not contrary (2)

M's will is contrary (3)

T dominates M

M's will conforms (4)

M's will does not conform

M's will is not contrary (5)

M's will is contrary (6)

The chart distinguishes six states of mind. I am using "will" very generally, to cover any mode of desire or volition. My will conforms to my situation (1, 4) if I enjoy what I am doing, if I feel fulfilled in it. If my will fails to conform (2, 3, 5, 6), this may be because I am opposed to what I am doing and I find it oppressive (3, 6) or because I merely acquiesce in my position, without investing my self in it (2, 5).

The images of capitalist and worker which we have examined both belong to the right-hand side of the schedule, for they are both alienated. Marx usually locates the worker under (6), portraying him as disposed to resent and react against his position. The worker never falls under (4): he never enjoys his alienated life. Some things Marx says about the worker warrant the application of (5). But (6) must be standard for the worker: he can satisfy (5) only provisionally, since otherwise his revolutionism would disappear.

In the *Holy Family* passage the capitalist is allocated to category (4): he enjoys his alienated life. I have found confirmation and explanation of this in the *Manuscripts*, although some of the texts I have used might be construed so as to deposit the capitalist in category (5), making him a dull and passive agent of his capital. But no interpretation could make him satisfy (6).

What would satisfy the descriptions on the left-hand side of the schedule? It seems that (1) applies to the energetic capitalist presiding in the early phases of bourgeois society. Such a capitalist is as close as any can be to being nonalienated. I hesitate to say that he would be regarded as fully nonalienated, since Marx would perhaps consider him too removed from concrete productive processes to deserve this title. Items (2) and (3) could represent resourceful industrialists who, in different ways, get no satisfaction out of their activity. Such types do not occur in Marx's writings, at any rate not as central characters for the purposes of theory.

A worker who fell under (1) would be a genuinely nonalienated man. There cannot be workers of types (2) and (3), for that would violate the principle that it is satisfying to live in accordance with the definition of one's essence. Nevertheless many contemporary alienation-hunters are prepared to find cases of (2) and (3), and to declare that they instantiate alienation, since psychological indices are now often treated as sufficient for that designation. Again, much of what is now identified as alienation falls under (4), another category containing no workers for Marx. This is the worker as described by semi-Marxist radicals who make concessions, like those I referred to in II-1. C. Wright Mills' "cheerful robot"[43] probably belongs in this category.

2. The present paper can be read as a reply to a recent article by D. C. Hodges, who claims that the only party to alienation in the *Manuscripts* is the worker, and that the capitalist is free in the measure that the worker is alienated. I do not know what Hodges would say about the *Holy Family* passage, for he does not mention it. That his case with respect to the *Manuscripts* is weak has, I think, been demonstrated here.

Hodges[44] deals with the power of money by saying that "to the enlightened bourgeois, it is a means and not an end."[45] But we find no such enlightened bourgeois in the *Manuscripts.* Hodges exploits Marx's assertion that "if the worker's activity is a torment to him, to another it must be *delight* and his life's joy."[46] But the *Holy Family* passage shows that Marx took this kind of delight to be compatible with the deepest alienation. I am in qualified agreement with one of Hodges' theses: Marx's doctrine of alienation does not refer to "the human situation as such."[47] He is concerned with the alienation of particular kinds of men. But I deny that the worker is the only kind of man who is alienated.

I do not agree with Hodges that to embrace the capitalist within the alienated fold is to reduce emphasis on the proletariat as the agency of revolutionary social change. I am against drawing this inference, for I have sought to explain (in I) why the capitalist cannot be expected to revolt against his situation.

3. I would like to suggest that, in proposing his concept of the capitalist who merely owns, Marx adumbrates the idea of the separation of ownership and management, which has been so popular since Berle and Means.[48] It might be thought that in making this attribution I am trying to vault across an impassable gulf between metaphysics and economics, but it is significant that Marx refers to an ownership/management cleavage in the third volume of *Capital*,[49] and assigns a crucial importance to it.

But why, it may be asked, do I suppose that there can be a connection between the phenomenological study of the abstract capitalist, considered in this paper, and the remarks Marx made on a more empirical basis about the tendencies in capitalist development which lead to the atrophy of the capitalist as far as the production process is concerned? To generalize the objection: Why is it supposed that from the sort of analysis provided in this paper one can reach an understanding of real capitalists in the real world?

I believe I can answer these questions, but here I shall only outline the steps I would take: (1) It can be shown that the worker whose alienation Marx describes is also a product of abstraction, and was known to be such by Marx. (2) The justification of treating both worker and capitalist abstractly is that bourgeois political economy implicitly does so. (3) The justification of beginning with the abstractions of political economy in an enquiry which purports to be relevant to three-dimensional people is that, for Marx, science sums up, anticipates, and even prepares the future development of capitalism, for the movement of modern history is a movement toward abstraction, and political economy is the ideal expression of that movement.[50] Complete abstraction can never be achieved because men cannot become completely dehumanized. What halts the increasing alienation is the socialist revolution,[51] to which bourgeois economists are blind. But Marx thought and said that their vision was acute when they perceived the condition of man *under* capitalism.

NOTES

1. "Die besitzende Klasse und die Klasse des Proletariats stellen dieselbe menschliche Selbstentfremdung dar. Aber die erste Klasse fühlt sich in dieser Selbstentfremdung wohl und bestätigt, weiss die Entfremdung als ihre eigene Macht, und besitzt in ihr den Schein einer menschlichen Existenz; die Zweite fühlt sich in der Entfremdung vernichtet, erblickt in ihr ihre Ohnmacht und die Wirklichkeit einer unmenschlichen Existenz." *Karl Marx: Die Frühschriften,* ed. S. Landshut (Stuttgart, 1953), p. 317. Translations alternative to the one offered above are given by T. B. Bottomore, in Bottomore and Rubel (eds.), *Karl Marx: Selected Writings in Sociology and Social Philosophy* (London, 1956), p. 231; and by R. Dixon in *The Holy Family* (Moscow, 1956), p. 51. They translate the text less literally though without, I think, any gain in intelligibility.

2. To illuminate one work by means of passages drawn from another is often, exegetically speaking, problematical. In the present case the problems are multiplied, for a number of reasons:

(1) There is the alleged division of Marx's writings into those which belong to his "young" period and those which belong to his "mature" period. And if there is such a transition in Marx, it may reasonably be located within the time during which the three texts mentioned here were written. The *Manuscripts* were composed between April and August 1844; *The Holy Family* from September to November 1844; and *The German Ideology* in 1845-46. Their composition thus occupies a small number of months, but these were months of great ferment in Marx's thinking.

(2) Many of Marx's works were not published: The *Manuscripts* remained manuscripts, and *The German Ideology* was "left to the gnawing criticism of the mice." This fact reduced the pressure on Marx to signal shifts in his use of concepts or changes in his general orientation. Two other facts had the same consequence:

(3) The works which were published were often intended for a largely nonacademic audience.

(4) Marx did not view his own writings, both published and unpublished, as the work of someone undergoing an exclusively intellectual development. He often wrote in response to (what he conceived to be) the changing demands of the social struggle.

Notwithstanding these reasons for caution, I regard my exegetical procedure as legitimate, since I use the other writings not to embellish a passage which already has a clear meaning, but to embellish a meaning where Marx's intentions are somewhat dark. When a passage is very difficult the interpreter must be liberal in his choice of instruments; the main test of their validity will be their success in rendering the passage less puzzling. But it is also important that Marx wrote *The Holy Family* immediately after writing the *Manuscripts,* so that they constitute, in a sense, a continuous *oeuvre.* And although *The German Ideology* (the other work which flanks *The Holy Family*) is very different in theme from the *Manuscripts,* it echoes the latter's stress on man as an essentially productive being. Finally, I concede that there is a measure of artificiality in distributing so much additional material around the *Holy Family* passage. My main object is to depict a worker/capitalist contrast which runs inexplicitly through the *Manuscripts,* and I begin with *The Holy Family* because in that work the same contrast is explicitly, though obscurely, drawn.

3. *The German Ideology* (Moscow, 1964), p. 31. (Marx's emphasis.)

4. Marx's view should not be overassimilated to Sartrean existentialism. It is not an originally featureless being, or Nothingness, which makes its nature, but a certain kind of animal. Animalhood rather than mere existence precedes essence for Marx.

5. If he fails to behave in this way, he sometimes comes to resemble an animal; he slips back into animalhood, from which he is essentially distinguished. There are suggestions of this kind in the *Manuscripts.* See T. B. Bottomore, *Karl Marx: Early Writings* (London, 1963), p. 125 (Henceforth Bottomore).

6. The worker's activity is a paradigm of the activity of mankind throughout history, which is also conceived as alienated production. Mankind has revealed its essence through the "history of industry," which is "an open book of the human faculties," though it shows us the essential human faculties in an alienated form (Bottomore, 162-163).

7. They therefore feel themselves to be active and productive: see Georg Lukács, *Geschichte und Klassenbewusstsein* (Berlin, 1923), p. 182: "...für den Kapitalisten ist diese Verdoppelung der Persönlichkeit, dieses Zerreissen des Menschen in ein Element der Warenbewegung und in einen (objektiv-ohnmächtigen) Zuschauer dieser Bewegung vorhanden. Sie nimmt aber für sein Bewusstsein notwendig die Form einer—freilich objektiv scheinbaren—Tätigkeit, einer Auswirkung seines Subjekts auf."

8. That the worker has his essence in a warped form is suggested in the *Manuscripts* (Bottomore, p. 126), where we read that his activity manifests itself as passivity, his strength as powerlessness, his creation as emasculation. (The capitalist lacks activity, strength, and creation in *any* form.)

9. Bottomore, p. 69. For the original integration and its dissolution, see *Pre-Capitalist Economic Formations,* ed. E. J. Hobsbawm (London, 1964), pp. 67, 86-87, 97-99. On how capitalism prepares a future integration, see *Capital* I (Chicago edition), p. 554. For the most relevant passages in Smith, see *The Wealth of Nations* (Everyman's Library), Volume I, pp. 41-48, 57-60.

10. Bottomore, p. 71. What might be called the *empirical manifestation* of this is given on p. 76: "In the declining state of society, the worker suffers most. The particular severity of his hardship is due to his situation as a worker, but the hardship in general is due to the condition of society."

11. Landshut (ed.), *op. cit.,* p. 275: "Sinnlich sein ist *leidend* sein. Der Mensch als ein gegenständliches sinnliches Wesen ist daher ein *leidendes* und weil sein Leiden empfindendes Wesen ein *leidenschaftliches* Wesen. Die Leidenschaft, die Passion ist die nach seinem Gegenstand energisch strebende Wesenkraft des Menschen." For similar remarks, see Feuerbach, *Principles of the Philosophy of the Future* (New York, 1966), especially section 33. The latter work appeared in 1843.

12. We also say "I knew many years of happiness," which is replaceable not by "I suffered. . ." but by "I enjoyed many years of happiness." So knowledge has no special association with suffering, but only with passivity in general. The link with suffering is more obvious to Marx, since he treats passivity and suffering as equivalent.

13. Bottomore, p. 208.
14. See Hobsbawm (ed.), *op. cit.*, p. 108, where Marx asserts that money becomes convertible into capital just when labor becomes powerless, when workers cease to own their means of production. Hence the machine achieves its power over the worker just when capitalists become possible.
15. Bottomore, p. 124. (Marx's emphases.)
16. *Ibid.*
17. In this section alienation has been rooted in the fact that the worker does not receive the product he makes. Earlier, alienated labor was identified as work not performed for its own sake. These formulations seem at best independent, at worst, inconsistent. But they can be reconciled. Producing is not the worker's freely chosen end, because he is bound by contract to work, and he enters the contract to satisfy needs other than the need to exercise his powers. That the product is not his is a sign that his activity is alienated, though it does not and need not follow that if the product were his, he would not be alienated. If he does not receive the product, there can be no joy in his work, yet true joy in work is not to be had from the prospect of receiving the product.
18. Bottomore, p. 125.
19. Bottomore, p. 80. The quotation is from *Die Bewegung der Produktion. Eine geschichtlich-statistische Abhandlung* (Zurich, 1843), p. 69.
20. For the empirical content of this idea in contemporary factory work, see Robert Blauner, *Alienation and Freedom* (Chicago, 1964), pp. 19-22.
21. *Manifesto of the Communist Party*, p. 40, *Marx-Engels Selected Works* (Moscow, 1962), Volume I. "Appendage" is predicated of the worker in many places throughout Marx's writings. See for example *Capital* I (Chicago edition), pp. 371, 421, 458, 461, 708. But note that in *ibid.*, p. 463, "machine" rather than "appendage" is used.
22. *Attention* (Oxford, 1963), p. 123. (My emphasis.)
23. He offers other differentiae as well. See Bottomore, pp. 126-128; *Capital* I (Chicago edition), pp. 197-205, esp. pp. 199-200; Hobsbawm (ed.), *op. cit.*, p. 91.
24. This becomes less true in those modern industrial settings in which workers do not engage with machines but merely "tend" them. See Daniel Bell, *The End of Ideology* (New York, 1962), p. 270.
25. Bottomore, p. 171.
26. *Op. cit.*, p. 35. For the values latent in capitalist production, see Hobsbawm (ed.), *op. cit.*, pp. 84-85.
27. See also *Capital* (Chicago edition), p. 365 (quoted in note 34 below) and pp. 648-649.
28. Bottomore, p. 179. (Marx's emphases.) Cf. *Capital* I (Chicago edition), pp. 650-651.

It may also be possible to bind (ii) and (iv), and hence all the four images, thereby rendering unnecessary the concession that (i) excludes (iv). The relevant text is *The Critique of Political Economy* (Chicago edition), pp. 178-180, where Marx asserts that "the hoarding of money for the sake of money is the barbaric form of production for production's sake" (Cf. *Ibid.*, p. 217). This permits us to call capitalist productivity (iv) a sophisticated form of hoarding or miserliness (ii). Capitalist (ii) and capitalist (iv) both seek to collect as much exchange-value as possible, but the latter realizes that exchange-value can be acquired more effectively by producing than by hoarding.

29. Hobsbawm (ed.), *op. cit.*, p. 118, *q.v.* See also Schumpeter, *Capitalism, Socialism and Democracy* (New York, 1950), p. 45.

30. Marx plays in a similar way with the two senses of "property" in *The German Ideology, op. cit.*, pp. 248-249.

31. Bottomore, p. 191. Cf. Feuerbach, *op. cit.*, section 16: "The more qualities I have . . . the greater is the circumference of my effects and influence."

32. (a) Bottomore, p. 171. (Marx's emphases.) It should be noted that Marx is speaking of anyone's money, not just the capitalist's. I take the liberty of applying what he says to the capitalist in particular, since while the worker's money latently possesses similar powers, there is never enough of it for those powers to spring into action. (b) The next sentence but one after this excerpt reads: "But although it can do all this, it only *desires* to create itself, and to buy itself, for everything else is subordinated to it." This confirms and extends what was argued above, that the Scrooge notion of the capitalist subjugates and limits the Consumer idea. (c) For one sense in which money can travel, see *Capital* II (Chicago edition), pp. 169, 184.

33. Bottomore, p. 171.

34. Bottomore, p. 114. (Marx's emphasis. I have corrected the translation.) Note that here property assumes the features of its owner, rather than vice versa, as is the case in capitalism. The bond between a person and his property counts as personal if it depends on the person's characteristics. See *The German Ideology, op. cit.*, p. 93.

   At one point in *Capital* Marx refuses to offer special compliments to the feudal lord: "It is not because he is a leader of industry that a man is a capitalist; on the contrary he is a leader of industry because he is a capitalist. The leadership of industry is an attribute of capital, just as in feudal times the functions of general and judge were attributes of landed property" (Chicago edition), I, p. 365. Contrast *Ibid.*, III, p. 1027. For further nuances see Avineri, *The Social and Political Thought of Karl Marx* (Cambridge, 1968), p. 30.

35. Bottomore, p. 115. Cf. *Capital* I (Chicago edition), p. 101.

36. Bottomore, p. 115.

37. *Ibid.*, Cf. *Capital* (Chicago edition), I, note 163, III, p. 724. Similar to Marx's discussion is Hannah Arendt's distinction between property and wealth. See *The Human Condition* (New York, 1959), p. 56. The distinction between feudal lord and capitalist takes a radical turn in and is essential to the work of Schumpeter. See *Capitalism, Socialism and Democracy, op. cit.*, pp. 137ff.

38. Bottomore, p. 85. (Marx's emphases.)

39. Therefore I cannot even suffer. See pp. 105-106 above.

40. "Stupid" and "mind" are translations of *geistlos* and *Geist*.

41. Bottomore, p. 191. (Marx's emphases.) On the ignorant capitalist's ownership of knowledge, see *Capital* I (Chicago edition), pp. 397, 422n, 462.

42. For the meaning of real possession, see Bottomore, pp. 193-194.

43. *White Collar* (New York, 1951), p. 233. *The Sociological Imagination* (New York, 1959), p. 171.

44. "The Young Marx—A Reappraisal," *Philosophy and Phenomenological Research*, 1966-67. Reprinted in this volume as Chapter 2.

45. *Ibid.*, p. 228.

46. *Ibid.*, p. 227. Quoted from Martin Milligan's translation: *Economic and Philosophic Manuscripts of 1844* (Moscow, 1956), p. 79.

47. *Ibid.*, p. 224. The first sentence of the Holy Family passage ("...the *same* human self-estrangement") shows that the agreement must be qualified.
48. *The Modern Corporation and Private Property* (New York, 1932).
49. See pp. 449-459, 516-518 (Chicago edition). Avineri (*op. cit.*, pp. 174ff) provides an original and illuminating discussion of these passages.
50. The *Manuscripts* passages most relevant for establishing these interpretations are in Bottomore, pp. 76-77, 82, 137-139, 181.
51. In which the proletariat brings human existence into harmony with the human essence: *The German Ideology, op. cit.*, pp. 54-55.

7: *Marx as a Political Theorist*

ROBERT C. TUCKER

That Marx ranks among the major political theorists is a widely accepted opinion in our time. The histories of political thought commonly accord him a chapter or two, and the great age of political theory in the modern West is often viewed as running from Machiavelli to Marx. With the reservation that Marx's impact upon political thought may have been greater than his measurable contribution to it warranted, I see no reason to take issue with this view.

As one of the "greats" of Western political thought, Marx was in some ways a great dissenter. He radically rejected the civilization of which he was so much a part. He saw the state as coercive power wielded in the interests of property, and its legitimation was no part of his intellectual concern. Nevertheless Marx's political theory was closer to at least one main current in the classical Western tradition than might be supposed. A long line of eminent political thinkers, including Aristotle, Machiavelli, Locke, and James Madison, had preceded him in offering an economic interpretation of politics, in linking the state with class interest and the property system.[1]

Originally published in Nicholas Lobkowicz (ed.), *Marx and the Western World,* University of Notre Dame Press, 1967, pp. 103-131.

If justification is needed for returning to such familiar territory as Marx's political thought, it may lie in certain characteristic inadequacies of past treatments of this subject. First, exposition of the Marxist conception of history as a whole has loomed large in these accounts, and systematic analysis of the political aspect of Marxist theory has correspondingly suffered.[2] Secondly, Marx's political thought has mistakenly been equated with his theory of the state, which is only a part of it. And thirdly, his descriptive theory of the state has been emphasized to the neglect of his normative view, his position as a political philosopher. These comments define the tasks of the present essay. Starting with an analysis of the theory of the state in classical Marxism (by which I mean the Marxism of Marx and Engels), I will go on to present the thesis that the theory of the state, for all its importance in Marxist political theory, is not the whole of it and not even the most vital part; for Marx sees the economy as the prime historical locus of the political relationship between man and man. In conclusion I will attempt to formulate Marx's position as a political philosopher and to treat the philosophical relation between Marxism and anarchism.

THE STATE AS ALIENATED SOCIAL POWER

We find in the writings of Marx and Engels a twofold view of the nature of the state. On the one hand, they give the well-known functional definition of it as "an organization of the possessing class for its protection against the nonpossessing class."[3] On the other hand, the state is also defined in intrinsic terms as an embodiment in a special class of governors—politicians, bureaucracy, standing army, police, and so on—of society's power. As Marx puts it, "by the word 'state' is meant the government machine, or the state insofar as it forms a special organism separated from society through the division of labor. . . ."[4]

In so characterizing the state, Marx was expressing a view that he had developed in the formative period of his thought. Progressing toward his first formulation of the materialist conception of history in the Paris manuscripts of 1844, he had briefly applied himself to political theory. In 1843 he produced an unfinished critical commentary on Hegel's *Philosophy of Right* and some published articles summarizing the results. Applying a method of inversion of Hegelianism which he had learned from Ludwig Feuerbach, he constructed a theory of the political life as a sphere of man's alienation. Feuerbach had extracted from Hegelianism by his method of inversion the view that religious, i.e., God-oriented, man was man alienated from himself, for God was only an imaginary externalization of man's own idealized attributes.

Just so, reasoned Marx, man as citizen in the modern state, i.e., as a communal being or member of the political community, is but an idealization of real man and hence an "abstraction." Real man is not man *qua* citizen but man as a member of civil society (*bürgerliche Gesellschaft*), which Hegel himself, influenced by such thinkers as Adam Smith, represented as the arena of an economic war of all against all. Accordingly, the primary realm of human existence is the economy rather than the polity. Hegel's error was to treat the state as the foundation of civil society, whereas the truth is just the reverse: civil society is the foundation of the state. And the state, like Feuerbach's God, is an externalization of the powers of the species. It has a real, material existence, however, rather than a purely imaginary one in heaven. It exists as a special political organism separate from the rest of society and lording it over the latter. To overcome political alienation, therefore, man must repossess this alienated social power by revolutionary means. For "only when man recognizes and organizes his *'forces propres'* as *social* forces and so ceases to separate social power from himself in the form of *political* power—only then will human emancipation take place."[5]

As already indicated above, Marx's early image of the state as alienated social power, a creature of society that comes to dominate its creator, persists in mature Marxism. Once historically established, writes Engels, political power is "endowed with a movement of its own" and "strives for as much independence as possible."[6] Marx, for his part, describes the "special organism" of political rule as a parasitic growth on the social body. Speaking, for example, of the executive power in nineteenth-century France, "with its artificial state machinery embracing wide strata, with a host of officials numbering half a million, besides an army of another half million," he depicts this power as an "appalling parasitic growth, which enmeshes the body of French society like a net and chokes all the pores. . . ."[7] In a similar vein, Engels pictures the United States as a politician-ridden nation where "two great gangs of political speculators" alternate in power and at the public trough. "Nowhere do 'politicians' form a more separate section of the nation than precisely in North America," he elaborates. "It is precisely in America that we see best how there takes place this process of the state power making itself independent in relation to society, whose mere instrument it was originally intended to be."[8]

These remarks of Engels appear in his preface to a twentieth anniversary edition of Marx's pamphlet on the Paris Commune of 1871, *The Civil War in France,* and reflect one of its chief themes. Indeed, all that the two men wrote about the Commune calls for interpretation in the light of classical Marxism's conception of the state as alienated social power. They saw in the Commune a revolutionary movement to destroy the state as, in Marx's words, a "parasitic excrescence" on the body of society, and this was a reason for their rapturous response. The Commune, wrote Engels, signified a "shattering" (*Sprengung*) of the former state power. By filling all posts through elections on the basis of universal suffrage and by paying all officials, high or low, only the wages received by other workers, the Commune inaugurated the reversal of the historical transformation of the state and its organs from servants of society into masters of society.[9] This echoed what Marx had said twenty years before. "While the merely repressive organs of the old governmental power were to be amputated," he had written of the Commune, "its legitimate functions were to be wrested from an authority usurping pre-eminence over society itself, and restored to the responsible agents of society. . . . The Communal Constitution would have restored to the social body all the forces hitherto absorbed by the state parasite feeding upon and clogging the free movement of society."[10] For Marx, the Commune was an unsuccessful but portentous first attempt by man in the mass to repossess his alienated *"forces propres"* and to abrogate the historic externalization of social power into the state.

There appears to exist, if not an outright contradiction, then at any rate a definite tension in the thought of Marx and Engels between their conception of the state as alienated social power and their functional definition of it as an organ of class rule. Whereas the one view propounds a dichotomy of state versus society, the other treats the state as the instrumentality of a class which in turn is a *part* of society. How, then, is it possible to conceive the state as an entity "independent" of society and lording it over the latter? The two men seem to have been somewhat uneasily aware of this problem. Engels offered a partial solution in the hypothesis that the state acquires a certain independence of society at times when no one class is clearly dominant. Citing as examples the absolute monarchies of the seventeenth and eighteenth centuries, which held the balance between nobility and bourgeoisie, and the Bonapartism of the first and second French empires, which played off the proletariat against the bourgeoisie and *vice versa,* Engels offered the generalization that there are periods when "the warring classes balance each other so nearly that the state power, as ostensible mediator, acquires, for the moment, a certain degree of independence of both."[11] This, however, would at best explain only certain instances of something that Marx and Engels elsewhere in their writings describe as a universal historical tendency; consequently the tension between their two approaches to the state went unresolved.

THE STATE AS ORGANIZED COERCION

Inverting Hegel's political philosophy in his critical commentary of 1843, Marx postulated that civil society was the foundation of the state and economics the foundation of civil society. He thereby arrived at the first premise of historical materialism, namely the primacy of economics in human affairs. The deeper existential significance of this familiar Marxist tenet becomes apparent only in the full context of the materialist conception of history as Marx went on to expound it in his Paris manuscripts of 1844 and then in Part I of *The German Ideology* (1845-1846). Man, in Marx's image of him, is essentially a producing animal who has his historical being primarily in the realm of material production. The growth process of the human species is in substance a *Produktionsgeschichte*, a process of man's production of the world of material objects that surrounds him, the "nature produced by history." Since history is chiefly a production process, human society itself is basically a society of production, i.e., a set of social relations that men enter into in their productive activity. In a well-known, later formulation of historical materialism, Marx called these social relations of production the "basis" of society. All other institutions and forms of consciousness, including political institutions and political consciousness, he relegated to the social "superstructure" arising over this foundation.[12]

Marx's theory goes on to assert that the human society of production has been deeply divided throughout recorded history. The social relations of production have represented so many different forms of a "social division of labor" between a minority class of nonproducing owners of the means of production and a majority class of non-owning producers: slave-owners and slaves in ancient society, landowning nobles and serfs in feudal society, and capitalists and wage-earning proletarians in bourgeois society. Social revolutions, the transitions from one form of society to another, have been changes in the social division of labor and mode of production arising out of advances in technology, and each such historical revolution of the social "basis" has been accompanied by a complete revolutionizing of the social "superstructure."

Every social system based on the division of labor is necessarily, in Marx's view, a conflictual system. The social division of labor is not simply a division but an antagonism, and class-divided society is society in conflict. What makes it so, according to Marx, is a postulated rebelliousness of man as producer against his life-conditions in societies of production based on division of labor. The rebelliousness is explained by the inability of man as producer to develop his productive powers freely and to the full within any given social division of labor. Thus bourgeois man could not develop the new capitalist productive powers freely within the division of labor between lords and serfs and the feudal system of landed property. Now proletarian man, as Marx sees it, is increasingly restive because of his inability to develop freely the new productive powers of modern machine industry within the division of labor between capitalist and worker, i.e., within the confines of wage labor as the mode of production. Generalizing, we may say that for classical Marxism the rebelliousness of man as producer is a constant historical tendency which periodically rises to a peak of intensity, bursts out in a revolutionary upheaval and then subsides—but not for long—with the resulting transformation of society. The envisaged destination of the historical process is a classless society in which the social relations of production will no longer take the form of division of labor and hence will not become again a fetter upon man's powers of production.

The state, a key element in the social superstructure, is functionally defined for Marx and Engels in this theoretical context. It institutionalizes the conflict-situation in societies founded on division of labor in production, and consequently is "simply the official form of the antagonism in civil society."[13] The state according to this view is an instrumentality for waging the class struggle *from above*. The possessing class, as the beneficiary of an existing social order of production, will necessarily resist all efforts of the producer class to transform society. In doing so it will freely make use of organized coercion. To curb the ever rebellious producers and to protect the social order from the danger of overthrow, the state will use the police, prisons, the standing army, the courts and so on. Thus the state is seen by classical Marxism as fundamentally a repressive force. In Engels' words, "the state of antiquity was above all the state of the slave owners for the purpose of *holding down* the slaves, as the feudal state was the organ of the nobility for *holding down* the peasant serfs and bondsmen, and the modern representative state is an instrument of exploitation of wage labor by capital."[14]

In the work from which this passage is quoted, Engels also writes that the state historically arose as a force for keeping class conflict within certain tolerable bounds. In order that antagonistic classes might not consume themselves and society in sterile struggle, he says, "a power seemingly standing above society became necessary for the purpose of moderating the conflict, of keeping it within the bounds of 'order'...."[15] This statement must be kept in context to avoid misinterpretation. Engels does not mean that the state stands above class conflict but only that it seems to. Nor does he mean that the state is in essence a conflict-preventing or conflict-resolving force. Along with Marx, he sees the state as a *weapon* of class conflict but a weapon which, in the hands of the economically dominant class, is employed to prevent the underlying antagonism in the society from exploding into revolutionary violence. Only in this special sense does the state, in the Marxist theory of it, exist as a means of "moderating" conflict in society.

For Marx and Engels, the social history of man is a series of systemic conflicts in which the fundamental issue has been the social order itself—its preservation or its overthrow. The division of labor has bifurcated society to such an extent that the great question for every historical society has always been: How long can it hold itself together? Moreover the Marxist view of the state is governed by this underlying assumption about society. The repressive function that it assigns to state power arises logically out of the imperative needs of society as a conflictual system whose very persistence is always at stake. The state is the supreme defense mechanism of a threatened social structure; furthermore it is a mechanism that regularly must be used, often violently, because the internal threat to the system, for the reasons already explained, is continually manifesting itself in violent ways. Hence Lenin caught the spirit of classical Marxism and was merely accentuating a basic theme of its political theory when he defined the state as "organized and systematic violence."[16]

Marx's theory holds that class struggles, when they grow in intensity, become political struggles. The possessing class is ready to call out the police and the army at the slightest provocation from the producers. By the same token, the producers cannot fight their class struggles without pitting themselves against the existing state; and since the state is the social structure's defense mechanism, they cannot revolutionize the social order without overthrowing the state and taking political power, or more specifically the producers cannot transform the social foundation without tearing down the old political superstructure. Consequently Marx's political theory holds that all social revolutions necessitate political revolutions. It sees the French Revolution, for example, as the political expression of the deeper bourgeois revolution in French society. However for Marx the "Thermidor" too finds its explanation in the tendency of every revolutionary new form of statehood to become very quickly a conservative force, a repressive defense mechanism for *its* social order. The state *qua* state is thus seen as in essence a conservative force for preservation of the social *status quo*. The later Leninist notion of the Communist party-state as a force for social change, an instrumentality of a long-range revolutionary transformation of society from above, is in this respect a serious modification of Marxist theory and represents one of the significant points of divergence between classical and Communist Marxism.

It follows that Marx and Engels propounded an economic interpretation of politics in both a radical and special form. Politics, in their view, is fundamentally *about* economics as defined above, i.e., about modes and relations of production and their changes. They were well aware, of course, that this conception ran counter to the general assumption of participants in political life and of those who have written about it; for this latter group had stated that political history genuinely revolves around political and moral issues, such as constitutions, forms of state, human rights, the franchise and justice. To account for the discrepancy between the real meaning of politics and what people believe about it, Marx and Engels invoked their theory of ideological thinking as false consciousness. Not only did all class conflicts tend to take the form of political struggles, but all political conflicts were also class struggles in *ideological disguise*. Such ideological disguise of economic issues as political ones was a matter of genuine obfuscation in the heads of men, including political leaders. Thus the struggles in states between government and opposition were manifestations of class conflict, but the latter was reflected in them "in inverted form, no longer directly but indirectly, not as a class struggle but as a fight for political principles, and so distorted that it has taken us thousands of years to get behind it."[17] In the same vein, Marx wrote that "all struggles within the state, the struggle between democracy, aristocracy and monarchy, the struggle for the franchise, etc., etc., are merely the illusory forms in which the real struggles of the different classes are fought out among one another."[18] Elsewhere, in answering the objection that his economic interpretation of politics would not apply to ancient Greece and Rome, where political considerations really were the dominant ones, Marx declared that classical antiquity could no more live on politics than the Middle Ages could live on Catholicism, and went on: ". . . a very little knowledge of the history of the Roman republic suffices to acquaint us with the fact that the secret core of its history is formed by the history of the system of landed proprietorship."[19]

Therefore political consciousness became, for classical Marxism, a form of false consciousness, an upside-down view of reality, and common sense assumptions about political life were explained away as illusions. Marx's thinking in this regard presupposed a distinction of the Freudian type between "manifest" and "latent" meaning content. Political consciousness was in a manifest sense about moral-political issues, but latently it was about economic ones. The underlying meaning of politics, obscure to participants and scholars alike, lay in the basic inner conflicts in the human society of production, the conflicts over modes of productive activity.

HISTORICAL FORMS OF THE STATE

Much of what Marx and Engels wrote about the state was expressed in sweeping generalities typified by the *Communist Manifesto's* description of the state as "merely the organized power of one class for oppressing another." To what extent were they conscious of differences between forms of government, and what importance did they attach to them? For reasons already touched on, they were much more impressed by that which all forms of government have in common than by the features distinguishing one form from another. They were not, however, oblivious to differences and did not treat them as insignificant. Though this aspect of their political theory was never systematically elaborated in detail, they did propound a kind of Marxist "comparative politics."

Not surprisingly in view of the general historical structure of their thought, this was a comparative politics over time rather than across space. They tended, in other words, to assume that each successive epoch in the social history of mankind, each dominant socio-economic formation, has its own characteristic form of statehood.

On that basis there should be five different forms of government corresponding to the five forms of class society mentioned by Marx: Asiatic society, the slave-owning society of classical antiquity, feudal society, modern bourgeois society and future communist society in its lower phase during which the state would persist in the form of a "dictatorship of the proletariat." But Marx and Engels deal only very sketchily with the theme of the correlations between the types of class-divided society and the forms of government.

Influenced by the writings of British political economists, notably Richard Jones and J. S. Mill, Marx saw Asiatic society as a socio-economic formation based on irrigated agriculture. Since the obligation of seeing to the construction and maintenance of complex and costly canals and waterworks devolved upon the state in those conditions, the centralizing power of government expanded very greatly and the state took the form of "Oriental despotism." Marx had little further to say on the social order of Oriental despotism.[20] Nor did he and Engels designate a particular form of government as characteristic of the slave-owning society of classical antiquity—an omission that may find its explanation in the diversity of forms of government in ancient Greece and Rome. They saw monarchy as the typical political form of feudal society, however, and parliamentary democracy, variously called the "representative state" or "democratic republic," as the form of government proper to a capitalist society in its mature development. It was in this "last form of state of bourgeois society" that the class struggle was destined to be "fought out to a conclusion."[21]

The attitude of Marx and Engels toward the political institutions of liberal parliamentary democracy was ambivalent. On the one hand, they saw the democratic republic in bourgeois society as being, like all previous forms of the state, a class dictatorship. The liberal democratic state was a camouflaged "bourgeois dictatorship."[22] Its representative government and universal suffrage meant no more than the opportunity of "deciding once in three or six years which member of the ruling class was to misrepresent the people in parliament."[23] Yet Marx and Engels were not inclined to dismiss democratic political institutions as useless or unimportant. Rather they saw in them a school of political training for the working class in bourgeois society, a stimulus to the growth of revolutionary class consciousness in the proletariat. For the debate by which parliamentary democracy lived necessarily had to spread to the larger society outside: "The parliamentary regime leaves everything to the decision of majorities; how shall the great majorities outside parliament not want to decide? When you play the fiddle at the top of the state, what else is to be expected but that those down below dance?"[24]

But was it possible, as later Social Democratic Marxists came to believe, for an anticapitalist revolution and socialist transformation of bourgeois society to take place in a peaceful and orderly way through the electoral process in a parliamentary democracy? Could the workers achieve political power by democratic means and proceed by those means to change the mode of production? On one or two occassions Marx alluded to such a possibility, most notably when he allowed in a speech about the Congress at the Hague in 1872 that in England and America, and possibly in Holland as well, the workers might conceivably attain their revolutionary aim by peaceful means.[25] However it is uncertain how seriously he or Engels actually entertained such a belief, which was at variance with a fundamental tendency of their thought over the years. Addressing himself in 1874 to believers in a nonauthoritarian revolution, Engels inquired: "Have these gentlemen ever seen a revolution?" And he went on: "A revolution is certainly the most authoritarian thing there is; it is the act whereby one part of the population imposes its will upon the other part by means of rifles, bayonets, and cannon-authoritarian means, if such there be at all. . . ."[26] It is true that later in his 1895 introduction to a new edition of Marx's *Class Struggles in France,* Engels found the Social Democratic movement to be thriving on universal suffrage and the ballot box; but even there he did not assert that the working class could actually come to power by these means. He said nothing to suggest that he had altered the view, expressed some years earlier, that universal suffrage was not, and could not be, anything more than a "gauge of the maturity of the working class." Its mission was to herald the revolutionary *dénouement:* "On the day the thermometer of universal suffrage registers boiling point among the workers, both they and the capitalists will know what to do."[27]

Marx and Engels saw in the class state not only organized coercion but also an element of deception. In each of its historical incarnations the state had been the dictatorship of a minority class of owners of the means of production, but its class character had been camouflaged. In Europe, for example, monarchy had been "the normal incumbrance and indispensable *cloak* of class-rule."[28] In addition the modern democratic republic claimed to be a state ruled by the people as a whole through their elected representatives in parliament; the control of this state by the capitalist class, and their use of it for class purposes, was concealed. This theme of the manipulation of political forms to cover up minority class rule is a minor one in Marx and Engels but merits special attention because it influenced later elitist theories of the state. In the elitist theories of Mosca, Pareto, and others, the ruling class is no longer defined in Marx's manner, and the possibility of a future society without a ruling class is explicitly or implicitly denied. But notwithstanding the fact that the elitists were anti-Marxists and offered their view of the state in part as a rebuttal of Marx's, their thinking showed the impact of classical Marxist political theory. Pareto admitted as much when he praised the "sociological part" of Marx's teaching, the idea that societies are divided into classes of rulers and ruled.[29] This basic notion, along with the tendency to see minority class rule as something concealed behind external political forms, is something for which the elitist theory is largely indebted to Marx. And it may be through this channel that Marx has had his most enduring influence upon political thought in the contemporary West.

So strong was Marx's belief in the class essence of every historical form of the state that the reality of autocracy or personal rule at certain junctures in history seems to have escaped him. Engels, as noted earlier, suggested in one passage that there were times when autocratic rulers might have become independent powers owing to a balance of contending classes in society. Marx, however, was less inclined to think in this fashion. The point is best illustrated by his interpretation of the rule of Louis Bonaparte. France seemed, Marx wrote, to have escaped the despotism of a class only to fall back beneath the despotism of an individual. But it was not so: "Bonaparte represents a class, and the most numerous class of French society at that, the *small peasants.*" However the small peasants were not a unified class; and since they were incapable for this reason of cognizing and enforcing their class interest in their own name, they had to do it through a representative: "Their representative must at the same time appear as their master, as an authority over them, as an unlimited governmental power, that protects them against the other classes and sends them the rain and the sunshine from above. The political influence of the small peasants, therefore, finds its final expression in the executive power subordinating society to itself."[30]

It was an ingenious interpretation but also an arbitrary one and reflects Marx's incapacity to grasp government under any other aspect than that of rule on behalf of the economic interest of a social class. I am unable to agree with Professor Plamenatz, therefore, when he writes that Marx, in the *Eighteenth Brumaire*, showed an understanding of the phenomenon that later came to be known as fascism and, in particular, that he ". . . saw that classless adventurers could, by playing off the classes against one another, capture the State and use it to promote interests which were not class interests."[31] It seems, on the contrary, that Marx's interpretation of Louis Bonaparte as the political representative of an inarticulate small peasantry foreshadowed the grievous mistake of Marxism in the twentieth century when it interpreted the full-grown fascisms of Hitler and Mussolini as forms of class rule by the monopoly bourgeoisie. One of the serious deficiencies of Marxist political theory is the difficulty that it inevitably encounters when it takes up the problem of personal dictatorship.

THE PROLETARIAN STATE

Marx and Engels thought the state would disappear in the higher phase of the communist society, but in the transitional lower phase of communist society—society as it would exist in the aftermath of proletarian revolution—the state would survive as a dictatorship of the working class. The *Communist Manifesto* thus speaks of the proletariat constituting itself as the ruling class. In *The Class Struggles in France,* written in 1850, Marx proclaimed "the class dictatorship of the revolution, the class dictatorship of the proletariat as the inevitable transit point to the abolition of class differences generally, to the abolition of all the productive relations on which they rest, to the abolition of all the social relations that correspond to these relations of production, to the revolutionizing of all the ideas that result from these social connections."[32] Returning to the theme in a letter of 1852 to Joseph Weydemeyer, Marx declared that "the class struggle necessarily leads to the dictatorship of the proletariat" and that "this dictatorship itself constitutes only the transition to the *abolition* of all classes and to a *classless society.*"[33] Finally in his unpublished notes of 1875 on the Gotha Program, Marx wrote: "Between capitalist and communist society lies the period of the revolutionary transformation of the one into the other. There corresponds to this also a political transition period in which the state can be nothing but *the revolutionary dictatorship of the proletariat.*"[34]

The doctrine of proletarian dictatorship is undoubtedly an integral part of classical Marxism and its political theory. On the other hand, Marx and Engels were not inclined to go into detail on this theme and left it somewhat unclear how they concretely envisaged the future proletarian dictatorship. This paved the way for later Marxist controversy over the question. Although diverse schools of Marxist thought have recognized the doctrine of the proletarian dictatorship as an inalienable part of Marxism, they have differed, at times very deeply and bitterly, over the amount of importance to be attached to it and the proper interpretation to be placed upon it. Indeed, the theoretical and practical question of what the proletarian dictatorship would and should look like in practice, and the related question of what the founders believed on the point, directly underlay the great schism of 1917 and after between orthodox Social Democratic Marxism and the Communist Marxism of Lenin and his followers. The issue was whether or not the latter were acting as good Marxists in setting up the Soviet one-party state and calling it a Marxist "dictatorship of the proletariat." In an effort to prove in advance that this *would* be a valid Marxist action, Lenin in the summer of 1917 wrote *The State and Revolution,* his principal contribution to Marxist political theory. The doctrinal conflict was joined when the German Social Democratic leader Karl Kautsky published a Marxist criticism of the Bolshevik Revolution in his pamphlet of August 1918, *The Dictatorship of the Proletariat,* to which Lenin later responded with *The Proletarian Revolution* and the *Renegade Kautsky.*

In attacking the Russian Bolsheviks on Marxist grounds for setting up a dictatorial regime and ruling by force and violence in the name of the proletariat, Kautsky contended that democracy and Marxist socialism were inseparable. A Marxist dictatorship of the proletariat would not be a dictatorship in the "literal sense" of suspension of democracy and rule by a single person. Rather it would be class rule by the proletariat and, as such, it would be majority rule according to the generally accepted democratic procedures and with full protection of minorities. In the proletarian context, therefore, the term "dictatorship" was to be understood in a Pickwickian sense as referring *not* to a form of government but rather to "a condition which must everywhere arise when the proletariat has conquered political power, namely, the condition of proletarian "sovereignty" in a society composed of the majority of proletarians. Moreover to prove that this was the Marx-Engels' viewpoint as well as his own, Kautsky cited Marx's description in *The Civil War in France* of the Paris Commune as a polity that abolished a standing army and state officialdom and operated on the basis of general suffrage and citizen rotation in elective public office. Had not Marx himself called the Commune an essentially working-class government? And had not Engels, in his preface to a twentieth-anniversary edition of Marx's famous pamphlet, expressly held up the Commune as the first example of dictatorship of the proletariat?[35]

Testimony could thus be found for a Social Democratic interpretation of the founders' views on the proletarian dictatorship. Marx did portray the Commune as a libertarian new order and hailed it as "the political form at last discovered under which to work out the economic emancipation of labor."[36] Nor was this the only evidence in support of the Kautskyan case. The *Communist Manifesto* had, after all, described the predicted future establishment of proletarian class rule as the "winning of democracy" (*Erkämpfung der*

Demokratie). Much later in his criticism of the draft of the Erfurt Program of the German Social Democratic Party, Engels wrote that the working class could only come to power under the form of the democratic republic and added: "this is even the specific form for the dictatorship of the proletariat, as the great French revolution has already shown."[37]

Yet the Kautskyan interpretation of the founders' position was ultimately shaky and unconvincing, for it ignored important conflicting evidence. The very words of Engels just quoted show the untenability of Kautsky's view that Marx and Engels conceived the proletarian dictatorship not as a form of government but as a "condition" only. They saw it as the final form that the state was destined to take in history. And Engels' reference to the French revolution in this context is only one of many indications that the political *content* of the proletarian dictatorship, even within the frame of a democratic republic, was envisaged in a very different manner from Kautsky's as described above. There is adequate evidence to show that when Marx and Engels spoke of the future proletarian dictatorship, they were not using the term "dictatorship" in a merely Pickwickian sense but literally. It is true that they offered no such general definition of the term as Lenin's, according to which "Dictatorship is rule based directly upon force and unrestricted by any laws." Nor were they as explicit on the applicability of the general formula to the case of the proletarian state as Lenin was when he added: "The revolutionary dictatorship of the proletariat is rule won and maintained by the use of violence by the proletariat against the bourgeoisie, rule that is unrestricted by any laws."[38] Yet this appears to have been the direction of their thinking.

One of the indications of it is their critical reaction to the draft Gotha Program's call for a "free people's state." They objected to the idea that a "free state" should be a stated goal of the workers' party in Germany and did so on the explicit ground that a proletarian state could no more be a free one than any other form of state could. "As, therefore, the state is only a transitional institution which is used in the struggle, in the revolution, in order to hold down one's adversaries by force," declared Engels in his letter of

March 18-28, 1875, to Bebel about the draft Program, so "it is pure nonsense to talk of a free people's state: so long as the proletariat still *uses* the state, it does not use it in the interests of freedom but in order to hold down its adversaries, and as soon as it becomes possible to speak of freedom the state as such ceases to exist."[39] Like all previous historical forms of the state, the proletarian state was looked upon by the founders of Marxism as an instrumentality of class struggle, a means of "holding down" a class in society, a repressive force. Nor did they shrink, even in their mature years, from the corollary that the revolutionary dictatorship of the proletariat would have to resort to the weapon of terror. Engels insisted on the need for a revolution to maintain itself in power by means of terror and criticized the Communards of 1871 for not having done so resolutely enough. Could the Commune have lasted a single day, he inquired, without resorting to the "authority of the armed people" against the bourgeoisie? And: "Should we not, on the contrary, reproach it for not having used it freely enough?"[40] Marx, stating in a letter of 1881 that the majority of the Commune was in no sense socialist, made clear what, in his view, a genuinely socialist government should be prepared to do on assuming power: "One thing you can at any rate be sure of: a socialist government does not come into power in a country unless conditions are so developed that it can above all take the necessary measures for intimidating the mass of the bourgeoisie sufficiently to gain time—the first *desideratum*—for lasting action."[41]

All this speaks against one further argument that has been adduced in favor of the Social Democratic exegesis of classical Marxism on the proletarian dictatorship. The argument holds that the thinking of Marx and Engels underwent a democratic evolution over the years, that they moved from a youthful Blanquist tendency or Jacobinism in 1848 and its aftermath to a mature outlook that was sober, moderate, and genuinely democratic. According to the Russian Menshevik leader Martov, for example, Marx and Engels originally conceived the idea of proletarian dictatorship in the late 1840s under the influence of the Jacobin tradition of 1793, with its minority political dictatorship and the Terror. But later, as Marx and Engels became convinced that conscious support of the majority of the population was required for a socialist revolution, their conception of the proletarian dictatorship lost its Jacobin content and they envisaged proletarian class rule "only in the forms of a total democracy."[42]

The weakness of this line of argument is clear from testimony already cited above. Although the mature Marx and Engels were not the flaming revolutionists that they had been in their youth, they remained faithful to the Marxian revolutionary idea and vision. It is true that they envisaged proletarian rule as a majoritarian dictatorship, but also, as we have just had occasion to observe, that democratic protection of the rights of the class minority was no part of their image of it. In their later as well as their earlier years, they saw the class rule of the proletariat as essentially a regime of revolution (a "class dictatorship of the revolution," as Marx had called it). They took it for granted that as such it would have bourgeois class enemies whom the government of the proletarian majority would have to deal with—and in their view ought to deal with—by forcible means, not excluding terror. The proletarian government, like every other, would be repressive in nature.

Lenin was on strong textual ground in emphasizing this point in the controversy with Social Democratic Marxism, but that is not to say that his exegesis of the doctrine of proletarian dictatorship was correct in all details or even in all essentials. If Kautsky unduly deprecated the significance of this doctrine in classical Marxism, Lenin unquestionably exaggerated it. Not content with saying in *The State and Revolution* that to be a genuine Marxist one had to accept not only the class struggle but also the proletarian dictatorship as its outcome, he subsequently asserted that the conception of proletarian dictatorship was "the essence of Marx's doctrine" and "sums up the whole of his revolutionary teaching."[43] This was to blow up one important part of Marx's thought out of all true proportion. Furthermore if Kautsky overly "democratized" Marx's notion of the proletarian dictatorship, Lenin too construed it in a manner that Marx had not foreseen. There is nothing, for example, to indicate that Marx conceived the proletarian state as a party-state, a dictatorship of a single party ruling, or claiming to rule, *on behalf* of the proletariat. Nor did he picture it in Leninist fashion as a form of polity destined to endure through an entire historical epoch of transition to communism, for the transition itself was understood in different terms. Precisely because the proletarian state would be a regime of the immense majority in an advanced society, a majority of the process of abolishing private property and therewith the division of labor in production, it would soon lose its repressive *raison d'être* and wither away. As a "dictatorship of the revolution," it would have a short life at the close of man's prehistory. Such, at any rate, is the belief that Marx and Engels seem to have entertained.

THE ECONOMY AS POLITY

To our conventional way of thinking, Marx's political theory is summed up in the views treated in the foregoing pages. However the conventional view is misleading in this instance. Marx's theory of the state is an extremely important portion of his political theory and the part that has directly influenced the subsequent course of political thought. Yet a philosophical appreciation of Marx as a political thinker cannot rest at this point. It must proceed to examine the political aspect of his economic thought.

What, parenthetically, is political theory about? One answer would be that it is about the state, since most systematic political theorizing has addressed itself to questions concerning the origin, nature, functions, and limits of the state. Alternatively, one can say that the proper subject-matter of political theory is the realm of the political, which includes the state but at the same time greatly transcends it. The "realm of the political" may in turn be defined as the realm of power and authority relations among people. Such relations between man as ruler and man as subject occur not alone through the medium of the state as the sovereign political authority and public sphere of government in society. They occur in virtually every other form of society as well, starting with the family. All established human groups and institutions have their inner structure of authority, their pattern of ruler-subject relations. If they stand outside the institutional structure of the state, they are not on that account nongovernmental. Rather they belong to the sphere of private as distinguished from public government; moreover government itself, in the elementary sense of rulership of man over man, is pervasive in human society.

All this is more than ordinarily pertinent in an assessment of Marx as a political thinker. For more, perhaps, than any other important Western political theorist, either before his time or after, he was concerned with private government, particularly as expressed in the economic life of man in history. Indeed, private government in the economic life was for him the primary and decisive realm of the political, and public government—the sphere of the state—was a secondary and surbordinate political field. Marx's economic interpretation of politics went along with a political interpretation of economics. If politics was "about economics," economics was political through and through.

This attribute of Marx's thought reflected the Hegelian heritage of the materialist conception of history, the influence of *The Phenomenology of Mind* in particular. His inversion of Hegel's political philosophy in the critical commentary of 1843 led him to the view that civil society underlay the state. But Marx did not for long visualize this *bürgerliche Gesellschaft* in the manner of the classical political economists, for whom it was a society of free self-interested economic men interacting as equals in the marketplace. The image of it underwent a profound transformation in his mind, as shown by his original formulation of the materialist conception of history in the Paris manuscripts of 1844. There the "economic men" in civil society reduced themselves to two archetypal figures: the worker and the capitalist. And in conceptualizing the relation between them, Marx was guided by the section of the *Phenomenology* in which Hegel had depicted the dualization of spirit into "Master and Servant" (*"Herr und Knecht"*). This was shown by the terminology he employed. He spoke of the capitalist as *"Herr,"* the worker as *"Knecht,"* and the labor itself as a condition of *"Knechtschaft"* or bondage. The fundamental socioeconomic relationship in civil society was thus politicalized. The capital-labor relation became, in Marx's mind, a "politico-economic" relation of dominion and servitude, and always remained that. Indeed, this is one of the significant expressions of the underlying continuity in Marx's thought from the 1844 manuscripts to *Das Kapital.*

Not only capitalism but every previous socioeconomic order founded on division of labor came to be viewed as a realm of the political. The "social relations of production," which had formed the foundation of society in every historical epoch, were relations not simply of economic exploitation but also of domination and servitude; the pervasive form of government in history was private government in the society of production. And this followed logically from Marx's basic premises as analyzed earlier. Since each historical form of the division of labor in production had been a form of captivity for the producers, the domination of man by man was necessarily involved by the process of production. So, for Marx, man as possessor of the means of production was *ruler* over man as producer. He was so not simply as the force controlling the public government in the given society; rather his dominion over the producer was manifested first of all in the economic life itself. It was precisely as owners—of slaves in ancient society, land in feudal society and capital in bourgeois society—that men of one class tyrannized over men of another. Not surprisingly, then, Marx saw the quest for wealth and property as a kind of *Wille zur Macht*. The capitalist profit motive, in particular, was a politico-economic drive for power over man through the possession of money. "Accumulation is a conquest of the world of social wealth," wrote Marx. "It increases the mass of human material exploited by the capitalist, and thus amplifies his direct and indirect dominion (*Herrschaft*)." A footnote to this passage commented: "In this study of the usurer, the old-fashioned but perennially renewed form of the capitalist, Luther shows forcibly that the love of power is an element in the impulse to acquire wealth."[44] Thus the capitalist "economic man" was for Marx a special kind of *homo politicus,* and avarice, the ruling passion of capitalist society, was seen as a passion to conquer and dominate human beings, to rule over them in the process of exploiting their labor.

Adumbrated already in the 1844 manuscripts, Marx's political interpretation of capitalist economics received its fullest and clearest expression in *Das Kapital*. This book, which is seen as his chief treatise of political theory as well as economics, is a vast elaboration of his original picture of the relationship between capitalist and worker as *Herr* and *Knecht*. Although legally free to seek employment where he will and terminate it when he will, the worker is compelled by the necessity of earning a living for himself and his family to enter a relationship of servitude to the employer, a condition of "wage slavery." The language that Marx uses in portraying this capital-labor relation is replete with political terminology. Hence in *Das Kapital* he variously describes it as a "dictatorship of capital," "autocracy of capital," and "despotism of capital." The capitalist economic order appears here as a supremely authoritarian private realm of the political. It is a special form of command economy where the capitalist *qua* capitalist acts as a tyrannical ruling authority comparable to the great oriental despots of antiquity: "The power that used to be concentrated in the hands of Asiatic or Egyptian kings or of Etruscan theocrats and the like, has in modern society been transferred to the capitalists—it may be to individual capitalists; or it may be to collective capitalists, as in joint-stock companies."[45]

The despotism of capital is decentralized. The politicalized command economy is enclosed within the confines of the productive unit, which in modern society is the factory. Marx sees the capitalists ruling over men and their productive activity in the factories rather as feudal lords once ruled over serfs on their estates. He repeatedly likens the private government inside the factory to a military dictatorship. where "The command of the capitalist in the field of production has become no less indispensable than the command of the general in the battlefield."[46] We read in the *Communist Manifesto* that "masses of laborers, crowded into the factory, are organized like soldiers. As privates of the industrial army they are placed under the command of a perfect hierarchy of officers and sergeants. Not only are they slaves of the bourgeois class, and of the bourgeois state; they are daily and hourly enslaved by the machine, by the over-looker, and, above all, by the individual bourgeois manufacturer himself." The same theme repeatedly recurs in *Das Kapital*. Here again Marx describes the workers and overseers as "the private soldiers and noncommissioned officers of an industrial army." And speaking of the factory code, he says that in it "capital formulates its autocracy over its workers—in a private legislative system, and without the partition of authority and the representative methods which in other fields are so much loved by the bourgeoisie. . . . In place of the slave driver's lash, we have the overseer's book of penalties."[47]

Because he devoted relatively very little space in his voluminous writings to general discussion of the state, it is easy to infer that Marx was only secondarily a political thinker. But such a view would be a superficial one. His major work, *Das Kapital*, was in its special way a study in rulership. Its central theme was as much political as economic. It was the theme of tyranny in modern man's life of production and of an inevitable final revolt by the worker-subjects against the "despotism of capital." Marx's economics of capitalism was quite literally a "political economy"—the phrase that he himself always used in referring to economics. To analyze it in these terms is to see Marx as the essentially political thinker that he was. His vision of the political saw the productive process itself as the prime field of power relations between man and man. And his position as a political philosopher was basically determined by this fact.

THE ANARCHISM OF MARX

The central problem in the modern history of political philosophy in the West has been that of legitimizing state power, of specifying the conditions under which the sovereign ruling authority in society can be considered a rightful authority. Political theorists have addressed themselves to the basic question: What requirements must the sovereign state meet in order to be adjudged a good state? These diverse answers have generally been predicated upon the assumption that the state derives its legitimacy from fulfilling such universal needs of the citizens as the needs for security and liberty.

In these terms Marx both was and was not a political philosopher. On the one hand, he never addressed himself to the problem of legitimizing state power. But on the other hand, he did have a definite position with regard to this problem. He had a normative as well as descriptive theory of the state. Very simply and briefly, it stated that there are *no* conditions under which the state can be adjudged a good state. Marx believed that the sovereign political authority in society could not under any circumstances be considered a rightful authority. The state *qua* state was evil. Every historical example of the state, whether in the past, present or future, would inevitably partake of this evil. Accordingly, Marx's normative position with regard to the state was anarchism, which may be defined as the view that state power, being evil in essence, cannot possibly be legitimized.

This formulation of Marx's political philosophy may seem contradicted by his attitude toward the proletarian dictatorship that he believed to be historically imminent. Did he not devoutly desire the coming of this dictatorship? Must he not, then, have believed it to be something good? The answer to the first of these questions is quite clearly affirmative but does not imply an affirmative answer to the second. Marx, as we have already seen, did not hold the proletarian political order to be a good or just one; he considered it at best a necessary evil on the road of man's entry into a higher form of society which would be a good society and as such stateless. The proletarian dictatorship was only a way-station to something beyond and something different: society without a state. As a means to this end, it was desirable; as a form of state, it was not. Moreover as a state the proletarian state would doubtless be less evil than any other in history, but an evil it would be.

Marx's anarchism, like that of other political philosophers who have embraced the anarchist position, was grounded in a philosophical affirmation of freedom as the supreme human value and a belief that the existence of the state is incompatible with the realization of freedom. "Free state—what is this?" he caustically inquired in commenting on the draft Gotha Program's statement that the German workers' party aimed to create "the free state."[48] Freedom and the state, as he saw it, were mutually exclusive concepts. Insofar as any state existed, man would remain unfree, and liberated man would enjoy not freedom *in* the state but freedom *from* it. Mankind's leap from the kingdom of necessity to the kingdom of freedom would take place only with the advent of the higher phase of communist society. Certain functions of public administration and direction of the processes of production would still remain at that phase. They would not be performed, however, by a state in Marx's definition of the term ("a special organism separated from society through the division of labor"). To underline this point, Engels, in his letter to Bebel on the Gotha Program, suggested on behalf of himself and Marx that the word "state" be deleted from the statement of the party's goals: "We would therefore propose to replace 'state' everywhere by 'community' (*Gemeinwesen*), a good old German word which can very well represent the French word *'commune.'* "[49]

A final problem emerges with the recognition that classical Marxism is committed to an anarchist position in its political philosophy. For if we consider Anarchism not as an abstract political philosophy but as a revolutionary movement associated with a political philosophy, then we are confronted with the fact that Marxism was deeply at odds with it.[50] Marxism and Anarchism were rival strains in European left-wing radicalism in the middle and later years of the nineteenth century. The rivalry originated at the time of Marx's break with Proudhon in the 1840s and later witnessed the bitter feud between Marx and Bakunin and their respective followers. The depth of the resulting division in European socialism was mirrored in Marx's reaction to the outbreak of the Franco-Prussian War of 1870. "The French need a thrashing," he wrote to Engels, explaining that a Prussian victory would foster a transfer of the center of gravity of the Western European workers' movement from France to Germany, which "would also mean the predominance of *our* theory over Proudhon's, etc."[51]

If we assume, as I believe we must, that the rivalry between Marxism and Anarchism was grounded in serious theoretical as well as personal differences between their leaders, the theoretical differences require explanation. How is it that classical Marxism, while embracing anarchism as a political philosophy, disagreed with Anarchism as a socialist ideology? The question has generally been answered by reference to an extremely serious difference over the strategy of transition to a stateless society. The Anarchists did not propose to create a workers' state in the revolutionary process of leading humanity to a stateless future. Instead they viewed the dismantling of statehood as part and parcel of the revolutionary process. The workers' revolution itself was to be antistatist. Commenting on this position, Engels wrote: "The Anarchists put the thing upside down. They declare that the proletarian revolution must *begin* by doing away with the political organization of the state. . . . But to destroy it at such a moment would be to destroy the only organism by means of which the victorious proletariat can assert its newly-conquered power, hold down its capitalist adversaries and carry out that economic revolution of society without which the whole victory must end in a new defeat and a mass slaughter of the workers similar to those after the Paris Commune."[52] The two doctrines were thus at odds over the issue of whether a state was needed for the purpose of abolishing the state. As Lenin later put it on behalf of the Marxists, "We do not at all disagree with the Anarchists on the question of the abolition of the state as an *aim*. We maintain that, to achieve this aim, we must temporarily make use of the instruments, resources and methods of the state power against the exploiters. . . ."[53]

But a deeper theoretical cleavage underlay this significant strategic difference. Anarchism did more than declare the state *qua* state to be evil; it also singled out the state as the principal evil in society, the decisive cause and expression of human unfreedom. For reasons previously dealt with here, classical Marxism rejected such a view. Although it was anarchist in treating the state *qua* state as evil, it was opposed to the Anarchist doctrine on the state as the prime locus of evil. It saw man's unfreedom in the state as something secondary to, and derivative from, his unfreedom in the polity of production. The decisive cause and principal form of human bondage, and thus the supreme evil in history, was not subjection to the state but the imprisonment of man within the division of labor in production. The supreme end, therefore, was the "economic emancipation of labor" via the overthrow of the relations of domination and servitude in the economic life. The emancipation of man from the state would follow as a matter of course.

We have direct testimony from Engels showing that this was his and Marx's understanding of the opposition between Marxism and Anarchism. Bakunin's position, he said in a letter of January 24, 1872, to Theodor Cuno, was that capital existed by courtesy of the state, which was therefore the main evil to be abolished.

As, therefore, the state is the chief evil, it is above all the state which must be done away with and then capitalism will go to hell of itself. We, on the contrary say: do away with capital, the appropriation of the whole means of production in the hands of the few, and the state will fall away of itself. The difference is an essential one. Without a previous social revolution the abolition of the state is nonsense; the abolition of capital *is* in itself the social revolution and involves a change in the whole method of production.[54]

The special anarchism of Marx and Engels must thus be seen as an anarchism directed primarily against authoritarianism in the society of production and only secondarily against authoritarianism as exemplified in the state. The tyranny from which it aimed to deliver man chiefly was that which he endured as a subject of the sovereign state of capital—the "despotism of capital."

What communism ultimately signified to Marx was man's complete and perfect freedom in the life of production. The revolutionary abolition of private property and therewith of the social division of labor between classes would lead, he thought, to the overcoming of the division of labor in all its subordinate forms. Men would no longer be bound down for life to a single form of activity; the slavery of specialization would thereby be overthrown. Even within the modern factory, the abolition of the capitalist mode of production—wage labor—would bring emancipation of the worker from bondage to a particular form of specialized work. The shortening of the working day would give him leisure, and rotation of jobs within the factory would free him from the tyranny of specialization in what remained of factory work. The economic life-process of society would be carried on by "a free association of producers,"[55] undivided into *Herr* and *Knecht*.

In his short essay of 1872 "On Authority," which was written against the Anarchists, Engels implicitly contradicted Marx's vision of the factory of the future as a realm of freedom in the life of production. "The automatic machinery of a big factory is much more despotic than the small capitalists who employ workers have ever been," he wrote. "Wanting to abolish industry itself, to destroy the power loom in order to return to the spinning wheel."[56] Yet a nonauthoritarian existence in the factory was integral to communism itself in Marx's understanding of it, and this was a central message of his political philosophy.

NOTES

1. On this point, see, for example, Charles A. Beard, *The Economic Basis of Politics and Related Writings,* New York, 1957, Ch. III.
2. The chapter on "Marx and Dialectical Materialism" in George Sabine's *A History of Political Theory,* New York, 1950, is an illustration. There are, of course, exceptions, a notable one being John Plamenatz' systematic analysis of the political views of Marx and Engels in Ch. 6 of *Man and Society,* London, 1963, vol. II.
3. *MEW,* XXI, 167; cf. K. Marx-F. Engels, *Selected Works,* Moscow, 1962, vol. II, p. 321.
4. *MEW,* XIX, 29; cf. *Selected Works,* vol. II, p. 34.
5. *MEGA,* I, 1/1, 599; cf. K. Marx, *Early Writings,* ed. T. B. Bottomore, London, 1963, p. 31. For a fuller exposition of this argument, see the writer's *Philosophy and Myth in Karl Marx,* Cambridge, Mass., 1961, pp. 102-105. Marx's own recollection of his thought process in the critical commentary on Hegel is contained in his preface to *A Contribution to the Critique of Political Economy* (1859).
6. Letter to C. Schmidt of October 27, 1890, in *Selected Works,* vol. II, p. 492.
7. *MEW,* VIII, 150; cf. *Selected Works,* vol. I, p. 284.
8. *MEW,* XXII, 197ff.; cf. *Selected Works,* vol. I, pp. 483ff.
9. *MEW,* XXII, 198; cf. *Selected Works,* vol. I, p. 484.
10. *MEW,* XVII, 340ff.; cf. *Selected Works,* vol. I, pp. 520ff.
11. *MEW,* XXI, 167; cf. *Selected Works,* vol. II, pp. 320ff.
12. *MEW,* XIII, 8ff.; cf. K. Marx, *A Contribution to the Critique of Political Economy,* Chicago, 1904, p. 11.
13. *MEW,* IV, 182; cf. K. Marx, *The Poverty of Philosophy,* Chicago, n.d., p. 190.
14. *MEW,* XXI, 167; cf. *Selected Works,* vol. II, p. 320. Italics added.
15. *MEW,* XXI, 165; cf. *Selected Works,* vol. II, p. 319.
16. V. I. Lenin, *Selected Works,* Moscow, 1946-1947, vol. II, p. 197.
17. Engels' letter of October 27, 1890, to C. Schmidt, *Selected Works,* vol. II, p. 493.
18. *MEW,* III, 33; cf. K. Marx-F. Engels, *The German Ideology,* New York, 1947, p. 23.
19. *MEW,* XXIII, 96; cf. K. Marx, *Capital,* London, 1933, p. 57n.
20. See his article on "The British Rule in India" (*New York Daily Tribune,* June 25, 1853) for his views on this subject. In an essay on "The Ruling Bureaucracy of Oriental Despotism: A Phenomenon that Paralyzed Marx," in *The Review of Politics* (July 1953), Karl A. Wittfogel hypothesizes that Marx's reticence on this theme stemmed from a reluctance to discuss the class structure of Oriental society and comments that this in

turn probably stemmed from a fear of suggesting that a bureaucracy might prove the ruling and owning class in a future socialist society. This is a highly speculative explanation, particularly considering that Oriental society was not the only prebourgeois social formation concerning which Marx had very little to say. The only form of society that Marx showed any interest in analyzing in detail was, after all, bourgeois society.

21. *MEW*, XIX, 29; cf. *Selected Works*, vol. II, pp. 33-34.
22. *MEW*, VII, 33; cf. *Selected Works*, vol. I, p. 163.
23. *MEW*, XVII, 340; cf. *Selected Works*, vol. I, p. 520.
24. *MEW*, VIII, 154; cf. *Selected Works*, vol. I, p. 288.
25. *MEW*, XVIII, 160; cf. K. Kautsky, *The Dictatorship of the Proletariat*, Ann Arbor, Mich., 1964, p. 10. See also Marx's article "The Chartists," *New York Daily Tribune* for August 25, 1852, *MEW*, VIII, 342ff., suggesting that in England universal suffrage must inevitably result in the political supremacy of the working class.
26. *MEW*, XVIII, 308; cf. *Selected Works*, vol. I, p. 638.
27. *MEW*, XXI, 168; cf. *Selected Works*, vol. II, p. 322.
28. *MEW*, XVII, 341ff.; cf. *Selected Works*, vol. I, p. 522. Italics added.
29. Quoted by H. Stuart Hughes, *Consciousness and Society*, New York, 1961, pp. 79ff.
30. *MEW*, VIII, 198ff.; cf. *Selected Works*, vol. I, pp. 334ff.
31. *Man and Society*, vol. II, pp. 371ff.
32. *MEW*, VII, 88; cf. *Selected Works*, vol. I, p. 223.
33. *Selected Works*, vol. II, p. 452.
34. *MEW*, XIX, 28; cf. *Selected Works*, vol. II, pp. 32ff.
35. *The Dictatorship of the Proletariat*, pp. 30, 43-44, 46.
36. *MEW*, XVII, 342; cf. *Selected Works*, vol. I, p. 522.
37. Marx and Engels, *Selected Correspondence 1846-1895*, New York, 1942, p. 486.
38. Lenin, *Selected Works*, vol. II, p. 365.
39. *Selected Works*, vol. II, p. 42.
40. *MEW*, XVIII, 308; cf. *Selected Works*, vol. I, p. 638.
41. Marx to Domela Nieuwenhuis, February 22, 1881, *Selected Correspondence*, p. 386.
42. J. Martov, *The State and the Socialist Revolution*, New York, 1939, pp. 57, 63. The lingering influence of this line of argument in present-day Marx scholarship in the West is to be seen in George Lichtheim, *Marxism: An Historical and Critical Survey*, New York, 1961.
43. Lenin, *Selected Works*, vol. II, p. 362. For the passage referred to in *The State and Revolution*, see *ibid.*, p. 163.
44. *MEW*, XXIII, 619; cf. *Capital*, p. 651.
45. *MEW*, XXIII, 353; cf. *Capital*, p. 350.
46. *MEW*, XXIII, 350; cf. *Capital*, p. 346.
47. *MEW*, XXIII, 447; cf. *Capital*, pp. 452ff.
48. *MEW*, XIX, 27; cf. *Selected Works*, vol. II, p. 31.
49. *Ibid.*, 42.
50. To express this distinction, I here capitalize the word when referring to the movement but not when referring to the abstract philosophy.
51. *Selected Correspondence*, p. 292.
52. Engels to Van Patten, April 18, 1883, *Selected Correspondence*, p. 417. The Commune naturally caused intense controversy between the rival movements. The Anarchists saw the Paris insurrection as an antistatist revolution, and on this account Bakunin accused the Marxists of betray-

ing their principles in claiming that the program and aim of the Commune was theirs. They contended, on the other hand, that the Commune was a proletarian dictatorship.

53. Lenin, *Selected Works,* vol. II, p. 181. For a similar view, see Plamenatz, *Man and Society,* vol. II, pp. 374, 383.
54. *Selected Correspondence,* pp. 319-320.
55. *MEW,* XXIII, 92; cf. *Capital,* p. 54.
56. *MEW,* XVIII, 306; cf. *Selected Works,* vol. II, p. 637.

8 : *Marx and the State*

RALPH MILIBAND

I

As in the case of so many other aspects of Marx's work, what he thought about the state has more often than not come to be seen through the prism of later interpretations and adaptations. These have long congealed into *the* Marxist theory of the state, or into *the* Marxist-Leninist theory of the state, but they cannot be taken to constitute an adequate expression of Marx's own views. This is not because these theories bear *no* relation to Marx's views but rather that they emphasize some aspects of his thought to the detriment of others, and thus distort by oversimplification an extremely complex and by no means unambiguous body of ideas; and also that they altogether ignore certain strands in Marx's thought which are of considerable interest and importance. This does not, in itself, make later views better or worse than Marx's own: to decide this, what needs to be compared is not text with text, but text with historical or contemporary reality itself. This can hardly be done within the

Originally published in *The Socialist Register*, 1965, pp. 278-296.

compass of an essay. But Marx is so inescapably bound up with contemporary politics, his thought is so deeply buried inside the shell of official Marxism and his name is so often invoked in ignorance by enemies and partisans alike, that it is worth asking again what he, rather than Engels, or Lenin or any other of his followers, disciples or critics, actually said and appeared to think about the state. This is the purpose of the present essay.

Marx himself never attempted to set out a comprehensive and systematic theory of the state. In the late 1850s he wrote that he intended, as part of a vast scheme of projected work, of which *Capital* was only to be the first part, to subject the state to systematic study.[1] But of this scheme, only one part of *Capital* was in fact completed. His ideas on the state must therefore be taken from such historical *pièces de circonstance* as *The Class Struggles in France*, the *18th Brumaire of Louis Bonaparte* and *The Civil War in France*, and from his incidental remarks on the subject in his other works. On the other hand, the crucial importance of the state in his scheme of analysis is well shown by his constantly recurring references to it in almost all of his writings; and the state was also a central preoccupation of the "young Marx": his early work from the late 1830s to 1844 was largely concerned with the nature of the state and its relation to society. His most sustained piece of work until the 1844 *Economic and Philosophical Manuscripts*, apart from his doctoral dissertation, was his *Critique of the Hegelian Philosophy of Right*, of which only the *Introduction*, actually written after the *Critique* itself, has so far appeared in English.[2] It is in fact largely through his critique of Hegel's view of the state that Marx completed his emancipation from the Hegelian system. This early work of Marx on the state is of great interest; for, while he soon moved beyond the views and positions he had set out there, some of the questions he had encountered in his examination of Hegel's philosophy recur again and again in his later writings.

II

Marx's earliest views on the state bear a clear Hegelian imprint. In the articles which he wrote for the *Rheinische Zeitung* from May

1842 to March 1843, he repeatedly spoke of the state as the guardian of the general interest of society and of law as the embodiment of freedom. Modern philosophy, he writes in July 1842, "considers the state as the great organism in which must be realized juridical, moral and political freedom and where the individual citizen, in obeying the laws of the state only obeys the natural laws of his own reason, of human reason." [3]

On the other hand, he also shows himself well aware that this exalted view of the state is in contradiction with the real state's actual behavior: "a state which is not the realization of rational freedom is a bad state," he writes, [4] and in his article on the Rhineland Diet's repressive legislation against the pilfering of forest wood, he eloquently denounces the Diet's denial of the customary rights of the poor and condemns the assignation to the state of the role of servant of the rich against the poor. This, he holds, is a perversion of the state's true purpose and mission; private property may wish to degrade the state to its own level of concern, but any modern state, in so far as it remains true to its own meaning, must, confronted by such pretensions, cry out "your ways are not my ways, and your ideas are not my ideas." [5]

More and more, however, Marx found himself driven to emphasize the external pressures upon the state's actions. Writing in January 1843 on the plight of the wine growers of the Moselle, he remarks that "in the examination of the institutions of the state, one is too easily tempted to overlook the concrete nature of circumstances (*"die sachliche Natur der Verhältnisse"*) and to explain everything by the will of those empowered to act." [6]

It is the same insistence on the need to consider the "concrete nature of circumstances" which lies at the core of the *Critique of Hegel's Philosophy of Right,* which Marx wrote in the spring and summer of 1843, after the *Rheinische Zeitung* had been closed down. By then, his horizons had widened to the point where he spoke confidently of a "break" in the existing society, to which "the system of acquisition and commerce, of ownership and of exploitation of man is leading even more rapidly than the increase in population." [7] Hegel's "absurdity," he also writes in the *Critique,* is that he views the affairs and the activities of the state in an abstract fashion; he forgets that the activities of the state are human functions: "the affairs of the state, etc., are nothing but the modes of existence and activity of the social qualities of men."[8]

The burden of Marx's critique of Hegel's concept of the state is that Hegel, while rightly acknowledging the separation of civil society from the state, asserts their reconciliation in the state itself. In his system, the "contradiction" between the state and society is resolved in the supposed representation in the state of society's true meaning and reality; the alienation of the individual from the state, the contradiction between man as a private member of society, concerned with his own private interests, and as a citizen of the state finds resolution in the state as the expression of society's ultimate reality.

But this, says Marx, is not a resolution but a mystification. The contradiction between the state and society is real enough. Indeed, the political alienation which it entails is the central fact of modern, bourgeois society, since man's political significance is detached from his real private condition, while it is in fact this condition which determines him as a social being, all other determinations appearing to him as external and inessential: "real man is the private man of the present constitution of the state."[9]

But the mediating elements which are supposed, in Hegel's system, to ensure the resolution of this contradiction—the sovereign, the bureaucracy, the middle classes, the legislature—are not in the least capable, says Marx, of doing so. Ultimately, Hegel's state, far from being above private interests and from representing the general interest, is in fact subordinate to private property. What, asks Marx, is the power of the state over private property? The state has only the illusion of being determinant, whereas it is in fact determined; it does, in time, subdue private and social wills, but only to give substance to the will of private property and to acknowledge its reality as the highest reality of the political state, as the highest moral reality.[10]

In the *Critique,* Marx's own resolution of political alienation and of the contradiction between the state and society is still envisaged in mainly political terms, i.e., in the framework of "true democracy." "Democracy is the solution to the riddle of all constitutions"; in it, "the constitution appears in its true reality, as the free product of man." "All other political systems are specific, definite, particular political forms. In democracy, the formal principle is also the material principle." It constitutes, therefore, the real unity of the universal and the particular.[11] Marx also writes: "In all states which differ from democracy, the state, the law, the constitution are sovereign without being property dominant, that is to say without materially affecting the other non-political spheres. In democracy, the constitution, the law, the state itself are only the people's self-determination, a specific aspect of it, in so far as that aspect has a political constitution."[12]

Democracy is here intended to mean more than a specific political form, but Marx does not yet define what else it entails. The struggle between monarchy and republic, he notes, is still a struggle within the framework of what he calls the "abstract state," i.e., the state alienated from society; the abstract political form of democracy is the republic. "Property and all that makes up the content of law and the state is, with some modifications, the same in the United States as in Prussia; the republic of America is thus only a purely political form as is the monarchy in Prussia."[13] In a real democracy, however, the constitution ceases to be purely political; indeed Marx quotes the opinion of "some modern Frenchmen" to the effect that "in a real democracy the political state disappears."[14] But the concrete content of "true democracy" remains here undefined.

The *Critique* already suggests the belief that political emancipation is not synonymous with human emancipation. The point, which is, of course, central to Marx's whole system, was made explicit in the two articles which he wrote for the *Franco-German Annals,* namely the *Jewish Question,* and the *Introduction* to a *Contribution to the Critique of Hegel's Philosophy of Right.*

In the first essay, Marx criticizes Bruno Bauer for confusing political and human emancipation, and notes that "the limit of political emancipation is immediately apparent in the fact that the *state* may well free itself from some constraint, without man himself being *really* freed from it, and that the state may be a *free state,* without *man* being free."[15] Even so, political emancipation is a great advance; it is not the last form of human emancipation, but it is the last form of human emancipation within the framework of the existing social order.[16] Human emancipation, on the other hand, can only be realized by transcending bourgeois society, "which has torn up all genuine bonds between men and replaced them by self-ishness, selfish need, and dissolved the world of men into a world of atomized individuals, hostile towards each other."[17] The more specific meaning of that emancipation is defined in the *Jewish Question*, in Marx's strictures against "Judaism," here deemed synonymous with trade, money, and the commercial spirit which has come to affect all human relations. On this view, the political emancipation of the Jews, which Marx defends,[18] does not produce their social emancipation; this is only possible in a new society, in which practical need has been humanized and the commercial spirit abolished.[19]

In the *Introduction,* which he wrote in Paris at the end of 1843 and the beginning of 1844, Marx now spoke of "the doctrine, that man is for man the supreme being" and of the "categorical imperative" which required the overthrow of all conditions in which "man is a degraded, enslaved, abandoned and contemptible being."[20] But he also added another element to the system he was constructing, namely the proletariat as the agent of the dissolution of the existing social order[21]; as we shall see, this view of the proletariat is not only crucial for Marx's concept of revolution but also for his view of the state.

By this time, Marx had already made an assessment of the relative importance of the political realm from which he was never to depart and which also had some major consequence for his later thought. On the one hand, he does not wish to underestimate the importance of "political emancipation," i.e., of political reforms tending to make politics and the state more liberal and democratic. Thus, in *The Holy Family,* which he wrote in 1844 in collaboration with Engels, Marx describes the "democratic representative state" as "the perfect modern state,"[22] meaning the perfect modern *bourgeois* state, its perfection arising from the fact that "the public system is *not* faced with any privileged exclusivity,"[23] i.e., economic and political life are free from feudal encumbrances and constraints.

But there is also, on the other hand, a clear view that political emancipation is not enough, and that society can only be made truly human by the abolition of private property. "It is natural necessity, *essential human properties,* however alienated they may seem to be, and *interest* that holds the members of civil society together; *civil,* not *political* life is their *real* tie. It is therefore not the state that holds the *atoms* of civil society together ... only *political superstition* today imagines that social life must be held together by the state, whereas in reality the state is held together by civil life."[24] The modern democratic state "is based on emancipated slavery, on bourgeois society ... the society of industry, of universal competition, of private interest freely following its aims, of anarchy, of the self-alienated natural and spiritual individuality ..."[25]; the "essence" of the modern state is that "it is based on the unhampered development of bourgeois society, on the free movement of private interest."[26]

A year later, in *The German Ideology,* Marx and Engels defined further the relation of the state to bourgeois society. "By the mere fact that it is a *class* and no longer an *estate,"* they wrote, "the bourgeoisie is forced to organize itself no longer locally but nationally, and to give a general form to its mean average interest"; this "general form" is the state, defined as "nothing more than the form of organization which the bourgeois necessarily adopt both for internal and external purposes, for the mutual guarantee of their property and interest."[27] This same view is confirmed in the *Poverty of Philosophy* of 1847, where Marx again states that "political conditions are only the official expression of civil society" and goes on: "It is the sovereigns who in all ages have been subject to economic conditions, but it is never they who have dictated laws to them. Legislation, whether political or civil, never does more than proclaim, express in words, the will of economic relations."[28]

This whole trend of thought on the subject of the state finds its most explicit expression in the famous formulation of the *Communist Manifesto:* "The executive of the modern state is but a committee for managing the common affairs of the whole bourgeoisie"[29]; and political power is "merely the organized power of one class for oppressing another."[30] This is the classical Marxist view on the subject of the state, and it is the only one which is to be found in Marxism-Leninism. In regard to Marx himself, however, and this is also true to a certain extent of Engels as well, it only constitutes what might be called a primary view of the state. For, as has occasionally been noted in discussions of Marx and the state,[31] there is to be found another view of the state in his work, which it is inaccurate to hold up as of similar status with the first,[32] but which is none the less of great interest, not least because it serves to illuminate, and indeed provides an essential context for, certain major elements in Marx's system, notably the concept of the dictatorship of the proletariat. This secondary view is that of the state as independent from and superior to all social classes, as being the dominant force in society rather than the instrument of a dominant class.

III

It may be useful, for a start, to note some qualifications which Marx made even to his primary view of the state. For in relation to the two most advanced capitalist countries of the day, England and France, he often makes the point that, at one time or another, it is not the ruling class as a whole, but a fraction of it, which controls the state[33]; and that those who actually run the state may well belong to a class which is not the economically dominant class.[34] Marx does not suggest that this *fundamentally* affects the state's class character and its role of guardian and defender of the interests of property; but it obviously does introduce an element of flexibility in his view of the operation of the state's bias, not least because the competition between different factions of the ruling class may well make easier the passage of measures favorable to labor, such as the Ten Hours Bill.[35]

The extreme manifestation of the state's independent role is, however, to be found in authoritarian personal rule, Bonapartism. Marx's most extensive discussion of this phenomenon occurs in *The 18th Brumaire of Louis Bonaparte,* which was written between December 1851 and March 1852. In this historical study, Marx sought very hard to pin down the precise nature of the rule which Louis Bonaparte's *coup d'état* had established.

The *coup d'état,* he wrote, was "the victory of Bonaparte over parliament, of the executive power over the legislative power"; in parliament, "the nation made its general will the law, that is, made the law of the ruling class its general will"; in contrast, "before the executive power it renounces all will of its own and submits to the superior command of an alien will, to authority"; "France, therefore, seems to have escaped the despotism of a class only to fall back beneath the despotism of an individual and, what is more, beneath the authority of an individual without authority. The struggle seems to be settled in such a way that all classes, equally impotent and equally mute, fall on their knees before the rifle butt."[36]

Marx then goes on to speak of "this executive power with its enormous bureaucratic and military organization, with its ingenious state machinery, embracing wide strata, with a host of officials numbering half a million, besides an army of another half million, this appalling parasitic body which enmeshes the body of French society like a net and chokes all its pores."[37] This bureaucratic power, which sprang up in the days of the absolute monarchy, had, he wrote, first been "the means of preparing the class rule of the bourgeoisie," while "under the Restoration, under Louis Phillipe, under the parliamentary Republic, it was the instrument of the ruling class, however much it strove for power of its own."[38] But the *coup d'état* had seemingly changed its role: "only under the second Bonaparte does the state seem to have made itself completely independent"; "as against civil society, the state machine has consolidated its position so thoroughly that the chief of the Society of December 10 [i.e., Louis Bonaparte] suffices for its head. . . ."[39]

This appears to commit Marx to the view of the Bonapartist state as independent of any specific class and as superior to society. But he then goes on to say, in an often quoted phrase: "And yet the state power is not suspended in mid-air. Bonaparte represents a class, and the most numerous class of French society at that, *the small-holding peasants.*"[40] However, their lack of cohesion makes these "incapable of enforcing their class interests in their own name whether through a parliament or a convention"[41]; they therefore require a representative who "must at the same time appear as their master, as an authority over them, as an unlimited governmental power that protects them against the other classes and sends them rain and sunshine from above. The political influence of the small-holding peasants, therefore, finds its final expression in the executive power subordinating society to itself."[42]

"Represent" is here a confusing word. In the context, the only meaning that may be attached to it is that the small-holding peasants *hoped* to have their interests represented by Louis Bonaparte. But this does not turn Louis Bonaparte or the state into the mere instrument of their will; at the most, it may limit the executive's freedom of action somewhat. Marx also writes that "as the executive authority which has made itself an independent power, Bonaparte feels it his mission to safeguard 'bourgeois order.' But the strength of this bourgeois order lies in the middle class. He looks on himself, therefore, as the representative of the middle class and issues decrees in this sense. Nevertheless, he is somebody solely due to the fact that he has broken the political power of this middle class and daily breaks it anew"; and again, "as against the bourgeoisie, Bonaparte looks on himself, at the same time, as the representative of the peasants and of the people in general, who wants to make the lower classes of the people happy within the frame of bourgeois society. . . . But, above all, Bonaparte looks on himself as the chief of the Society of 10 December, as the representative of the *lumpen-proletariat* to which he himself, his *entourage,* his government and his army belong. . . ."[43]

On this basis, Louis Napoleon may "represent" this or that class (and Marx stresses the "contradictory task" of the man and the "contradictions of his government, the confused groping about which seeks now to win, now to humiliate first one class and then another and arrays all of them uniformly against him. . ."[44]); but his power of initiative remains very largely unimpaired by the specific wishes and demands of any one class or fraction of a class.

On the other hand, this does *not* mean that Bonapartism, for Marx, is in any sense neutral as between contending classes. It may *claim* to represent all classes and to be the embodiment of the whole of society. But it does in fact exist, and has been called into being, for the purpose of maintaining and strengthening the existing social order and the domination of capital over labor. Bonapartism and the Empire, Marx wrote much later in *The Civil War in France*, had succeeded the bourgeois Republic precisely because "it was the only form of government possible at a time when the bourgeoisie had already lost, and the working class had not yet acquired, the faculty of ruling the nation."[45] It was precisely under its sway that "bourgeois society, freed from political cares, attained a development unexpected even by itself."[46] Finally, Marx then characterizes what he calls "imperialism," by which he means Napoleon's imperial régime, as "at the same time, the most prostitute and the ultimate form of the State power which nascent middle-class society had commenced to elaborate as a means of its own emancipation from feudalism, and which full-grown bourgeois society had finally transformed into a means for the enslavement of labour by capital."[47]

In *The Origin of the Family, Private Property and the State*, written a year after Marx's death, Engels also notes: "By way of exception, however, periods occur in which the warring classes balance each other so nearly that the state power, as ostensible mediator, acquires, for the moment, a certain degree of independence of both."[48] But the independence of which he speaks would seem to go much further than anything Marx had in mind; thus Engels refers to the Second Empire, "which played off the proletariat against the bourgeoisie and the bourgeoisie against the proletariat" and to Bismarck's German Empire, where "capitalists and workers are balanced against each other and equally cheated for the benefit of the impoverished Prussian cabbage junkers."[49]

For Marx, the Bonapartist state, however independent it may have been *politically* from any given class, remains, and cannot in a class society but remain, the protector of an economically and socially dominant class.

IV

In the *Critique of Hegel's Philosophy of Right*, Marx had devoted a long and involved passage to the bureaucratic element in the state, and to its attempt "to transform the purpose of the state into the purpose of the bureaucracy and the purpose of the bureaucracy into the purpose of the state."[50] But it was only in the early fifties that he began to look closely at a type of society where the state appeared to be genuinely "above society," namely societies based on the "Asiatic mode of production," whose place in Marx's thought has recently attracted much attention.[51] What had, in the *Critique,* been a passing reference to the "despotic states of Asia, where the political realm is nothing but the arbitrary will of a particular individual, where the political realm, like the material, is enslaved,"[52] had, by 1859, become one of Marx's four main stages of history: "In broad outlines," he wrote in the famous Preface to *A Contribution to the Critique of Political Economy,* "Asiatic, ancient, feudal and modern bourgeois modes of production can be designated as progressive epochs in the economic formation of society."[53]

The countries Marx was mainly concerned with in this connection were India and China, and also Russia as a "semi-Asiatic" or "semi-Eastern" state. The Asiatic mode of production, for Marx and Engels, has one outstanding characteristic, namely the absence of private property in land: "this," Marx wrote to Engels in 1853, "is the real key, even to the Oriental heaven...."[54] "In the Asiatic form (or at least predominantly so)," he noted, "there is no property, but individual possession; the community is properly speaking the real proprietor"[55]; in Asiatic production, he also remarked, it is the state which is the "real landlord."[56] In this system, he also wrote later, the direct producers are not "confronted by a private landowner but rather, as in Asia, [are] under direct subordination to a state which stands over them as their landlord and simultaneously as sovereign"; "the state," he went on, "is then the supreme lord. Sovereignty here consists in the ownership of land concentrated on a national scale. But, on the other hand, no private ownership of land exists, although there is both private and common possession and use of land."[57]

A prime necessity of the Asiatic mode of production, imposed by climate and territorial conditions, was artificial irrigation by canals and waterworks; indeed, Marx wrote, this was "the basis of Oriental agriculture." In countries like Flanders and Italy the need of an economical and common use of water drove private enterprise into voluntary association; but it required "in the Orient, where civilization was too low and the territorial extent too vast to call into live voluntary associations, the interference of the centralized power of Government. Hence an economical function devolved upon all Asiatic governments, the functions of providing public works."[58]

Finally, in the *Grundrisse,* Marx speaks of "the despotic government which is poised above the lesser communities,"[59] and describes that government as the *"all-embracing unity* which stands above all these small common bodies . . . since the *unity* is the real owner, and the real pre-condition of common ownership, it is perfectly possible for it to appear as something separate and superior to the numerous real, particular communities . . . the despot here appears as the father of all the numerous lesser communities, thus realizing the common unity of all."[60]

It is therefore evident that Marx does view the state, in the conditions of Asiatic despotism, as the dominant force in society, independent of and superior to all its members, and that those who control its administrations are society's authentic rulers. Karl Wittfogel has noted that Marx did not pursue this theme after the 1850s and that "in the writings of the later period he emphasized the technical side of large-scale waterworks, where previously he had emphasized their political setting."[61] The reason for this, Professor Wittfogel suggests, is that "obviously the concept of Oriental despotism contained elements that paralysed his search for truth"[62]; hence his "retrogressions" on the subject. But the explanation for Marx's lack of concern for the topic would seem much simpler and much less sinister; it is that he was, in the sixties and the early seventies, primarily concerned with Western capitalism. Furthermore, the notion of bureaucratic despotism can hardly have held any great terror for him since he had, in fact, worked through its nearest equivalent in capitalist society, namely Bonapartism, and had analyzed it as an altogether different phenomenon from the despotism encountered in Asiatic society. Nor is it accurate to suggest, as does Mr. Lichtheim, that "Marx for some reason shirked the problem of the bureaucracy" in post-capitalist society.[63] On the contrary, this may be said to be a crucial element in Marx's thought in the late sixties and in the early seventies. His concern with the question, and with the state, finds expression in this period in his discussion of the nature of political power in post-capitalist societies, and particularly in his view of the dictatorship of the proletariat. This theme had last occupied Marx in 1851-1852; after almost twenty years it was again brought to the fore by the Paris Commune, by his struggles with anarchism in the First International and by the programmatic pronouncement of German Social Democracy. It is to this, one of the most important and the most misunderstood aspects of Marx's work on the state, that we must now turn.

V

It is first of all necessary to go back to the democratic and representative republic, which must be clearly distinguished from the dictatorship of the proletariat: for Marx, the two concepts have nothing in common. An element of confusion arises from the fact that Marx bitterly denounced the class character of the democratic republic, yet supported its coming into being. The contradiction is only apparent; Marx saw the democratic republic as the most advanced type of political régime in *bourgeois society,* and wished to see it prevail over more backward and "feudal" political systems. But it remained for him a system of class rule, indeed the system in which the bourgeoisie rules most directly.

The limitations of the democratic republic, from Marx's point of view, are made particularly clear in the *Address of the Central Committee of the Communist League* which he and Engels wrote in March 1850. "Far from desiring to revolutionize all society for the revolutionary proletarians," they wrote, "the democratic petty bourgeois strive for a change in social conditions by means of which existing society will be made as tolerable and comfortable as possible for them." They would therefore demand such measures as "the diminution of state expenditure by a curtailment of the bureaucracy and shifting the chief taxes on to the big landowners and bourgeois . . . the abolition of the pressure of big capital on small, through public credit institutions and laws against usury . . . the establishment of bourgeois property relations in the countryside by the complete abolition of feudalism." But in order to achieve their purpose they would need "a democratic state structure, either constitutional or republican, that will give them and their allies, the peasants, a major- ity; also a democratic communal structure that will give them direct control over communal property and over a series of functions now performed by the bureaucrats."[64] However, they added, "as far as the workers are concerned, it remains certain that they are to remain wage workers as before; the democratic petty-bourgeois only desire better wages and a more secure existence for the workers . . . they hope to bribe the workers by more or less concealed alms and to break their revolutionary potency by making their position tolerable for the moment."[65]

But, Marx and Engels go on, "these demands can in no wise suffice for the party of the proletariat"; while the petty-bourgeois democrats would seek to bring the revolution to a conclusion as quickly as possible, "it is our interest and our task to make the revolution permanent, until all more or less possessing classes have been forced out of their position of dominance, until the proletariat has conquered state power, and the association of proletarians, not only in one country but in all the dominant countries of the world, has advanced so far that competition among the proletarians of these countries has ceased and that at least the decisive productive forces are concentrated in the hands of the proletarians. For us the issue cannot be the alteration of private property but only its annihila- tion, not the smoothing over of class antagonisms but the abolition of classes, not the improvement of existing society but the founda- tion of a new one."[66]

At the same time, while the demands and aims of the proletarian party went far beyond anything which even the most advanced and radical petty-bourgeois democrats would accept, the revolutionaries must give them qualified support and seek to push the democratic movement into even more radical directions.[67] It was, incidentally, precisely the same strategy which dictated Marx's later attitude to all movements of radical reform, and which led him, as in the *Inaugural Address* of the First International in 1864, to acclaim the Ten Hours

Act or the advances of the cooperative movement as the victories of "the political economy of labour over the political economy of property."[68]

In 1850, Marx and Engels had also suggested that one essential task of the proletarian revolutionaries would be to oppose the decentralizing tendencies of the petty-bourgeois revolutionaries. On the contrary, "the workers must not only strive for a single and indivisible German republic, but also within this republic for the most determined centralization of power in the hands of the state authority. . . ."[69]

This is not only the most extreme "statist" prescription in Marx's (and Engels') work—it is the only one of its kind, leaving aside Marx's first "Hegelian" pronouncements on the subject. More important is the fact that the prescription is intended *not* for the proletarian but for the bourgeois democratic revolution.[70] In 1850, Marx and Engels believed, and said in the *Address,* that the German workers would not be able "to attain power and achieve their own class interest without completely going through a lengthy revolutionary development."[71] The proletarian revolution would see the coming into being of an altogether different form of rule than the democratic republic, namely the dictatorship of the proletariat.

In a famous letter to J. Wedemeyer in March 1852, Marx had revealed the cardinal importance he attached to this concept by saying that, while no credit was due to him for discovering the existence of classes in modern society or the struggles between them, "what I did that was new was to prove (1) that the *existence of classes* is only bound up with *particular historical phases in the development of production,* (2) that the class struggle necessarily leads to the *dictatorship of the proletariat,* (3) that this dictatorship itself only constitutes the transition to *abolition of all classes* and to a *classless society.* "[72]

Unfortunately, Marx did not define in any specific way *what* the dictatorship of the proletariat actually entailed, and more particularly what was its relation to the state. It has been argued by Mr. Hal Draper in an extremely well documented article that it is a *"social description,* a statement of the class character of the political power. It is not a statement about the forms of the government machinery."[73] My own view, on the contrary, is that, for Marx, the dictatorship of the proletariat is *both* a statement of the class character of the political power *and* a description of the political power itself; and that it is in fact the nature of the political power which it describes which guarantees its class character.

In the *18th Brumaire,* Marx had made a point which constitutes a main theme of his thought, namely that all previous revolutions had "perfected this [state] machine instead of smashing it. The parties that contended in turn for domination regarded the possession of this huge state edifice as the principal spoils of the victors."[74] Nearly twenty years later, in *The Civil War in France,* he again stressed how every previous revolution had consolidated "the centralized State power, with its ubiquitous organs of standing army, police, bureaucracy, clergy and judicature"; and he also stressed how the political character of the state had changed "simultaneously with the economic changes of society. At the same pace at which the progress of modern history developed, widened, intensified the class antagonism between capital and labour, the State power assumed more and more the character of the national power of capital over labour, of a public force organized for social enslavement, of an engine of class despotism. After every revolution marking a progressive phase in the class struggle, the purely repressive character of the State power stands out in bolder and bolder relief."[75]

As Mr. Draper notes, Marx had made no reference to the dictatorship of the proletariat in all the intervening years. Nor indeed did he so describe the Paris Commune. But what he acclaims above all in the Commune is that, in contrast to previous social convulsions, it sought not the further consolidation of the state power but its destruction. What it wanted, he said, was to have "restored to the social body all the forces hitherto absorbed by the State parasite feeding upon, and clogging the free movement of society."[76] Marx also lays stress on the Commune's popular, democratic and egalitarian character, and on the manner in which "not only municipal administration but the whole initiative hitherto exercised by the State was laid into the hands of the Commune."[77] Moreover, while the communal form of government was to apply even to the "smallest country hamlet," "the unity of the nation was not to be broken, but, on the contrary, to be organized by the Communal Constitution, and to become a reality by the destruction of the State power which claimed to be the embodiment of that unity independent of, and superior to, the nation itself, from which it was but a parasitic excrescence."[78]

In notes which he wrote for *The Civil War in France*, Marx makes even clearer than in the published text the significance which he attached to the Commune's dismantling of the state power. As contributing evidence of his approach to the whole question, the following passage from the Notes is extremely revealing: "This [i.e., the Commune] was," he wrote, "a Revolution not against this or that, legitimate, constitutional, republican or Imperialist form of State power. It was a Revolution against the *State* itself, of this supernaturalist abortion of society, a resumption by the people for the people of its own social life. It was not a revolution to transfer it from one fraction of the ruling class to the other but a Revolution to break down this horrid machinery of Classdomination [*sic*] itself . . . the Second Empire was the final form (?) [*sic*] of this State usurpation. The Commune was its definite negation, and, therefore, the initiation of the social Revolution of the nineteenth century."[79] It is in the light of such views that Marx's verdict on the Commune takes on its full meaning: this "essentially working-class government," he wrote, was "the political form at last discovered under which to work out the economic emancipation of labour."[80]

It is of course true that, while Engels, long after Marx's death, did describe the Paris Commune as the dictatorship of the proletariat,[81] Marx himself did not do so. The reason for this would seem fairly obvious, namely that, for Marx, the dictatorship of the proletariat would be the outcome of a socialist revolution on a national scale; the Commune, as he wrote in 1881, was "merely the rising of a city under exceptional conditions," while "the majority of the Commune was in no wise socialist, nor could it be."[82] Even so, it may justifiably be thought that the Commune, in its de-institutionalization of political power, did embody, for Marx, the essential elements of his concept of the dictatorship of the proletariat.

Precisely the opposite view has very generally come to be taken for granted; the following statement in Mr. Lichtheim's *Marxism* is a typical example of a wide consensus: "His (Marx's) hostility to the state was held in check by a decidedly authoritarian doctrine of political rule during the transition period: prior to being consigned to the dustbin of history, the state was to assume dictatorial powers. In different terms, authority would inaugurate freedom—a typically Hegelian paradox which did not worry Marx though it alarmed Proudhon and Bakunin. . . ."[83]

The trouble with the view that Marx had a "decidedly authoritarian doctrine" is that it is unsupported by any convincing evidence from Marx himself; and that there is so much evidence which directly runs counter to it.

Marx was undoubtedly the chief opponent of the anarchists in the International. But it is worth remembering that his central quarrel with them concerned above all the manner in which the struggle for a socialist revolution ought to be prosecuted, with Marx insisting on the need for political involvement within the existing political framework, against the anarchists' all or nothing rejection of mere politics; and the quarrel also concerned the question of the type of organization required by the international workers' movement, with Marx insisting on a *degree* of control by the General Council of the International over its affiliated organizations.

As for the role of the state in the period of transition, there is the well-known passage in the "private circular" against the anarchists issued by the General Council in 1872, *Les Prétendues Scissions dans l'Internationale,* and most probably written by Marx: "What all socialists understand by anarchism is this: as soon as the goal of the proletarian movement, the abolition of class, shall have been reached, the power of the state, whose function it is to keep the great majority of the producers beneath the yoke of a small minority of exploiters, will disappear, and governmental functions will be transformed into simple administrative functions. The Alliance [i.e., Bakunin's Alliance of Socialist Democracy] turns the thing upside down. It declares anarchism in the ranks of the workers to be an infallible means for disrupting the powerful concentration of social and political forms in the hands of the exploiters. Under this pretext, it asks the International, when the old world is endeavouring to crush our organization, to replace organization by anarchism. The international police could ask for nothing better. . . ."[84]

This can hardly be construed as an authoritarian text; nor certainly is Marx's plaintive remark in January 1873 quoted by Lenin in *State and Revolution* that "if the political struggle of the working class assumes violent forms, if the workers set up this revolutionary dictatorship in place of the dictatorship of the bourgeoisie, they commit the terrible crime of violating principles, for in order to satisfy their wretched, vulgar, everyday needs, in order to crush the resistance of the bourgeoisie, instead of laying down their arms and abolishing the state, they give the state a revolutionary and transitory form. . . ."[85]

Nor is there much evidence of Marx's "decidedly authoritarian doctrine" in his marginal notes of 1875 on the Gotha Programme of the German Social-Democratic Party. In these notes, Marx bitterly attacked the programme's references to "the free state" ("free state—what is this?") and this is well in line with his belief that the "free state" is a contradiction in terms; and he then asked: "What transformation will the state undergo in communist society? In other words, what social functions will remain in existence there that are analogous to present functions of the State?" Marx, however, did not answer the question but merely said that it could only be answered "scientifically" and that "one does not get a flea-hop nearer to the problem by a thousandfold combination of the word people with the word state."[86] He then goes on: "Between capitalist and communist society lies the period of the revolutionary transformation of the one into the other. There corresponds to this also a political transition period in which the state can be nothing but *the revolutionary dictatorship of the proletariat.*"[87]

This does not advance matters much but neither does it suggest the slightest "authoritarian" impulse. In the *Critique of the Gotha Programme,* Marx as always before, made a sharp distinction between the democratic republic and the dictatorship of the proletariat, and Engels was clearly mistaken when he wrote in 1891 that the democratic republic was "even the specific form of the dictatorship of the proletariat."[88] On the contrary, Marx's critical attitude toward the democratic republic in the *Critique of the Gotha Programme* shows that he continued to think of the dictatorship of the proletariat as an altogether different and immeasurably freer form of political power. "Freedom," he wrote in the *Critique of the Gotha*

Programme, "consists in converting the state from an organ super-imposed upon society into one completely subordinated to it...."[89] This would seem a good description of Marx's view of the state in the period of the dictatorship of the proletariat. No doubt, he would have endorsed Engels' view, expressed a few weeks after Marx's death, that "the proletarian class will first have to possess itself of the organized political force of the state and with this aid stamp out the resistance of the capitalist class and reorganize society."[90] But it is of some significance that, with the possible exception of his remark of January 1873, referred to earlier, Marx himself always chose to emphasize the liberating rather than the repressive aspects of post-capitalist political power; and it is also of some interest that, in the notes he made for *The Civil War in France,* and which were not of course intended for publication, he should have warned the working class that the "work of regeneration" would be "again and again relented [*sic*] and impeded by the resistance of vested interests and class egotisms," but that he should have failed to make any reference to the State as an agent of repression. What he did say was that "great strides may be [made] at once through the communal form of political organization" and that "the time has come to begin that movement for themselves and mankind."[91]

The fact is that, far from bearing any authoritarian imprint, the whole of Marx's work on the state is pervaded by a powerful anti-authoritarian and anti-bureaucratic bias, not only in relation to a distant communist society but also the period of transition which is to precede it. True, the state is necessary in this period. But the only thing which, for Marx, makes it tolerable is popular participation and popular rule. If Marx is to be faulted, it is not for any authoritarian bias, but for greatly understating the difficulties of the libertarian position. However, in the light of the experience of socialist movements since Marx wrote, this may perhaps be judged a rather less serious fault than its bureaucratic obverse.

NOTES

1. K. Marx to F. Lassalle, 22 February 1858, and K. Marx to F. Engels, 2 April 1858 (*Selected Correspondence,* Moscow, n.d.), pp. 125, 126.
2. For the *Critique,* see *Marx/Engels Gesamtausgabe* (MEGA) (Moscow, 1927), I 1/1, pp. 403-553; for the *Introduction,* first published in the *Franco-German Annals* of 1844, *ibid.,* I 1/1, pp. 607-21, and T. B. Bottomore, Ed., *K. Marx, Early Writings* (London, 1963).
3. MEGA, *ibid.,* p. 249.
4. *Ibid.,* p. 248.
5. *Ibid.,* p. 283.
6. *Ibid.,* p. 360. Note also his contemptuous reference in an article of May 1842 on the freedom of the Press to "the inconsistent, nebulous and timorous reasoning of German liberals, who claim to honour freedom by setting it up in an imaginary firmament, rather than on the solid ground of reality" (*ibid.,* p. 220; A. Cornu, *Karl Marx et Friedrich Engels. Leur Vie et leur Oeuvre* [Paris, 1958] II, p. 17).
7. K. Marx to A. Ruge, May 1843, MEGA, p. 565; see also K. Marx to A. Ruge, March 1843, *Sel. Cor., op. cit.,* p. 25.
8. MEGA, *ibid.,* p. 424.
9. *Ibid.,* pp. 498-9. See also J. Hyppolite, *Etudes sur Marx et Hegel* (Paris, 1955), pp. 123ff., and M. Rubel, *K. Marx. Essai de Biographie Intellectuelle* (Paris, 1957), pp. 58ff.
10. MEGA, *ibid.,* p. 519.
11. *Ibid.,* pp. 434-5.
12. *Ibid.,* p. 435.
13. *Ibid.,* p. 436.
14. *Ibid.,* p. 435.
15. *Ibid.,* p. 582. Italics in original.
16. *Ibid.,* p. 585.
17. *Ibid.,* p. 605.
18. See S. Avineri, "Marx and Jewish Emancipation" in *Journal of the History of Ideas,* vol. XXV (July-September 1964), pp. 445-50.
19. MEGA, *op. cit.,* p. 606.
20. *Ibid.,* p. 615.
21. *Ibid.,* pp. 619ff.
22. K. Marx and F. Engels, *The Holy Family* (Moscow, 1956), p. 154.
23. *Ibid.,* p. 157. Italics in original.
24. *Ibid.,* p. 163. Italics in original.
25. *Ibid.,* p. 164.
26. *Ibid.,* p. 166.
27. K. Marx and F. Engels, *The German Ideology* (New York, 1939), p. 59. Italics in original.
28. K. Marx, *The Poverty of Philosophy* (London, 1936), p. 70.
29. K. Marx and F. Engels, *Selected Works,* hereafter noted as *S.W.* (Moscow, 1959), I, p. 35.
30. *Ibid.,* p. 51.
31. See, e.g., J. Plamenatz, *German Marxism and Russian Communism* (London, 1954), pp. 144ff.; J. Sanderson, "Marx and Engels on the State" in the *Western Political Quarterly,* vol. XVI, no. 4 (December 1963), pp. 946-55.

32. As is suggested by the two authors cited above.
33. See, e.g., *The Class Struggles in France, passim, The 18th Brumaire of Louis Bonaparte, passim.*
34. See, e.g., "The Elections in Britain" in K. Marx and F. Engels, *On Britain* (Moscow, 1953), pp. 353ff. "The Whigs are the *aristocratic representatives* of the bourgeoisie, of the industrial and commercial middle class. Under the condition that the bourgeoisie should abandon to them, to an oligarchy of aristocratic families, the monopoly of government and the exlusive possession of office, they make to the middle class, and assist it in conquering, all those concessions, which in the course of social and political developments have shown themselves to have become *unavoidable* and *undelayable.*" (*Ibid.*, p. 353. Italics in original.)
35. *Ibid.*, p. 368.
36. *S.W.*, I, p. 300.
37. *Ibid.*, p. 301.
38. *Ibid.*, p. 302.
39. *Ibid.*, p. 302.
40. *Ibid.*, p. 302. Italics in original.
41. Marx also notes that the identity of interest of the smallholding peasants "begets no community, no national bond and no political organization among them," so that "they do not form a class" (*ibid.*, p. 302). For an interesting discussion of Marx's concept of class, see S. Ossowski, *Class Structure in the Class Consciousness* (London, 1963), ch. V.
42. *S.W.*, I, p. 303.
43. *Ibid.*, pp. 308-9.
44. *Ibid.*, p. 309.
45. K. Marx, *The Civil War in France, S.W.*, I, p. 470.
46. *Ibid.*, p. 470.
47. *Ibid.*, p. 470.
48. F. Engels, *The Origin of the Family, Private Property and the State, S.W.*, II, p. 290.
49. *Ibid.*, pp. 290-1. For further comments on the subject from Engels, see also his letter to C. Schmidt, 27 October 1890, in *S.W.*, II, pp. 446-7.
50. MEGA, *op. cit.*, I, 1/1, p. 456.
51. See, e.g., K. Wittfogel, *Oriental Despotism* (Yale, 1957), ch. IX; G. Lichtheim, "Marx and the 'Asiatic Mode of Production'" in *St. Antony's Papers*, no. 14, Far Eastern Affairs (London, 1963). Also K. Marx, *Pre-Capitalist Economic Formations*, with an introduction by E. J. Hobsbawm (London, 1964). This is a translation of a section of Marx's *Grundrisse Der Kritik der Politischen Okonomie* (*Rohentwurf*) (Berlin, 1953).
52. MEGA, I, 1/1, p. 438.
53. *S.W.*, I, p. 329.
54. K. Marx to F. Engels, 2 June 1853, *Sel. Cor.*, p. 99.
55. K. Marx, *Pre-Capitalist Formations, op. cit.*, p. 79.
56. *New York Daily Tribune*, 5 August 1853, in Lichtheim, *op. cit.*, p. 94.
57. K. Marx, *Capital* (Moscow, 1962), III, pp. 771-2.
58. K. Marx and F. Engels, *The First Indian War of Independence* (1857-9) (Moscow, n.d.), p. 16. In *Capital* (Moscow, 1959), I, p. 514, ft. 2, Marx also notes that "one of the material bases of the power of the State over the small disconnected producing organisms in India, was the regulation of the water supply"; also, "the necessity for predicting the rise and fall of the Nile created Egyptian astronomy, and with it the dominion of the priests, as directors of agriculture" (*ibid.*, p. 514, ft. 1); for some further

elaborations on the same theme, see also F. Engels, *Anti-Dühring* (Moscow, 1962), p. 248.

59. K. Marx, *Pre-Capitalist Economic Formations, op. cit.*, p. 71.
60. *Ibid.*, p. 69. Italics in original.
61. K. Wittfogel, *Oriental Despotism, op. cit.*, p. 381.
62. *Ibid.*, p. 387.
63. Lichtheim, *op. cit.*, p. 110.
64. K. Marx and F. Engels, *Address of the Central Committee to the Communist League, S.W.*, I, p. 101.
65. *Ibid.*, p. 101.
66. *Ibid.*, p. 102.
67. *Ibid.*, p. 101.
68. *Ibid.*, pp. 307-9.
69. *Ibid.*, p. 106.
70. It is, in this connection, of some interest that Engels should have thought it necessary to add a Note to the 1885 edition of the Address, explaining that this passage was based on a "misunderstanding" of French revolutionary experience and that "local and provincial self-government" were not in contradiction with "national centralization." (*Ibid.*, p. 107.)
71. *Ibid.*, p. 108.
72. K. Marx to J. Wedemeyer, 5 March 1852, *Sel. Cor.*, p. 86. Italics in original.
73. H. Draper, "Marx and the Dictatorship of the Proletariat" in *New Politics*, vol. I, no. 4, p. 102. Italics in original.
74. *S.W.*, I, p. 301.
75. *Ibid.*, pp. 468-9.
76. *Ibid.*, p. 473.
77. *Ibid.*, p. 471.
78. *Ibid.*, p. 472.
79. *Marx-Engels Archives* (Moscow, 1934), vol. III (VIII), p. 324. Italics in original. I am grateful to Mr. M. Johnstone for drawing my attention to these Notes. Note also, e.g., the following: "Only the Proletarians, fired by a new social task to accomplish by them for all society, to do away with all classes and class rule, were the men to break the instrument of that class rule—the State, the centralized and organized governmental power usurping to be the master instead of the servant of society. . . . It had sprung into life against them. By them it was broken, not as a peculiar form of governmental (centralized) power, but as its most powerful, elaborated into seeming independence from society expression and, therefore, also its most prostitute reality, covered by infamy from top to bottom, having centred in absolute corruption at home and absolute powerlessness abroad" (*ibid.*, p. 326). The peculiar English syntax of such passages is obviously due to the fact that they are only notes, not intended for publication.
80. *S.W.*, I, p. 473.
81. "Of late," Engels wrote in an Introduction to the 1891 edition of *The Civil War in France*, "the Social-Democratic philistine has once more been filled with wholesome terror at the words: Dictatorship of the Proletariat. Well and good, gentlemen, do you want to know what this dictatorship looks like? Look at the Paris Commune. That was the Dictatorship of the Proletariat." (*S.W.*, I, p. 440.)
82. K. Marx to F. Domela-Nieuwenhuis, 22 February 1881, in *Sel. Cor.*, p. 410.

83. G. Lichtheim, *Marxism* (London, 1961), p. 374.

84. G. M. Stekloff, *History of the First International* (London, 1928), pp. 179-80, and J. Freymond, ed., *La Première Internationale* (Geneva, 1962), II, p. 295.

85. V. I. Lenin, *State and Revolution* (London, 1933), p. 54.

86. K. Marx, *Critique of the Gotha Programme, S.W.,* II, p. 30.

87. *Ibid.,* p. 30. Italics in original.

88. Quoted in Lenin, *The State and Revolution,* p. 54. Lenin's own comment is also misleading: "Engels," he writes, "repeats here in a particularly striking manner the fundamental idea which runs like a red thread through all of Marx's works, namely, that the democratic republic is the nearest approach to the dictatorship of the proletariat" (*ibid.,* p. 54). Engels' phrase does not bear this interpretation; and whatever may be said for the view that the democratic republic *is* the nearest approach to the dictatorship of the proletariat, it is not so in Marx.

89. *S.W.,* II, p. 29.

90. F. Engels to P. Van Patten, 18 April 1883, *Sel. Cor., op. cit.,* p. 437.

91. *Marx-Engels Archives, op. cit.,* p. 334.

9
Marx and the "Asiatic Mode of Production"

GEORGE LICHTHEIM

I

Since the appearance in 1957 of Professor Wittfogel's important work on Oriental society[1] it has gradually become known in academic circles that there exists a problem in Marxist sociology which has to do with Marx's and Engels' views on Asiatic society, and with the gradual abandonment of these views in the Soviet Union, notably during the so-called Stalinist era. In what follows I propose to take for granted some awareness of the standard Soviet approach in these matters, with the obvious proviso that one cannot foretell the possible consequences in the theoretical sphere of a more thorough de-Stalinization, let alone of an open conflict between the USSR and China. A partial return to genuine Leninism, as distinct from Stalinism, is a possibility which must be taken into account, but for reasons which cannot be elaborated in this space even this would not help much toward a restoration of the authentic Marxian approach, to say nothing of a critical interpretation of Marx's and

Originally published in *St. Anthony's Papers*, XIV, Oxford-London, 1963.

182

Engels' writings on the subject of Asiatic society. The reader who is interested in Leninism, as distinct from Marxism, must be referred to Professor Wittfogel.[2]

It has to be admitted at the outset that this distinction is not quite watertight, inasmuch as Lenin—at any rate down to 1917—did operate within the Marxian concept of an "Asiatic society" and an "Asiatic mode of production." It is apparent, however, that even in those early writings of his in which he characterized the Tsarist regime as semi-Asiatic, he did not relate this concept clearly or systematically to the dominant role of the bureaucracy, but rather tended to overstress the role of the landowners, or even to describe the Tsarist government as one dominated by the landed nobility. The resulting medley of genuinely theoretical concepts and merely political slogans revolved around the question whether Russia might or might not relapse into what Lenin himself at times described as "the restoration of our old 'semi-Asiatic' order" or as "the restoration of the Asiatic mode of production." The most one can say is that he was aware of the problem, both as a theoretical issue having to do with the character of Oriental society and as a practical concern for those who wished to break with Russia's semi-Asiatic past. The matter was complicated by the factional debates in which he was involved, and which at various times led him to stress one aspect rather than another. Thus in 1905 he was quite ready to advocate a bourgeois development and even to suggest that the revolution then in progress would, if it were victorious, "for the first time really clear the ground for a widespread and rapid European, not Asiatic, development of capitalism" in Russia (cf. *Two Tactics,* in *Selected Works,* London, 1947, vol. I, p. 375); whereas from 1906 onwards he showed a tendency to water down the "Asiatic" concept and to employ the ambiguous terms "medieval," "patriarchal," or "pre-capitalist."[3] In 1911, in a comment on Tolstoy's writings, he reverted once more to the theme, this time to suggest that down to the revolution of 1905 Russia was a country where "the Oriental system, the Asiatic system" predominated. By this he evidently meant more than that Russia had until then been governed autocratically, since that would also have been true of Bourbon France, or of Prussia before 1848; but what exactly he did mean is not quite clear, though he went on to say that the upheaval of 1905 was "the beginning of the end of 'Oriental' stagnation," which rather suggests that he was thinking along lines familiar to Marxists at that time.

The opposite of "stagnation" is "progress" and most Socialists—following Marx—were then in the habit of giving qualified approval to the capitalist form of progress, though without idealizing it and while stressing its catastrophic impact on backward countries and exploited classes. The roots of this attitude are clearly traceable to the *Communist Manifesto,* where it is observed that capitalism "batters down all Chinese walls" and "compels all nations on pain of extinction to adopt the bourgeois mode of production" (cf. Marx-Engels, *Selected Works,* Moscow, 1958, vol. I, p. 38). The reference to Chinese walls is scarcely accidental: when Marx drafted the *Manifesto* the first Opium War had recently been fought, and there is a characteristic remark in the same passage on "the barbarians' intensely obstinate hatred of foreigners," which "the bourgeoisie" has to overcome in its relentless march to world domination: the process whereby it "draws all, even the most barbarian, nations into civilization." Whatever they thought of the means whereby this result was accomplished, the distinction between Eastern barbarism (or "stagnation") and Western progress ("civilization") was one that Marx and Engels in 1848 had no intention of questioning.

II

When we turn to the writings composed by Marx—with some assistance from Engels—in the early 1850s, we encounter the same ambivalent attitude toward "progress" that had already characterized the *Manifesto,* plus a special undertone arising from the fact that both men were then settled in England and commenting upon British colonial affairs in a leading American newspaper.[4] Though one would not gather as much from the Soviet editors of their works, their strictures upon British rule in India, or the British Government's behavior toward China, are substantially in tune with the "bourgeois" radicalism of the period, and in some respects anticipate the standard anti-colonialism of later American writing.

Marx's caustic comments on British colonial policy clearly went down well with his American readers for reasons which had little to do with his own theoretical approach. In some respects indeed he took a more tolerant view of British rule than they did, since he tended to regard the impact of capitalism upon Oriental society as beneficial in the long run, whereas the *Tribune's* line reflected an anti-industrial bias which he did not share. Thus on June 14, 1853, we find him writing to Engels (*Selected Correspondence,* Moscow, 1956, pp. 101-102):

> The *Tribune* of course trumpets Carey's book with all its might. Both indeed have this in common that under the guise of Sismondian-philanthropic-socialistic anti-industrialism they represent the protectionist, i.e., the industrial bourgeoisie of America. This also explains the secret why the *Tribune,* despite its "isms" and its socialistic humbug, can be the "leading journal" in the United States. . . . I have continued this camouflaged warfare in a first article on India, in which the destruction of the native industry by England is described as *revolutionary*. This will be very shocking to them.

The reference is to an article entitled "British Rule in India" which appeared in the *Tribune* on June 25, 1853,[5] and in which Marx for the first time expressed a considered opinion about the nature of Oriental society. It is amusing to find that one of the key ideas of this important article had been suggested by an impromptu remark dropped by Engels. On June 6, 1853, in a letter to Marx on the general subject of Oriental history,[6] Engels had thrown out the suggestion that "an Oriental government never had more than three departments: finance (plunder at home), war (plunder at home and abroad), and public works (provision for reproduction). The British Government in India has administered Nos. 1 and 2 in a rather more philistine fashion[7] and dropped No. 3 entirely, so that Indian agriculture is being ruined." Marx incorporated these observations in his article, and went on to outline some ideas on the genesis of Oriental society and the "Asiatic mode of production":

> Climate and territorial conditions, especially the vast tracts of desert extending from the Sahara through Arabia, Persia, India and Tartary, to the most elevated Asiatic highlands, constituted

artificial irrigation by canals and waterworks the basis of Oriental agriculture. . . . This prime necessity of an economical and common use of water, which in the Occident drove private enterprise to voluntary association, as in Flanders and Italy, necessitated in the Orient, where civilization was too low [*sic*] and the territorial extent too vast to call into life voluntary association, the interference of the centralizing power of Government. Hence an economical function devolved upon all Asiatic Governments, the function of providing public works.[8]

For Marx and Engels this state of affairs ("the Hindu . . . leaving like all Oriental peoples to the Central Government the care of the great public works . . .") was connected with a circumstance to which Marx refers in the same article, namely the dispersion of the population "in small centres by the domestic union of agricultural and manufacturing pursuits," i.e., in self-governing villages; now these small units, "inoffensive though they may appear, had always been the solid foundation of Oriental despotism," their inhabitants being totally indifferent to whatever went on around them, including massacres and foreign invasions.[9] It was this passivity which had made despotism possible in the first place. But how had "this undignified, stagnatory, and vegetative life . . . this passive sort of existence" come into being? The exchange of letters hints at an answer. On June 2, 1853, Marx observes apropos of François Bernier's eighteenth-century *Travels Containing a Description of the Dominions of the Great Mogul:* "Bernier rightly considers the basis (*Grundform*) of all Oriental phenomena—he refers to Turkey, Persia, Hindustan— to be the *absence of private property in land.* This is the real key, even to the Oriental heaven" (cf. MEGA *Briefwechsel,* III/I, p. 447; SC, p. 99). Engels echoes this judgment in his answering letter of June 6: ". . . The absence of property in land is indeed the key to the entire Orient. Herein lies the political and religious history. But how does it come about that the Orientals did not arrive at landed property, even in its feudal form? I think it is mainly due to the climate, taken in connection with the nature of the soil, especially the great stretches of desert. . . . Artificial irrigation is here the first condition of agriculture, and this is a matter either for the communes, the provinces, or the central government." Follow the remarks about the character of Oriental rule which have already been quoted and which Marx reproduced in his article.

At this state, then, Marx and Engels are agreed that (1) there is no Oriental feudalism; (2) its absence is synonymous with the non-existence of private landed property, which in turn is due to climatic conditions; (3) the centralized Oriental despotism has arisen from the need to provide artificial irrigation; (4) the forcible destruction of the system by the British, whatever its motivation, is about to introduce the preconditions of 'progress' in the Western sense, albeit at immense cost. In the Hegelian manner, Marx in his article poses the historical problem philosophically ("The question is, can mankind fulfill its destiny without a fundamental revolution in the social state of Asia? If not, whatever may have been the crimes of England, she was the unconscious tool of history in bringing about that revolution"), but in our context this is immaterial, except insofar as it supplies the explanation of his readiness to include the destruction of Indian handicrafts among the *faux frais* of history. The real theoretical problem lies elsewhere. When Marx, in a subsequent article on India (*New York Daily Tribune,* August 8, 1853; cf. Marx-Engels *Selected Works,* vol. 1, p. 356), looks forward to the time when the Indians will "reap the fruits of the new elements of society scattered among them by the British bourgeoisie," he is simply being "progressive" in a manner which today permits every Asian nationalist to applaud him, especially since he also alludes to the time when "the Hindus themselves shall have grown strong enough to throw off the English yoke." But if Marx had merely been another nineteenth-century progressive his views would not command special interest. The question is what can be made of his scattered and unsystematic notions about Oriental society and the "Asiatic mode of production."

Before turning to this theme it may be as well to round off the factual account with some quotations from Marx's references to China which date from roughly the same period, i.e., the 1850s. In this connection little weight need be given to his (or Engels') humorous forecast of a time to come when the last European reactionaries, having taken refuge in Asia and finally reached that ancient bastion of conservatism, the Great Wall of China, would find inscribed upon its gates the dreadful words: *"République chinoise—Liberté, Egalité, Fraternité."*[10] If the joke shows anything, it is that to Marx and Engels in 1850 "the revolution" signified more or less what it did to all their democratic contemporaries.[11] "Chinese socialism," they observe with a touch of condescension, "may stand in the same relation to European socialism as does Chinese philosophy to that of Hegel. But it is nonetheless an amusing circumstance [*sic*] that the oldest and most unshakeable empire on earth should within eight years have been brought by the cotton-bales of the English bourgeoisie to the eve of a social revolution which cannot fail to have the most important consequences for civilization."[12] That Marx and Engels regarded this prospect as "amusing" as well as inevitable testifies not only to the sense of security and superiority which they shared with most other Europeans but also to their intellectual descent from Hegel, who in his lectures on world history had drawn an unflattering picture of the Celestial Empire.[13] Marx's essential Hegelianism, whenever he has occasion to discuss the probable fate of an ancient and now stagnant civilization, is well exemplified by the concluding passage of one of his articles on China in the late 1850s:

> While the semi-barbarian stood on the principle of morality, the civilized opposed to him the principle of self. That a giant empire, containing almost a third of the human race, vegetating in the teeth of time, insulated by the forced exclusion of general intercourse, and thus contriving to dupe itself with delusions of Celestial perfection—that such an empire should at last be overtaken by fate on the occasion of a deadly duel in which the representative of the antiquated world appears prompted by ethical motives, while the representative of the overwhelming society fights for the privilege of buying in the cheapest and selling in the dearest markets—this indeed is a sort of tragical couplet, stranger than any poet would ever have dared to fancy.[14]

This elegiac note is struck repeatedly in the writings he devoted to China in 1858/9, while the struggle to "open up" the Treaty Ports was in progress, but it is only toward the end of this period that Marx—by now in the throes of drafting his major economic work and with the *Critique of Political Economy* already behind him—pulls the strands of his theoretical argument together:

> It is the same combination of husbandry with manufacturing industry which for a long time withstood, and still checks, the

export of British wares to East India; but there the combination was based upon a peculiar constitution of the landed property which the British, in their position of the supreme landlords of the country, had it in their power to undermine, and thus forcibly convert part of the Hindu self-sustaining communities into mere farms producing opium, cotton, indigo, hemp, and other raw materials, in exchange for British stuffs. In China the English have not yet wielded this power, nor are they likely ever to do so.[15]

Oriental society clearly is something more complex than a system of canals. It has to do, on the one hand, with centralized, i.e., despotic, regulation of the basic economic functions and, on the other, with the prevalence of the self-sufficient village economy. But still the key, as we have seen earlier, has to be sought in the "absence of private property in land."

III

In January 1859, when writing the *Preface* to the *Critique of Political Economy,* Marx for the first (and last) time gave a summary of his method that indicates the exact relationship in which the economic process ("the mode of production of material life") stands to the historical process generally; and it is here, toward the close of the now classic formulation of the "materialist conception of history," that he introduces his four historical stages: "In broad outlines, Asiatic, ancient, feudal, and modern bourgeois modes of production can be designated as progressive epochs in the economic formation of society."[16] He was never again to display a similar degree of certainty in assigning their relative place to those forms of society which had embodied their characteristic features in definite stages of recorded history. Yet the general standpoint laid down in the *Preface* was not superseded or even substantially modified. (The qualifications introduced by Engels in the *Anti-Dühring* and the *Origins of the Family* are not, in my opinion, of basic importance.)[17] There are four, and only four, major historical epochs, the Asiatic being the first, and each corresponds to a definite social order which in turn lays the foundation for the succeeding one.

These two aspects are internally related, but must nonetheless for analytical purposes be considered separately.[18]

To start, then, with the "Asiatic mode" taken by itself, we have already seen what features can be said to distinguish it. In his unsystematic fashion, Engels had suggested two: climatic conditions and the pervasive habits of an Oriental government. Marx expanded these hints into a system by tracing the peculiar character of Oriental society to the absence of private ownership in land.[19] He related this to the overriding role of the central government by suggesting that under the "Asiatic system" the State was the "real landlord."[20] So far as private property in land is concerned we are left in no doubt what Marx thought of its role in dissolving the "Asiatic mode," since in the second and concluding of his important *Tribune* articles on British rule in India he expressly describes it as "the great *desideratum* of Asiatic society,"[21] for the sake of which the infamies practiced by the Indian *zamindar* and *ryotwar* systems, "abominable as they are," should nonetheless be regarded as a step toward the emancipation of Indian society. Now what of the role played by the State? That in Asia it was the "real landlord" Marx never doubted. For proof we have the passage in *Capital*, volume III, where he refers to the situation of the producers being confronted not by a private landowner, "but rather, as in Asia, under direct subordination to a state which stands over them as their landlord and simultaneously as sovereign."[22] These characteristics of "Asiatic society"—state control over the producer, and absence of private property in land—are presumably related to the strategic role of the central government in administering the irrigation system, but how does this complex interrelationship come about *historically?* Engels never bothered about such difficult questions, but from Marx we are entitled to expect an answer. Let us see how far he has provided one.

An indirect clue is afforded by his observation that where the small peasants "form among themselves a more or less natural production community, as they do in India . . . the surplus labour for the nominal owner of the land can only be extorted from them by other than economic pressure, whatever the form assumed may be."[23] This is followed by the remark about the state-sovereign doubling as landlord, so that taxes and ground-rents coincide. Marx then continues: "Under such circumstances there need exist no harder political or economic dependence than that common to all subjection to that state. The state is here the supreme landlord. Sovereignty here consists in the ownership of land concentrated on a national scale. Conversely, no private ownership of land exists, although there is both private and common possession and use of land."[24]

Does this point in the direction of a theory of conquest or some other form of political usurpation which blocks the emergence of true "private ownership" of land, leaving the subject peasant population only with "possession and use"? The puzzling thing is that the immediately following sentence states: "The specific economic form in which unpaid surplus labour is pumped out of (the) direct producers determines the relationship of rulers and ruled, as it grows directly out of production itself and in turn reacts upon it as a determining element. Upon this, however, is founded the entire formation of the economic community which grows up out of the production relations themselves, (and) therewith simultaneously its specific political form."[25] Other parts of the same lengthy passage refer to serfdom and similar forms of socioeconomic bondage. It must be borne in mind that volume III of *Capital* was pieced together by Engels from unfinished drafts. Even so it remains uncertain how Marx envisaged the historical genesis of a relationship which counterposes the State as supreme landlord to the peasant-producer. He makes it quite clear, however, that it is the dominance of the State which excludes genuine private ownership of land, i.e., the precondition of feudalism. If anything defines "the Orient" according to Marx (and Engels) it is this supremacy of the State, which reduces the landowners to the role of merely "nominal landlords" as Marx calls them.[26] There cannot then have been any genuine Oriental feudalism, at any rate not in India and China, the two Asian countries to which Marx had given some systematic attention. That he regarded their problems as broadly similar appears from a passage in *Capital,* volume III, where he refers to the impact of European commerce upon Eastern societies:

The obstacles presented by the internal solidity and organization of pre-capitalistic, national modes of production to the corrosive influence of commerce are strikingly illustrated in the intercourse of the English with India and China. The broad basis of the mode of production here is formed by the unity of small-scale agriculture and home industry, to which in India we should add the form of village communities built upon the common ownership of land, which incidentally was the original form in China as well. In India the English lost no time in exercising their direct political and economic power, as rulers and landlords, to disrupt these small economic communities. English commerce exerted a revolutionary influence on these communities and tore them apart only insofar as the low prices of its goods served to destroy the spinning and weaving industries which were an ancient integrating element of this unity of industrial and agricultural production. Even so this work of dissolution proceeds very gradually. And still more slowly in China, where it is not reinforced by direct political power. The substantial economy and saving in time afforded by the association of agriculture with manufacture put up a stubborn resistance to the products of the big industries whose prices include the *faux frais* of the circulation process which pervades them. Unlike the English, Russian commerce, on the other hand, leaves the economic ground-work of Asiatic production untouched.[27]

The interest of this passage is that it shows Marx, in the 1860s and while at work on *Capital*, reverting to the theme of his early newspaper articles. He does so also in a footnote in which the "absurd (in practice infamous) economic experiments" conducted by the British in India are duly condemned, with special reference to the creation of "a caricature of large-scale English estates" in Bengal.[28] Yet we have seen that in 1853 he had described private property in land as "the great *desideratum* of Asiatic society," and expressly mentioned the *zamindars*. There is of course no contradiction if one bears in mind that for Marx the rupture of India's ancient stagnation involved the payment of a terrible price in exploitation and dislocation. But the new stress in *Capital* on the futility and absurdity of these "economic experiments," together with the reference to the solidity of the ancient social structure built upon the union of farming and handicrafts, does strike rather a different note. When he remarks that "in the north-west they (sc. the English) did all they could to transform the Indian economic community with common ownership of the soil into a caricature of itself,"[29] he seems to be saying, or at least hinting, that but for this outside interference the village community might have evolved in a sounder direction. Then there is the passing reference to the economic savings inherent in small-scale enterprise, as against the *faux frais* of modern large-scale industry—this last a familiar theme in socialist literature since Fourier, but one to which Marx normally did not give a great deal of attention. Altogether the tone of this passage seems to anticipate his well-known observations upon the prospects of the Russian village community in the 1880s: there is a hint of "Narodism" about it.[30]

It is, I think, a fair inference from these passages that while in the 1850s Marx was inclined to emphasize the progressive role of Western capitalism in disrupting Oriental stagnation, by the time he came to draft his major economic work he was less certain that traditional society embodied no positive factors. At any rate, it may be said that by the 1860s his attitude had become ambivalent. We now find him remarking upon the stability of the ancient village communities, in a manner suggesting that he saw some genuine virtue in their peculiar mode of life. At the same time his hostility to capitalism had deepened. This is worth stressing as a qualification of the familiar statement that he had by the 1860s lost some of his early revolutionary ardor. If one has in mind his early attachment to a rather Jacobinical view of the coming European revolution, it is true to say that he grew more moderate in the measure that he became the theorist of a genuine labor movement with democratic aims. But at the same time he sharpened his critique of bourgeois society and the operation of capitalism as an economic system. The *Manifesto*, rather paradoxically, had celebrated the triumphant march of capitalism at the same time that it proclaimed the proletariat's coming victory. By the time Marx wrote *Capital* he was more concerned with factory legislation than with the proletarian revolution, but this did not make him more tolerant of "the system"; rather less so. The note of indulgence had vanished, and the tone has become one of unqualified hostility and contempt. In 1847 the bourgeoisie still gained some plaudits for battering down the Chinese walls of barbarism; by 1867 even the "Asiatic mode" comes in for favorable comment, at any rate so far as the village community is concerned: it is valued as a bulwark against social disintegration.

IV

Here, then, is something like a hiatus in the argument. To some extent the difficulty arises from the fact that the more strictly historical part of Marx's theory of Oriental society is to be found in the posthumously published draft for *Das Kapital,* the so-called *Grundrisse.*[31] Before turning to this theme it may be as well to note where he departs from his predecessors. There was an eighteenth-century and early-nineteenth-century view of Asian society with which Marx was thoroughly familiar. It is briefly but succinctly set out in the *Wealth of Nations,* and it is amusing to find that Smith, like Marx, refers to Bernier's travels as a source.[32] Chinese isolationism and indifference to foreign trade attracted the unfavorable attention of Smith who thought that "upon their present plan they have little opportunity of improving themselves by the example of any other nation; except that of the Japanese"[33]: a nice example of historical foresight. China is classed with "ancient Egypt and Indostan," and Smith makes the pertinent point that in both these countries the government paid much attention to the canal system.[34] He also observes that "the sovereigns of China, of ancient Egypt, and of the different kingdoms into which Indostan has at different times been divided, have always derived the whole, or by far the most considerable part, of their revenue from some sort of land-tax or rent. . . . It was natural, therefore, that the sovereigns of those countries should be particularly attentive to the interests of agriculture, upon the prosperity or declension of which immediately depended the yearly increase or diminution of their own revenue."[35] Later he remarks that "the sovereigns of China, those of Bengal while under the Mahometan government, and those of ancient Egypt, are said accordingly to have been extremely attentive to the making and maintaining of good roads and navigable canals, in order to increase, as much as possible, both the quantity and value of every part of the produce of the land. . . ."[36] He then goes on to discuss "the loss of the sovereign from the abuse and depredation of his tax-gatherers" and the interest of "the Mandarins and other tax-gatherers" in maintaining a system of payment in kind that enabled them to fleece the peasants and defraud the central government.[37] There are the elements here of a theory of Oriental society, but it cannot be said that Smith makes much of them. He is content to register various features of Indian or Chinese administration, without inquiring to what extent they constitute a whole. In the following generation, we find James Mill, in his *History of British India* (1820), referring to an "Asiatic model of government" (vol. I, pp. 175ff.), while John Stuart Mill (*Principles of Political Economy,* 1848) already employs the term "Oriental society" as distinct from European.[38] Marx was familiar with these writers. Where does he diverge from them?

Principally, it seems to me, in expanding their hints into a theory that is both historical and sociological.[39] Unfortunately the theory was never formulated in systematic fashion, but has to be pieced together from his published and unpublished writings, notably the *Grundrisse* of 1857-58, where it is, however, chiefly employed to bring out the contrast between Oriental society and Graeco-Roman antiquity. By drawing upon all these scattered sources (including a very early work, the *German Ideology* of 1845-46, which throws out some interesting hints about slavery and feudalism), we arrive at something like the following:

The various stages in the development of the social division of labor correspond to different forms of property.[40] The "first form" is communal and proper to "the undeveloped stage of production where a people sustains itself by hunting and fishing, by cattle-raising or at most by farming."[41] At this stage, the division of labor is rudimentary and consists for the most part in a further development of the primitive division of functions inherent in the family. "The social order therefore limits itself to an extension of the family: patriarchal tribal chiefs, below them the members of the tribe, finally slaves. The slavery latent in the family develops gradually with the growth of population and needs, and with the extension of external intercourse, both of war and barter trade."[42] This primitive tribal or communal organization is succeeded historically by a "second form" which in the 1845-46 sketch is equated with "the communal and state property of antiquity." This is said to arise particularly "from the union of several tribes to a city through contact or conquest, and while retaining slavery. Side by side with communal property, mobile and subsequently immobile private property develops, but as an abnormal form subordinated to communal property. The citizens of the state possess power over their labouring slaves only collectively, and for this reason alone they are tied to the form of communal ownership. It is the joint private property (*das gemeinschaftliche Privateigentum*) of the active citizens who are compelled *vis-à-vis* the slaves to remain in this primitive (*naturwüchsige*) manner of association. Hence the entire organization of society based thereupon, and therewith the power of the people, decays in the same degree in which especially immobile property develops. The division of labour is more highly developed. We already find the contrast of town and country. . . . The class relationship as between citizens and slaves is fully developed."[43] Marx notes as a possible objection that "the fact of conquest appears to contradict this whole conception of history," and goes on to demonstrate that "for the conquering barbarian people, war itself is . . . a regular form of intercourse, which is exploited all the more energetically the more the growth of population together with the traditional . . . primitive mode of production arouses the demand for new means of production."[44] This organization finds its ultimate development in Roman society, where "slavery remains the basis of the entire production" and the plebeians "stationed between free citizens and slaves never got beyond a *Lumpenproletariat.*" It is succeeded by the "third form" of property, namely, "feudal or estate ownership."[45] In other words, by the European Middle Ages.

In 1845-46 Marx had not yet discovered Oriental society and the "Asiatic mode"; consequently he mentions only three pre-modern stages: tribal society is succeeded by classical antiquity founded on slavery, and the latter by European feudalism. By 1859 the *Preface* to the *Critique of Political Economy* presents four stages corresponding to different forms of property: Asiatic society, antiquity, feudalism, and modern bourgeois society. Tribal society has disappeared, to be subsequently resurrected by Engels.[46] Now the 1859 work is based on the unpublished *Grundrisse* of 1857-58, and when we turn to this much-neglected source we obtain some light on how Marx had in the meantime come to regard the relationship of the Orient and the "Asiatic mode" to primitive tribal society on the one hand, and to classical antiquity and European feudalism on the other. His economic studies had acquainted him with the researches of the British school, and what we now get is a picture in which the skeleton of the "materialist conception of history" is fleshed out with economics.

True to his method, the approach remains historical. Marx begins by asking what are the "forms which precede capitalist production,"[47] and he replies that the historical presupposition of the latter is the "separation of free labour from the objective preconditions of its realization. . . . Hence above all separation of the toiler from the soil as his natural laboratory: thus dissolution of small free landed property, as well as of the joint (*gemeinschaftlichen*) landed property resting upon the Oriental commune."[48] "In the first form of this landed property there appears a primitive (*naturwüchsige*) commonwealth as the precondition: (the) family and its extension to the tribe . . . or a combination of tribes. . . ." "Tribal community (*die Stammgemeinschaft*), the natural community, appears not as the result but as the precondition of joint appropriation . . . and utilization of the soil." "The earth is the great laboratory, the arsenal, which provides the means as well as the materials of work, and likewise the location, the basis, of the community."[49] The individual participates in ownership of the soil and the instruments of production only insofar as he is a member of this primitive commonwealth held together by the ties of consanguinity. "The real appropriation through the process of labour occurs under these presuppositions which are themselves not the product of labour, but appear as its natural or divine preconditions. This form, based on the same primitive relationship, can realize itself in many different ways. Thus it is not contradicted by the fact that in most of the Asiatic patterns (*Grundformen*) the encompassing unity, which stands above all these small communities, appears as the superior or as the sole proprietor, (and) the real communities only as hereditary possessors. Since the unity is the true owner and the real precondition of common ownership, it can appear as a particular something (*als ein Besonderes*) above the many real particular communities, where the individual is then in fact without property, or property . . . appears as though mediated for him through a grant by the total unity (*der Gesamteinheit*)—which is realized in the despot as the father of the many communities—to the individual through the intermediacy of the particular community. The surplus product . . . thus belongs inherently to this supreme unity. In the midst of Oriental despotism, and of the absence of ownership (*Eigentumslosigkeit*) which juridically seems to obtain therein, there thus exists in fact as the basis this tribal or communal ownership, generally produced by a combination of manufacture and agriculture within the small community, which thus becomes entirely self-sustaining and contains within itself all the conditions of reproduction and surplus production. Part of its surplus labour belongs to the higher unity which at last exists as a person, and this surplus labour makes its appearance both in tribute, etc., and in common labours for the glorification of the unity: in part the real despot, in part the imaginary tribal being, the god."[50]

This kind of common ownership, held together at the top by the "higher unity which at last exists as a person," appears under different historical variants: either the small communities maintain a separate existence and the individual works his plot independently, together with the members of his family; or again, "the unity may extend to communalism at work itself, which may be a formalized system, as in Mexico, notably in Peru, among the ancient Celts, (and) some Indian tribes. Further, the communal form (*die Gemeinschaftlichkeit*) within the tribal organization may appear realized in a head of the tribal family, or rather as the mutual interrelationship of the heads of families. Thence either a more despotic or more democratic form of this commonwealth. The common preconditions of genuine appropriation through labour, *waterworks* (Marx's emphasis), very important among the Asiatic people, means of communication, etc., thus appear as a work of the superior unity, the despotic government suspended above the small communities. Towns come into existence here only where there is a particularly favourable location for foreign trade; or where the head of state and his satraps exchange their revenue (surplus product) against labour, expend it as labour-funds."[51]

As against this centralized system—historically typified above all by the various Oriental despotisms—Graeco-Roman antiquity, with its development of private property in land, represents what Marx describes as "the second form" wherein the original communal (tribal) organization raises itself to a higher socio-historical level. The lengthy process whereby the urban patriciate of independent land-owners, which here monopolizes political power, builds up its peculiar institutions (ultimately resting upon slave labor, and constant war to acquire more slaves) and eventually brings about its own downfall, is described with many fascinating details, and—quite in accordance with Hegel, but also with Niebuhr and nineteenth-century historiography generally—the decline and fall of antiquity leads straight on to the Germanic Middle Ages:

"An (other) form of ownership by the labouring individuals, self-sustaining members of the community, of the natural conditions of their work, is the *German*. Unlike the specifically Oriental form, the member of the community is not as such a co-owner of the com-munal property . . . nor, unlike the Roman or Greek form . . . is the soil occupied by the community . . ." (follows a brief analysis of the *ager publicus* as the specifically Roman institution, whereby the individual Roman citizen exercises his sovereign private ownership over a particular area of Roman soil).[52] As against these earlier forms, "the German community"—which is treated by Marx as the original cell of the medieval body politic—represents something new: "Ancient classical history is a history of cities, but of cities founded upon landed property and agriculture; Asiatic history is a kind of indifferent union of town and country (the great cities are to be regarded merely as princely camps, as superfetations above the economic construction proper); the Middle Ages (German age) starts from the countryside as the seat of history, whose further develop-ment then proceeds through the antagonism of town and country; modern (history) is urbanization of the land, not as in antiquity ruralization of the town."[53] Among the Germans, the coming-together of the clan chiefs does not subvert their original inde-pendence: "The community appears as union, not as unity (*als Vereinigung, nicht als Verein*)," the (originally tribal, later feudal) landowners constituting themselves as "independent subjects."[54] "The community does not therefore in fact exist as a *state* . . . as in antiquity, because it does not exist as a *city*. For the community to come into real existence, the free landed proprietors must come together in a meeting, whereas, e.g., in Rome it existed apart from these meetings, in the being of the city itself and the officials standing at its head."[55] True, the medieval Germans also had their *ager publicus,* their commons, but it did not, as in Rome, appear "as the peculiar economic existence of the state, side by side with the private owners." It merely served as a "supplement to individual ownership" and thus represents the sharpest possible contrast to the "Asiatic form" where the individual has "no ownership, only possession"[56]; but it also contrasts sharply with the Graeco-Roman system, where the city has a life of its own, being the collective organization and quasi-ideal representation of the citizens in their public capacity, as distinct from their private existence. Thus, in the European Middle Ages, private property predominates from the start. "The community exists only in the mutual relation of these individual landowners."[57] Our modern liberties (Marx might have added, but did not) have their roots in the Germanic forests.

What he does add is an extremely interesting and subtle analysis of tribal and communal ownership in antiquity, interlarded with polemical excursions against Proudhon[58] which need not concern us here. When he returns to his original theme—tribal organization as the source of the subsequent threefold differentiation into Oriental, Graeco-Roman, and German-medieval forms of private and common ownership—it is to emphasize once more that the tribal system, "wherein the community originally dissolves itself," recognizes no property save that held by members of the tribe, so that conquered tribes are automatically deprived of it. "Slavery and serfdom are thus only further developments of the property rooted in the tribal system. They necessarily modify all its forms," though least of all in the "Asiatic form," with its "self-sustaining union of manufacture and agriculture on which this form rests."[59] What Marx describes as "the general slavery of the Orient" (as distinct from the personal slavery of classical antiquity) appears as a special case of the institutions of property. The latter—"in its Asiatic, Slav, antique, German, form"[60]—originally signifies "the relation of the labouring (producing) . . . subject to the conditions of his production or reproduction."[61] Historically this relationship takes different forms, depending upon the existence of the individual "as a member of a tribe or community (whose property he is up to a certain point)": an interesting hint which hardly squares with the rather more idyllic picture subsequently painted by Engels. Man originally makes his appearance on earth as part of a primitive collective: "a generic being, tribal being, herd animal—though by no means a *zoon politikon* in the political sense."[62] He individualizes himself through the historical process, which is primarily a process of evolving various forms of communal and private property, i.e., various ways of organizing his social intercourse with nature and the—natural or artificial—preconditions of work. The different forms of this metabolism correspond to different stages of society, among which Oriental society is historically closer to man's primitive origins, having conserved some elements of primitive communism "in the midst of Oriental despotism." Hence the succession of stages—Asiatic, antique, feudal, modern—mirrors the gradual dissolution of the "primitive unity," and the evolution of private ownership properly so called. The forcible disruption of the Indian or Chinese village community by European capital completes the process by rendering it truly global.

V

With this historical sketch in mind we can now return to our starting point and try to establish whether Marx's and Engels' utterances on the subject of Oriental society are reducible to a consistent pattern.[63]

The picture in some ways is a puzzling one. Reference has already been made to the gradual change in Marx's attitude toward the Asian village community and its resistance to the battering rams of Western capitalism. Now when one turns to the other structural element of the "Asiatic mode of production," the centralized governmental despotism, it would seem as though Marx and Engels gradually deepened their hostility to this form of rule, to the point of discovering some positive virtues not only in private property but even in European feudalism and the Germanic Middle Ages. How else to account for Marx's 1859 statement about "Asiatic, ancient, feudal, and modern bourgeois modes of production" being "progressive epochs in the economic formation of society"? It must be remembered that these words were written shortly after he had composed his unpublished draft of 1857-58, with its quasi-Hegelian stress on the element of personal freedom inherent in the rude institutions of the European Middle Ages. It must also be recalled that for Marx "progressive" does not signify "whatever happens to be going on," as it later did for his more thoughtless followers. "Progress" in his sense stands for the unfolding of man's dormant powers. European feudalism is "progressive" compared with Asiatic or Graeco-Roman society because, thanks to its relatively healthy starting point, it embodies new potentialities of growth and human development; in Hegel's terminology, it represents "a new principle." These potentialities clearly have to do with a circumstance to which Marx alludes in passing in the *Grundrisse:* the fact that among the Germans political power did not at first exist separately from the individuals, but was simply the result of joint decisions taken in public. Engels was subsequently to go further by implying that the German barbarians rejuvenated Europe by infusing the remnants of their clan organization into the decaying fabric of the Roman Empire.[64] Sound Teutonic orthodoxy, one might say, as well as containing an indubitable amount of truth.[65] But exactly how does it relate to the more strictly theoretical concepts formulated by Marx and Engels?

There is no question that both men maintained and even accentuated their original aversion to Oriental rule considered as a political system. As we have seen, their first tentative utterances go back to the 1850s, when Marx was still inclined on occasion to play off the moral superiority of the decaying Confucian empire against the crude materialist aims of the encroaching Europeans. These polemical sideswipes are, however, scarcely to be taken seriously. They relate back to the familiar eighteenth-century habit of contrasting the virtuous Chinese with the hypocritical Europeans: an amiable fantasy which Marx commonly ranked with other childish naiveties of the Rousseauist age. When he speaks as a theorist, the term "semi-Asiatic" carries connotations which are both precise and un-

flattering. Moreover, it was gradually extended to Russia and became the standard reproach addressed to the Government of that
country. In this respect Engels took the lead[66] but Marx followed
suit in contrasting "Russia" with "Europe,"[67] and thereafter consistently referred to the Tsarist Government as a despotism suspended above an unfree peasantry. The references are too numerous
and familiar to need citing. Later in 1875 we find Engels classing
Russia with the "Asiatic mode" in an article where incidentally he
comments on the village community.[68] The same point is briefly
made in a better-known work, the *Anti-Dühring:* "Where the ancient
communes have continued to exist, they have for thousands of years
formed the basis of the most barbarous form of state, Oriental despotism, from India to Russia."[69] Lastly, there are Engels' writings
of the 1890s, in which it is indeed suggested that Tsarist despotism
is crumbling (and even that "the young Russian bourgeoisie has the
State entirely in its power"), but here too the surviving "despotic
autocracy of the Tsar" is related to "the old communistic village
community"—now in process of breaking up.[70]

In between, he and Marx had, however, given qualified support to
the notion that the village community might become the starting
point of a socialist development. How was this to be accomplished?
We have two statements by Marx, both regrettably brief. In his letter
to Vera Zasulich of March 8, 1881, we find him ready to go some
distance in accepting the Populist idea that the resistance of the
village community to private capitalism might offer the emerging
socialist movement a unique opportunity; though after stating that
"this community is the *point d'appui* of social regeneration in
Russia," he is at pains to add that "the pernicious influences which
attack it from all sides" must be eliminated, so as "to assure it of
normal conditions for a spontaneous development."[71] Then there is
the preface to the Russian edition of the *Communist Manifesto,*
dated January 21, 1882, with the quasi-Trotskyist suggestion that
"if the Russian Revolution becomes the signal for a proletarian revolution in the West, so that both complement each other, the present
Russian common ownership of land may serve as the starting point
for a communist development."[72] These hints point in the direction
of a controversy which was destined to convulse the Russian socialist

movement for decades, but they do not contribute much to the strictly theoretical concept of the "Asiatic mode." At most they imply that for Marx socialism offered a way out of the uncomfortable dilemma suggested by his researches into Oriental society: the element of personal freedom, so plainly lacking in that society and equally so plainly at the roots of West European feudalism (and capitalism), might enter the system after the collapse of its "political superstructure." In different terms, the approaching fall of Tsarism presented an opportunity to develop the healthy core of the ancient communal organization, instead of disrupting it completely in the interest of capitalism.

It is noteworthy that Marx—and to some extent Engels—saw such an opportunity latent in Russia, but not in India or China: presumably because Russia was only "semi-Asiatic." It was not a genuinely European country, but it nonetheless possessed the germ of development, whereas "the East" proper was stagnant. For the same reason, unfortunately, Russia was a permanent menace to Europe, and even its internal progress tended to make it more dangerous, because more aggressive and powerful.[73] The way out lay in a form of Europeanization which did away with the autocracy without—as the liberals would have it—simultaneously introducing Western capitalism. The commune—or what was left of it—was to be preserved as the future basis of a socialist society, or at any rate as an element of such a society. With this analysis the Populists were in agreement, and those among them who in the 1880s and 1890s gradually transformed themselves into Marxists could feel that they had not renounced the ideals and values which had originally brought them to socialism. Conversely, Marx for his part might think that by relating socialism back to pre-individualist, communal forms of ownership, he had closed the circle of his argument: bourgeois society, so far from being "natural" and permanent, was revealed to be simply one socioeconomic formation among others.

The unsolved, or half-solved, problem lay in the genesis of the Oriental State. In his writings of the early 1850s Marx had stressed both its centralized character and its independence from the vast mass of scattered village communes. In the 1857-58 draft the roots of despotism in general are traced back to the tribal organization, with its tendency to "realize" its internal unity in a personal ruler. Subsequently we find references to "the state" as "the supreme landlord," but no analysis of the means whereby the despotic sovereign builds up his power by surrounding himself with an administrative apparatus. From all this it is not difficult to conclude that Marx for some reason shirked the problem of the bureaucracy. Yet the latter's role is frequently alluded to in his other writings, notably in his diatribes against Bonapartism. His failure to make more of it in connection with the "Asiatic mode" remains an oddity. Perhaps the fact that he thought of it as a "caste" as distinct from a "class" of society lessened his interest in the subject; but though a possible explanation this is hardly an adequate defense.[74]

In his *Theories of Surplus Value* (1861-63) Marx quotes Richard Jones to the effect that "the surplus revenue from the soil, the only revenues except those of the peasants of any considerable amount, were (in Asia and more especially in India) distributed by the state and its officers."[75] Taken together with his own previous observations on the importance of centrally controlled irrigation in Asia, and with Engels' subsequent remarks (mainly in the *Anti-Dühring*) about the emergence of a ruling class from within primitive society, the elements of a complete theory of Oriental despotism appear to be present. Why were they not fully exploited? Perhaps an indirect answer is afforded by a somewhat lengthy passage from Engels which demonstrates at once the enormous advance in understanding he and Marx had actually effected in relation to earlier writers, and the point where their investigations tailed off into an uncritical acceptance of the prevalent Victorian attitude in regard to state and society:

> It is not necessary for us to examine here how this independence of social functions in relation to society increased with time until it developed into domination over society; how he who was originally the servant, where conditions were favourable changed gradually into the lord; how this lord, depending on the conditions, emerged as an Oriental despot or satrap, the dynast of a Greek tribe, chieftain of a Celtic clan, and so on; to what extent he subsequently had recourse to force in the course of this transformation; and how finally the individual rulers united into a ruling class. Here we are only concerned with establishing the fact

that the exercise of a social function was everywhere the basis of political supremacy; and further, that political supremacy has existed for any length of time only when it discharged its social functions. However great the number of despotisms which rose and fell in Persia and India, each was fully aware that above all it was the entrepreneur responsible for the collective maintenance of irrigation throughout the river valleys, without which no agriculture was possible there. It was reserved for the enlightened English to lose sight of this in India; they let the irrigation canals and sluices fall into decay, and are now at last discovering, through the regularly recurring famines, that they have neglected the one activity which might have made their rule in India at least as legitimate as that of their predecessors.[76]

Setting aside the polemical glance at the British Government in India, what does this passage suggest, if not that Engels—and by implication Marx, since he had seen the text before publication—thought of the "ruling class" in political terms, as the governing caste responsible for the exercise of those superior functions without which social life must come to a stop? The *Anti-Dühring* admittedly is a semi-popular tract primarily addressed to a working-class audience, but if Engels on this occasion expresses himself rather loosely, he does not contradict his or Marx's previous utterances. Political power arises from the exercise of a necessary social function: it then becomes independent of society (and of its own origins), but retains its roots in a collective need which it serves, *tant bien que mal,* until the social organism itself changes its character so as to require a different kind of "superstructure." The state, in short, is an epiphenomenon. Although it does have a life of its own, it is subservient to the real basic needs of society; consequently the long-run process can be analyzed in terms of the latter.

In passing, it may be observed that Engels in the above passage identifies the "ruling class" so completely with the governing caste as to provoke the rejoinder that on his assumptions Bismarck might have claimed to be a more legitimate representative of German society than the elected Reichstag. It is not at all clear how Engels would have met the argument that the political elite of a given society is, and must always remain, something different from, and superior to, the socially dominant class. It is true that in nineteenth-century Germany—and to some extent in Victorian England—the two coincided, inasmuch as the landed aristocracy had retained its political and social role, while steadily yielding economic power to the bourgeoisie. But this symbiosis was a peculiarity of European history, and its roots—as Marx observed in his 1857-58 sketch—lay in the relatively free and autonomous development of public life during the early Middle Ages. The Orient had never experienced anything of the kind, and since Engels had put his finger on the crucial role of the state—i.e., the bureaucracy—in administering the central economic functions, it was really incumbent upon him to explain in what sense the governing caste was a "ruling class." Failure to clarify this matter was bound to obscure the entire problem of political power and the state in general.

At this point, however, we are on the threshold of the modern age, and for the same reason at the end of our brief investigation into the manner in which Marx and Engels, at the peak of the Victorian era, saw the problem of political power in an Eastern setting. It can hardly surprise a contemporary reader to find that they did not seriously examine the possibility of despotic rule in an industrial society: in other words, the problem of what we have learned to call totalitarianism. To have done so would have meant to overstep the presuppositions they shared with their contemporaries: chief among them the confident belief that in Europe, anyhow, the despotic reorganization of society from the top was excluded by the very nature of that society. If we have in recent years begun to doubt this certainty, we may nevertheless extract what comfort we can from Marx's belief that the inner principle of Western historical development has from the start been quite different from that of the East or of Graeco-Roman antiquity. For my own part I am inclined to think that—in this as in most other matters—he was right, and that we are entitled to look upon European history as an evolution propelled by a dialectic of its own, to which there is no parallel in Oriental history. Needless to say, this Hegelian-Marxist view is incompatible with the notion that European, or Western, society is subject to a general law of growth and decay (or "challenge and response" to employ the currently fashionable jargon) applicable to *all* major civilizations. On the contrary, it insists upon the West's uniqueness; and to that extent the present writer has no hesitation in calling himself a Hegelian.

NOTES

1. *Oriental Despotism: A Comparative Study of Total Power.* Yale University Press and Oxford University Press, 1957.
2. *Ibid.,* pp. 372ff. For a reasonably intelligent and scholarly restatement of the orthodox Leninist standpoint cf. the Introduction to the selection entitled "Marx on China 1853-1860," ed. Dona Torr (London, 1951). Anyone curious to sample a specimen of authentic Soviet writing, as distinct from what might be called Anglo-Leninism, is advised to compare this doctrinaire but scholarly piece of editing with the characteristically dishonest and imbecilic Introduction to the Marx-Engels selection on India issued by the Moscow Institute of Marxism-Leninism in 1959 under the title *The First Indian War of Independence.*
3. Wittfogel, p. 394. In a pamphlet written in 1907 he even used the term "state feudalism" which had apparently been coined by one of his Menshevik opponents a year earlier to designate the peculiar character of Russian medievalism.
4. Cf. *Marx on China;* there is still no adequate English-language edition of the mass of articles contributed by Marx and Engels to the *New York Daily Tribune* (NYDT) between 1852 and 1862. The two-volume edition arranged by D. Ryazanov (*Gesammelte Schriften von Karl Marx und Friedrich Engels 1852-62,* Stuttgart, 1920) only covers the first four years of that period; the official East German *Gesammelte Werke* presents the complete text, but laboriously translated into German, instead of the original English-language version, and must therefore be treated with caution.
5. Cf. "Die britische Herrschaft in Indien," *Gesammelte Werke,* Berlin 1960, vol. 9, pp. 127ff; *The First Indian War of Independence 1857-1859,* Moscow, 1959, London, 1960, pp. 14ff; quotations are from the latter work which presumably reproduces the original text; cf. also the photo-offprint facing p. 128 of the Berlin edition.
6. *Selected Correspondence,* pp. 99ff; cf. *Marx-Engels Gesamtausgabe* (MEGA), Third Department, vol. I, pp. 480ff., for the full text.
7. Cf. *Selected Correspondence:* "in a rather narrow-minded spirit"; this is clearly a mistranslation due to the translator's failure to appreciate irony.
8. *Op. cit.,* p. 16. For a critical comment, cf. Wittfogel, pp. 374ff.
9. *Ibid.,* pp. 18-20. Cf. Marx to Engels, June 14, 1853, MEGA III/I, p. 487, *Selected Correspondence,* pp. 103-104: "I believe one cannot imagine a more solid foundation for a stagnant Asiatic despotism. And however much the English have Hibernicized the country, the breaking up of these stereotyped archaic forms was the *sine qua non* of Europeanization."
10. *Neue Rheinische Revue,* London, January 31, 1850 (reprinted in book form, Berlin, 1955, see p. 121); cf. also *Marx on China,* p. xvii.

11. *Ibid.*
12. *Ibid.*
13. Cf. *Vorlesungen über die Philosophie der Weltgeschichte,* ed. Lasson, Leipzig, 1920-23; especially vol. I, pp. 232ff.; vol. II, pp. 275ff.
14. NYDT, September 20, 1858; cf. *Marx on China,* p. 52; *Gesammelte Werke,* Berlin, 1961, vol. 12, p. 552.
15. NYDT, December 3, 1859; cf. *Marx on China,* pp. 91-92; *Gesammelte Werke,* vol. 13, p. 544.
16. *Selected Works,* vol. I, p. 363. The translation fails to convey the Hegelian ring of the original. Since an exact rendering of Hegel's observations on world history into English is a stylistic impossibility, one is left with the bare statement that Marx echoes Hegel not only in distinguishing four major epochs of world history but also in the confident Europeanocentrism with which he pronounces sentence upon the three preceding ones.
17. For a different view cf. Wittfogel, pp. 382ff.
18. It seems to me to be a decided weakness of Wittfogel's treatment of the subject that he fails to do this.
19. Engels' notion that the failure of Oriental society to develop private landed ownership was "mainly due to the climate" is a trifle naive, and looks back to Hegel, or even Montesquieu: one of the many instances of his tendency to relapse into ordinary cause-and-effect explanation, in the manner of the Enlightenment. The point cannot be pursued here; the reader of Hegel's *Vorlesungen,* vol. I, pp. 178ff., can easily discover where Engels obtained his basic notions about Oriental history. Marx, though equally inclined to take a Hegelian view of the historical process, relied for his factual information upon the classical economists, down to and including J. S. Mill, and upon British Blue Books and other official or semi-official sources.
20. NYDT, August 5, 1853; cf. *Gesammelte Werke,* vol. 9, p. 218; this article has for some reason not been included in any English-language collection known to the writer.
21. NYDT, August 8, 1853; cf. *Selected Works,* vol. I, p. 353.
22. Quoted after the Moscow, 1960, English-language edition, p. 771.
23. *Capital,* vol. III, p. 771. Marx here appends a footnote which adds: "Following the conquest of a country, the immediate aim of the conqueror was also to convert its people to his own use. Cf. Linguet (*Théorie des lois civiles, etc.,* London, 1767). See also Möser." It is not quite clear whether this refers to Indian conditions or whether it is meant to stand indifferently for all cases where peasant proprietors fall under some form of noneconomic exploitation.
24. *Ibid.,* pp. 771-72 (cited after the German text).
25. *Ibid.,* p. 772; for the original text, cf. *Das Kapital,* Berlin, 1949, vol. III, 841-42. The authorized English translation published in Moscow is both wooden and inaccurate.
26. The context makes it clear that this refers to the original pre-conquest Indian landowners, and not only to the *zamindars,* as might be supposed from Marx's characterization of the latter as tax-gatherers imposed by the British Government upon the wretched Bengali peasants (cf. NYDT, August 5, 1853).
27. Cited after the Moscow edition, pp. 328-29; Engels' qualifying footnote (appended in 1894, i.e., almost thirty years after Marx had written these lines), about Russian commerce having in the meantime become genuine-

ly capitalistic, does not affect the substance of the argument. Incidentally, the Soviet translation is not merely scandalously bad but in parts positively misleading; e.g., the key sentence really ought to run as follows: "Insofar as their commerce here revolutionizes the mode of production, it does so only as through the low price of their merchandise they destroy the spinning and weaving which constitutes an ancient and integrating part of this union of industrial-agricultural production and thus disrupt the communities."

28. *Loc. cit.,* p. 328n.
29. *Ibid.*
30. For Lenin's view on this issue, which of course was central to the gradual emergence of Russian Marxism from its Populist chrysalis, see his rather agitated defense of the "real" Marx against the Narodniks (who naturally quoted *Capital,* vol. III, when it suited them) in *The Development of Capitalism in Russia* (1900; new ed., Moscow, 1956, pp. 340ff.); cf. Lichtheim, *Marxism: An Historical and Critical Study,* London, 1961, pp. 325ff.
31. Cf. *Grundrisse der Kritik der politischen Ökonomie (Rohentwurf) 1857-1858,* Berlin, 1953; originally published in two volumes (Moscow, 1939-41); part of this draft (over 1,000 pages in print) was revised and published by Marx in 1859 under the title *Zur Kritik der politischen Ökonomie;* the bulk was reworked from 1863 onwards into what is now called *Das Kapital.*
32. Cf. *Wealth of Nations* (Modern Library, New York, 1937), p. 688, where the title of Bernier's *Voyages contenant la description des états du Grand Mogol,* etc. (Amsterdam, 1710), is given as *Voyages de François Bernier.*
33. *Ibid.,* p. 64.
34. *Ibid.,* p. 646.
35. *Ibid.,* p. 647.
36. *Ibid.,* p. 789.
37. *Ibid.,* p. 790.
38. *Op. cit.* (1909 edition), p. 20; Marx on the whole prefers the term "Asiatic society," perhaps first used by Richard Jones in *An Essay on the Distribution of Wealth* (1831); cf. Wittfogel, p. 373.
39. I am obliged to refer the reader to the chapter on Historical Materialism in *Marxism,* pp.141ff., for a discussion of Marx's methodology. (The originality of his approach, and the basic difference between his theory and the unsystematic hints thrown out by his predecessors, seems to me to have been understressed by Wittfogel.)
40. Cf. *Die deutsche Ideologie,* MEGA, vol. V, pp. 11ff.
41. *Ibid.*
42. *Ibid.,* p. 12.
43. *Ibid.*
44. *Ibid.,* pp. 12-13.
45. *Ibid.,* p. 13.
46. Cf. the latter's *Origin of the Family* (1884). In passing it may be observed that Marx's sketch of 1845-46 supplies a very realistic hint at the emergence of slavery from within the tribal organization. Compare this with Engels' account of how and why "the old classless gentile society" with its "simple moral grandeur" succumbs to "civilized" pressure from outside; cf. *Selected Works,* vol. II, p. 231.
47. *Grundrisse,* p. 375.
48. *Ibid.*

49. *Ibid.*, pp. 375-76.
50. *Ibid.*, pp. 376-77.
51. *Ibid.*, p. 377.
52. *Ibid.*, pp. 380-81.
53. *Ibid.*, p. 382.
54. *Ibid.*, p. 383.
55. *Ibid.*
56. *Ibid.*
57. *Ibid.*, p. 384.
58. *Ibid.*, pp. 384-92.
59. *Ibid.*, p. 392.
60. *Ibid.*, p. 395.
61. *Ibid.*
62. *Ibid.*, pp. 395-96.
63. I express a mere personal opinion when I say that the argument outlined in pp. 375-96 of the *Grundrisse* seems to me to be among the most brilliant and incisive of Marx's writings. Unfortunately it remained a mere sketch and, what is worse, it did not see the light until 1939-41. Had it been published around 1900, instead of remaining unknown until our days, one may suppose that Max Weber and his school would have found even better reason for relating themselves to Marx's researches. Marx in fact anticipates a good deal of what Weber had to say about Oriental society.
64. *Origin of the Family;* cf. *Selected Works*, vol. II, p. 277.
65. Cf. Marc Bloch, *Feudal Society*, London, 1961, pp. 145ff.
66. The article in the *New York Tribune* of April 19, 1853, in which Russia is first described as "semi-Asiatic," was signed by Marx, but actually written by Engels; cf. *Gesammelte Werke*, vol. 9, p. 23.
67. NYDT, August 5, 1853; cf. *Gesammelte Werke*, vol. 9, p. 215.
68. "Such a complete isolation of the individual (village) communities from each other . . . is the natural foundation of Oriental despotism, and from India to Russia this societal form, wherever it prevailed, has always produced despotism and has always found therein its supplement." Cf. *Internationales aus dem Voksstaat (1871-5)*, Berlin, 1894, p. 56.
69. *Anti-Dühring* (German ed.), Moscow, 1935, p. 165; cf. Foreign Languages Publishing House ed., Moscow, 1954, p. 251.
70. Cf. *Volkstaat*, l.c., pp. 61-72.
71. Full text in *Marx-Engels Archiv*, vol. I, Frankfurt¸ 1926, pp. 309-42; cf. Blackstock and Hoselitz, *The Russian Menace to Europe*, London, 1953, pp. 275ff.
72. *Selected Works*, vol. I, p. 24. In his 1894 gloss on this text, Engels pours a good deal of water into this heady wine; cf. "Russia and the Social Revolution Reconsidered," in Blackstock and Hoselitz, *op. cit.*, pp. 229ff.
73. Cf. Marx, *Herr Vogt* (1859), in *Gesammelte Werke*, vol. 14, especially pp. 497-98: "Incidentally, the emancipation of the serfs *in the sense of the Russian government* would multiply the aggressiveness of Russia a hundredfold. Its aim is simply the completion of the autocracy through the elimination of the barriers hitherto opposed to the great autocrat by the many little autocrats of the serf-based Russian gentry; as well as by the self-governing peasant communes whose material basis, the common ownership, is to be destroyed by the so-called emancipation."
74. For a critique of Marx's and Engels' views on the subject of Oriental

despotism, see Wittfogel, pp. 380ff.; it seems to me, though, that Witt-fogel overdoes the theme of Marx's alleged theoretical backsliding in his later writings. The most one can say is that the earlier suggestions were not systematically developed.

75. R. Jones, *Literary Remains, Consisting of Lectures and Tracts on Political Economy*, London, 1859, pp. 448ff.; cf. Marx, *Theorien über den Mehrwert*, Stuttgart, 1921, vol. III, p. 501.

76. *Herr Eugen Dühring's Revolution in Science*, Moscow, 1954, p. 249.

For Further Reading

Shlomo Avineri, *The Social and Political Thought of Karl Marx* (Cambridge, 1968).

Shlomo Avineri, "From Hoax to Dogma: A Footnote on Marx and Darwin," *Encounter* (March 1967), 30-32.

Isaiah Berlin, *Karl Marx,* 2nd ed. (London, 1952).

Auguste Cornu, *The Origins of Marxian Thought* (Springfield, Ill., 1957).

Louis Dupré, *The Philosophical Foundations of Marxism* (New York, 1966).

Jean Hyppolite, *Studies on Marx and Hegel* (London, 1967).

Eugene Kamenka, *The Ethical Foundations of Marxism* (London, 1962).

George Lichtheim, *Marxism* (London, 1961).

David McLellan, *Marx Before Marxism* (London, 1970).

Karl Marx, *Selected Works,* 2 vols. (Moscow, 1962).

Karl Marx, *Early Writings,* trans. T. B. Bottomore (London, 1963).

Karl Marx, *Writings of the Young Marx on Philosophy and Society,* eds. L. Easton and K. Guddat (Garden City, 1967).

Karl Marx, *Grundrisse,* ed. D. McLellan (London, 1971).

Karl Marx, *On Colonialism and Modernization,* ed. S. Avineri (Garden City, 1968).

Karl Marx, *Critique of Hegel's "Philosophy of Right,"* ed. J. O'Malley (Cambridge. 1970).

István Mészáros, *Marx's Theory of Alienation* (London, 1970).

John Plamenatz, *German Marxism and Russian Communism* (London, 1954).

Nathan Rotenstreich, *Basic Problems of Marx's Philosophy* (Indianapolis/New York, 1965).

Robert C. Tucker, *Philosophy and Myth in Karl Marx* (Cambridge, 1961).

213

Index

215